The Gazebo Narratives

Writing Ourselves into History

I0555340

By
Wilfred Komoh Winn, Sr.

Copyright © 2025 by Wilfred Komoh Winn, Sr.
All rights reserved.
No portion of this book may be reproduced in any form
without written permission from the publisher or author
except as permitted by U.S. copyright law.

Dedication

I am grateful to many people, including many family members, whose names I would rather not mention for fear of leaving others out. You know yourselves. I know you, too. But above all, God, the Source of all blessings, knows you very well. Had it not been for your help and contributions, this way of telling our stories to much larger audiences, using prose, as opposed to word-of-mouth, would have remained simply a perpetual dream. So, I appreciate you.

I am dedicating this book to my beautiful wife, Mrs. Annie P. Winn. You are the reason I am smiling again. Only the almighty God can pay and will reward you. And to all our children: Victoria, Toe, Simeon, Jerry, Amos, Wilfred Junior, and AJ. You are the world to your mother and me; you add new meanings to our lives.

Mrs. Annie Paytee Winn & Mr. Wilfred Komoh Winn, Sr.

Table of Contents

Preface

For centuries, we—many of us in Liberia, especially in the southeast—relied on oral narratives as the primary means of information transfer between generations. So, history in this part of the world is poor; it doesn't go far back because it is not written.

Saylee Sayjolo, my older brother, is one of many people without whose efforts this book would have remained a perpetual dream. He played a pivotal role in our collective effort to begin the act of writing ourselves into history. On January 19, 2004, Sayjolo braced the early morning dew along the Jarkaken-Wodaiken route and sat down with our father, Mr. Josiah Saylee Winn, Sr., a renowned oral historian. Their conversation took place in the village of **Wodaiken**, a tiny farming outpost in Jarkaken's Dilamo farming reservation. The old man himself established the hamlet in the year 1975 while he was still living in the village of Puwaiken, River Gee.

It—narrating on record—was a long-awaited opportunity for the old man. The old man used the opportunity to talk about the things he cared about. He went on and on with hardly any interruptions for ninety minutes. He discussed several topics, including a lengthy family tree, historical events, the Dilamo region, the Dilamo Road (a footpath), the historical peoples in the greater Jarkaken area (and beyond), and much, much more.

Going from word-of-mouth narratives to written narratives is a huge transition. Note that the oral form of communication, for some apparent reasons, has always been the standard for our people for a time extending beyond the reach of memory, record, or tradition. So, I am certain that information transferred in this mode (word-of-mouth) will remain the predominant means by which we get and share stories in our region, especially if we—the current generations—do little or nothing to improve the way we communicate between our generations of people. I caution my readers, however, to understand me on this point. I have a genuine fear of being misconstrued. This mode of communication— oral narration—is important. In fact, a significant portion of this book is possible because of a buildup or collection of many fireside chats or narratives, presented not only by old man Saylee but by many of his kinsmen.

For his part, old man Saylee talked about the people of Chedepo, a district in River Gee County, Liberia, where his hometown, Chedepo Jarkaken, is located. He later expanded on the topic by not only talking about the major residential areas (Chedepo towns), the ones with governmental services, but he also discussed the tiny satellite hamlets that are dotted around the area's major settlements.

He spent a significant time on his *Bocuwao family*—a collection of more than two hundred nuclear families who are believed to be blood-related and are impressively skilled in tracing their common roots, lineages, or relations. (Any semblance of courtship is forbidden—an absolute taboo— within this mammoth of a family.)

He discussed their hamlets (such as Wodaiken), the ones in existence, and the ones that once existed. He also spent much of his time on one key road: the Dilamo Road, along which family members of the Bocuwao line their lives: their villages, their huts, their farms. He named the original pioneers—the people who were the first to establish hamlets on the Dilamo farming reservation, which is located outside the key town of Chedepo Jarkaken. He also talked about their roads, their important hamlets—such as their once therapeutic hamlet: Weltehken—and their relations.

2

In "*The Gazebo Narratives*," we read the history of the area, to include River Gee and beyond, from another perspective: Newton Gbeh Chea Nyanley Winn, the baby brother of old man Josiah Saylee Winn. (I call him Uncle, Old Man, or Nyanley, interchangeably.)

Uncle dived much deeper in other areas; his senior brother ventured not, and he— this baby brother—is detail-oriented. But he is conscious about being misinterpreted, or his antidotes being misused in ways that could breed conflicts, instead of readers just reading for historical knowledge. Readers will find that Uncle is quite conscious throughout his narratives. In a few areas, he displayed a reluctance to dive deeper into some of the topics.

While his narratives on his subjects or topics of choice were true—with many of the events occurring in the lives of some people who are still alive—Uncle was a bit timid about exploring some of the details he considered to be sensitive in nature.

One particular issue was on Sanma, a prominent Bocuwao forefather. Oral historians trace his roots to the family of Tarwiao, in the town of Jaykwiken, where he was reportedly experiencing hardship and decided to seek resettlement elsewhere. He (Uncle) was reluctant to explain the details about this man, whose children's children constitute more than a quarter of the families who make up today's Bocuwao family.

My approach to this is a regret because stories tend to die out when narrators hold out or refuse to share them. When a narrator is concerned that some people in his or her audience might apply their stories in the wrong context, that narrator may fear being blamed for any potential consequence. That was Uncle's fear. In fact, he offered this preamble:

"We do not explain some of these things [stories] in detail because some chatty mouths may use the information in the

3

wrong context. And when someone asks tomorrow, 'Where did you get that kind of information?' The answer might be, 'My father, Nyanley, told me.'"

Anyway, the above was the firmed prelude he offered before telling the story of Sanma, one of Bocuwao's prominent, respected forefathers.

Uncle also narrated a story on Klosoken, a one-time prominent community in the land of Chedepo that was destroyed in the late eighteenth century by a fire. He said in matter-of-fact terms who was culpable and the family in which the culprit belonged. In essence, the locals blamed the entire family for the acts of their relative. It is an interesting story; readers will learn more about Klosoken, culpabilities, and even some nagging, stubborn, and enduring Bocuwao family stereotypes.

Other topics explored in this book include the transcripts of Wleh Snoteh, who paid an early morning visit to his great uncle, Winn Saylee. The transcripts included the opinions of not just Snorteh but Gbayi Puwai, Snorteh's cousin and one of the sons of old man Gbayi Wliya, who lived to be the oldest in the entire family.

The visit coincided with the presence of some of the old man's own children: Tinpan, Woday, Saylee Junior, and Sayjolo. The old man's wife, Kanbo Snoh, was at home during the stopover. Her brother, Kanbo Wiah, had arrived earlier and had been paying his own visit before the arrival of Snoteh, Puwai, and other family members. They had a rather fascinating and memorable dialogue.

Then there is the "Echoes of Sorrow," which I can only describe as "an informed childhood recollection" on the major Bocuwao family's tragedies; the family of Bocuwao experienced significant emotional pains due to the mass slaughter of some members of its elderly. Brace yourself.

4

I—the author—also talk about recent activities. In "War in Jarkaken," I talk about how Charles Taylor's war affected Chedepo Jarkaken, its people, and its environs. I also ventured into the grouping of peers, a Grebo tribal or cultural phenomenon that groups, trains, and assigns collective names (epithets) to equals (social classes) as part of a rite of passage. Then there is a lengthy piece on Jumayee Dance, a youth dance which had a "turbulent" historical beginning, but is now considered a catalyst for social cohesion across numerous age groups in the land of Chedepo, River Gee County, and elsewhere in southeastern Liberia, West Africa.

Moreover, no Jarkaken stories are completed without one involving their favorite son, Colonel William G. Cholopray. I had my share of interactions with Hon. Cholopray, who—during his time in the USA—lived with us in New York City for more than three years before moving to his own place in the city of Trenton, New Jersey. I was privileged to have helped him with political asylum paperwork during his time with us. While this aspect of his life in the USA is briefly discussed in my piece on him, how he gained his legal status in the United States is not included in my brief biography on the life of this renowned colonel.

On oral history, my own attitude has always been to first acknowledge that our people, such as many of the subjects in this book—Saylee, Nyanley, Wleh Snorteh, as well as Gbayi Wliya's Puwai (just to name a few)—and all the others who were before them, had done their best to preserve our history through the narrative form. But while there are great benefits to sharing information in this primitive, yet valuable, mode of communication (e.g., one does not have to know how to read or write in order to transmit oral narratives, and it is possible to ask the storyteller rear time questions), there are detrimental aspects associated with this mode of information transfer.

The information we receive from our oral narrators, for instance, does not go very far back into our past; it is short-

5

lived. The quality of the information that is transmitted depends on the power of memories (i.e., how well they had remembered the stories) from one generation (or one storyteller) to another. Moreover, transmitted stories differ in their consistency or trustworthiness. In general, all oral accounts are not reliable because their values change with time itself.

Oral history also tends to be biased because of the nature of the transmission itself; other concerns with this mode of information sharing are their being too prone to exaggeration, the tendencies of the storyteller to "blow things out of proportion" as he or she tells the stories; creativity, the storyteller may change the original story; and selectivity, the storyteller may pick or choose to talk about only the favorable aspects of the stories. Of all these disadvantages, the inclination for oral history to die as rapidly as it forms is, in my view, the most harmful characteristic.

So, as we begin the new era of writing our people into history, my hope is that this book, *The Gazebo Narratives*, will serve multiple purposes in furthering that goal—writing ourselves into history.

When oral historians, such as the narrators in this book, die, there is a general understanding that many countless stories effectively die with them. This is why I often say that oral history is "prone to rapid death." Every time an oral historian dies, stories die, too. Thus, the intent of this book is to serve as a pioneer, if you like, in the quest to slow the "rapid death" of our historical accounts. This book begins the loss prevention by picking up where our fireside narrators left off—by using text or prose to communicate with this and future generations.

In conclusion, this book seeks to be an inspirational tool to those who are thinking of writing themselves, others, or our domain into history, that it can be done, regardless of the overwhelming nature of the task.

6

Chapter I:
The Chedepo Domain

Chedepo is a district in River Gee County, Liberia. The people who live here are called Chedepo. They are members of the Grebo tribe, and the version of the Grebo language they speak here is called Chedepo. The land on which they live is, well, you get the picture.

The names of some Chedepo communities, such as Geeken or Putuken, are common regional designations. To avoid any confusion, the people in this district have a unique solution, which leaves no room for doubt. The names of their towns are often, if not always, preceded by the word Chedepo: Chedepo Geeken, Chedepo Putuken, and so on.

The land of Chedepo is divided into two main sections. These sections are **Nyenawleken** and **Kaytoken**. Old man Winn Saylee (1931–2015), an oral historian from the Bocuwao family of Chedepo Jarkaken (Kaytoken), explained that the two sections— Nyenawleken and Kaytoken—are names for two historic foothills on which the Chedepo people lived a long, long time ago. He said both foothills are not too far from each other. He was explaining all of this to his family in the village of Wodaiken, a hamlet in the Dilamo region of Chedepo Jarkaken, during an early morning fireside chat that was primarily on the history of Bocuwao, one of six mega families in the town. With his elder son, Saylee Sayjolo, recording the conversation, the old man described the location of an ancient Bocuwao village called Sindoloken, an outlier from many of the families' other villages.

"There is a once-settled foothill we call Nyenawle," the old man said, "and next to it [Nyenawle] is the foothill we call Polo. Between these two foothills—Nyenawle and Polo—is the foothill we call Sindolo. It was on this foothill [Sindolo], the Bocuwao man we call Wiah Chie built his Sindoloken settlement a long, long time ago. Sindolo and the foothill we call Kayto lie side by side. While Wiah Chie was living in his Sindoloken village, another man we call Blisa, who was a member of the Magwulu family [in today's Jarkaken and Geeken], built a settlement on the foothill of Kayto. Blisa's settlement was called Kaytoken."

Each of the major Chedepo subdivisions—Nyenawleken and Kaytoken—comprises several towns in which large family groups reside. Some of the towns have larger family groups than others. In the Kaytoken subdivision, for example, there are several settlements scattered all over the area's landscape, but only the communities with vital government services (schools, clinics, government offices) are recognized there. Therefore, Kaytoken, which is the most populated of the Chedepo subdivisions, has only two towns: Chedepo Jarkaken and Chedepo Geeken. These two cities lie near each other. In fact, Jarkaken is 14.8 km (9.2m) from Chedepo Geeken. The people who live in these towns once lived in one village, historically speaking. Their ancestors were the residents in the village or settlement of Kaytoken, which was founded by Blisa (whom the old man talked about in the previous paragraph).

To this day, the ruins of the ancient village of Kaytoken, such as its still-standing hut poles in the middle of countless circular mount formations, which indicate where the huts used to be, are clearly visible on the top of the Kaytoken foothill. Kaytoken, the foothill, overlooks Chedepo Jarkaken no more than five miles away. Geeken is a relatively large town. It is smaller than Jarkaken. It is probably smaller than Putuken, if not equal.

Nyenawleken, like Kaytoken, has a great many settlements, too. They are dotted over its entire landscape, but only three essential towns—Chedepo Putuken, Chedepo Klaboken, and Chedepo Bletiken—are recognized. The folks in Nyenawleken, especially those in the area's three major population centers, used to live together in the ancient community of Nyenawleken.

Of the three communities in Nyenawleken, Putuken is the largest. It is a main road community. In fact, Putuken is the only Chedepo town along the Zwedru-Harper Highway; hence, it is, arguably, the most popular Chedepo town. The town is the commercial center for the district because of its location. It is a market town. People from across Chedepo go to Putuken every Saturday to sell and purchase a variety of local products, including arts, local produce, clothes, electronics, and so on.

In Putuken, the marketplace is along the major highway mentioned above. People, mostly from Chedepo towns, set up tables at the junction where the route from Jarkaken, which is the most populous of the Chedepo towns, merges with the Zwedru-Harper Highway. The market basically straddles this Kaytoken-bound route.

The last two communities in Nyenawleken—Klaboken and Bletiken—are not as popular as the market town. Klaboken is a small town, tucked away from all the major thoroughfares in the area. Its neighbor, Bletiken, is even tinier (smaller). Bletiken, like many of the Chedepo towns, is isolated within the Chedepo jungles.

In summary, the three communities that resulted from the collapse of Nyenawle (*Putuken, Klaboken,* and *Bletiken*), along with two of the several towns established after the collapse of Kayto (*Jarkaken* and *Geeken*), are officially the five principal communities recognized in the land of Chedepo.

After the town of Kaytoken fell (most likely caught on fire), several of its nearby communities saw their populations increase. Tiny hamlets that had a very small number of people gained more people after the tragic fall of Kaytoken. There were many communities that benefited from the tragedy, in terms of population increase, but these are the ones that come to mind: Klosoken, Chiken (Geeken), Chutuken, Chelateken, Blaliken (Blalorken), Weltehken, Cheboken, Wotuken, and Jarkaken. These places (and more) saw increases in their local populations. While all the villages at the time of Kayto's collapse received refugees, the majority of those who left Kaytoken town, according to local historians, went to three nearby communities: Klosoken, Chutuken, and Geeken. In fact, it was during this time that the settlements of Klosoken, Chutuken, Cheboken, and Geeken gained town statuses.

It was not until the beginning of the second quarter of the twentieth century that Jarkaken, the hamlet, gained real town status (in the early 1930s) following yet another tragic fiery accident in the key town of Klosoken [a fired destroyed it in 1931]. The survivors from Klosoken went to the towns of Jarkaken and Chutuken in droves. Also, in due course, many area communities, the likes of Chutuken, Weltehken, Cheboken, Chelateken, and so on, were absorbed into today's Chedepo Jarkaken. In fact, it is no surprise that the people in

Chedepo Jarkaken officially refer to themselves as "Klosokwen" because they still embrace the ruined hilltop community of Klosoken. Its tragic fall benefited the people of Jarkaken in many ways. The fall of Kloso really raised Jarkaken from a small farming outpost to what it is today—one of the major population centers not just in Chedepo District but in River Gee County, Liberia.

Today, Jarkaken is the largest of all Chedepo towns. It is the headquarters of the Chedepo District. The town has six major families: Bowionpo, Ponwaon, Magwulu, Bocuwao, Dowao, and Kaytiao. And some of the families are broken up into smaller units because of their huge sizes. Some of these families are composed of as many as two hundred or more smaller families (nuclear families or households). The family of Bowionpo is a good example. It is the largest in Kaytoken, if not the entire Chedepo domain. In Jarkaken alone, the Bowionpo mega family is broken up into five subfamilies. They include Chenchipo, Karpehpo, Kpatorpo, Teatypo, and Wionnyenpanpo. Some of the smaller units within the Bowionpo family are large enough to surpass a few of Jarkaken's other primary families in terms of population.

Chedepo Geeken comprises many of the same mega families found in Chedepo Jarkaken because of the communities' historic contacts or connections. In fact, there are only two families found in Jarkaken that are absent in Geeken. There are no Bocuwao and Dowao families in Chedepo Geeken. The only common-sense explanation for the absent families could be this: after the downfall of Kaytoken, a clear majority of the absent families went to nearby Klosoken, Chutuken, and Jarkaken. Unlike other primary families, very few elements from the absent families branched out far enough to get to Geeken. The few that did either died out or rejoined their families in Jarkaken and its immediate surroundings. On the other hand, the families of

11

Kaytiao and Ponwaon, which are collectively known as "Ponwaon Daisu"—allegedly with shared heritage—went in droves to Geeken along with Magwulu. Thus, the mega families in Geeken, listed from most popular households to least popular households, are as follows: Ponwaon, Bowionpo, Kaytiao, and Magwulu.

Some of the smaller family units flirt with breakaway ideas. They want to be stand-alone families, with primary mega-family status. This is not an easy status to assign to a portion of any family; in fact, it is frowned upon, and for good reason. Mega families are made up of people who are generally believed to belong to the same genetic line. The elders within each family group, for example, make it their responsibility to teach younger generations so they see or know others within their mega family as relatives.

Pronouncing a sector as a primary or a stand-alone entity will mean that its members will be at liberty to get married to members within other mega families. And this, ironically, will include taking wives or husbands from within the very family that had granted the new family its primary status. There is very little chance that such a pronouncement will ever happen.

The Grebo people have a complete ban on intra-family courtship. Granting a stand-alone status to a portion of a mega family will open the door to intra-family courtship, a gross violation of a major norm.

In Chedepo, families are assigned farming reservations. Each family is assigned a huge enclave of land for their farming needs. The locals call these reservations **Sonjigbae**, literally, "the faces of farming."

Old man Nyanley explained the reservations this way:

12

"Where do we go to farm? Where are our hamlets? For the families of Bocuwao and Dowao, our farming reservation is **Dilamo** (also known as Deorken or Deormo). The reservation begins from Tarwulu, which is a small, once-settled foothill just outside the main town. A traveler from Jarkaken will first see Kloso, another once-inhabited foothill. This foothill (Kloso) is about three-quarters of a mile outside the town. From Kloso, the next foothill is Tarwulu. This is the official beginning or start point of the Dilamo road. In truth, Tarwulu is a tiny mount; it is technically not even a foothill, especially when compared to Kloso, which is more vertical and steeper.

It is on this mount that the first Bocuwao hamlet was established a long time ago. That first settlement, as I said, belongs to us because it was one of our forefathers who first settled the area. His name was Teh.

He was the first to build and live on the foothill of Tarwulu. The tiny village he established at Tarwulu was called Chutu or Chutuken. In due course, however, the settlement transformed into a sizable community, particularly after fired destroyed Klosoken, which was a nearby community, as I said earlier."

From time to time, that location has always been a major source of food in the entire Kaytoken area, the greater Jarkaken-Geeken area.

The meaning of *Dilamo* is twofold: "a region for eating [a region of plenty]" is one meaning. The other meaning of *Dilamo* is "this is the way." The former term boasts of the yields from the region's farms, so that the place or the locals are not plagued with hunger.

Similarly, the latter version is more welcoming and invitational. Ironically, however, the second meaning is used with a bit of arrogance, a chest-pounding way of saying the

Dilamo location is superior to neighboring locations. That it is the place to visit—as opposed to other locations—because it is tremendously beneficial to the locals and anyone who calls the place home. That "this is the place to live, and this is the place to simply be." The locals say this with the impression that no other place compares to the Dilamo reservation. They use Dilamo in that sense.

Anyway, it is the road we take as we set out for Chedepo Geeken. Once we get to the foothill of Chutu (Tarwulu), we take a slight left turn while the person going to Geeken continues straight. We continue until we get to and beyond Killepo Torwloken. We continue to and beyond a place we call *'Twinwulojaemo'* until we get to Kunnehpo, a location in Grand Gedeh. All that area—from here to the Krahn line—is ours: we, the people or family of Bocuwao.

In fact, by tradition, when something bad happens here, the people of Klosoken call on us to petition for calm and peace. And we are often there with the family of Dowao. They are not charged with that role—the role to petition for calm and peace. Instead, it is we, the family of Bocuwao, the core (*'jelsowel'*) owners of the Dilamo reservation, who petition. When someone dies in the bushes—such as a traumatic death, say as a result of a fallen tree—it is our role to petition for calm and peace. If women go into the local creeks to fish, and they cannot catch their desired fish, it falls on Bocuwao to petition for a turnaround. We do that [the petitioning] at a location near Chichi, the northern section of the River Gee. And we call that location 'Deorblemgehn,' under a [tlalala] tree. It takes the family of Bocuwao, not Dowao (and definitely not Magwulu), to petition the wild for peace.

We, the Bocuwao family, are the owners of that road [the Dilamo road], as I said earlier. We are here with people from the mega family of Dowao. Dowao family members are our

14

partners. We inter-marry because we live together. There are permanent Dowao hamlets in the Dilamo reservation. For starters, the village of Wlehpotogbe, which belongs to a Dowao man. His name was Sanyonoh Chelene. Even Gbetohken (now a Bocuwao hamlet)—that was built initially by a Dowao man, the grandfather of Alexander Boyah.

His name was Nyenkan Kosolo. He took Quayee Swen [the father of David Karwolo Swen] with him to serve as the 'nyansunupoi' (pioneer) from the Bocuwao family, as was sometimes required. Wolodolo—another Dowao village. The man we call Teah, along with Tinyan Toe—these are Dowao folks. They were over there. Even the village of 'Kwelehken'— old man Paytee Cholo and other Dowao people were over there.

But we, the family of Bocuwao, are the principal owners of that farming location. Our hamlets start from the village of Chutuken—it was an actual, full-fledged town until its fall in the year 1942. Locals in the greater Kaytoken area (the Jarkaken-Geeken area) also refer to this village as Tarwulu because it sits over an aptly-named foothill (Tarwulu). The man who was the first to settle the village of Chutuken (Tarwulu) was our great father Tebateh. He built Chutu. We also have Welteh (Weltehken); it was built by our father, Tehfueh, whose wife we know historically as 'Karfor Paytee.' We have Puwai (Puwaiken); our father, Wedlyn Chea, the son of Kaji Choloplay Sloboh, is the pioneer at Puwai. We have Wotu (Wotuken), which was built by our father, Wiah Nyonoh Nowinnie, the father of Jenkins Adjaphie Norrington; he once lived in the western Ivorian town of Tabou.

Those are some of the Bocuwao villages on the Dilamo farming reservation. Most of our villages are along the Dilamo route, which is the major thoroughfare that snakes through the vast farming enclave.

For the people who live in the farming reservation of Tartymo, where our father Teaty Saylee's townhouse is located, it belongs to the mega family of Bowionpo.

Specifically, the family members from the Karpehpo branch of Bowionpo are the owners of Tartymo. But near those Karpehpo families is the Magwulu family. [Note that the Magwulu family is also in the Dilamo region. That region is historically not theirs. In the year 1931, the Magwulu family went to the Dilamo area during the reign of Chief Gbagba Toe, who went through one of the Bocuwao family's forefathers, Panteah, son of Jorpoh Chea Fueh.] Magwulu went over there [in the Tartymo farming reservation] a long time ago through Wulopoi Swen, a Magwulu man. Additionally, there are a lot of other Jarkaken families in the Tartymo area. Together, all the families built the hamlet of Cheboken. It is a joint community (*'Klordie'*). The village of Cheboken actually belongs to no one family; it is a group town. So, that is Tartymo (or Tartyken) in a nutshell.

The old Putuken road: when you go through Karwea, a borough in Jarkaken — just a stone's throw after the giant kola tree, turn on the path that goes towards Mr. Jeffery Saylee's place, [this turn is well before the Prime Timber Products' sawmill (or PTP Yard)—before you get to Neplen Creek]. If you continue and pass Mr. Saylee's area and follow that road [a foot path, really], it will take you to Klaboken. In fact, this road ends in the town of Klaboken, which is one of the five major towns that are in the land of Chedepo. Anyway, this road—the one through Karwea that eventually ends in Klaboken—is an old, historic road. It has a name: Seayorken. It is not the main Putuken road; instead, it branches off the main road to the Putuken, a main road community in Chedepo, which is the area's commercial hub.

16

There is a road behind Dweh Kargbe Nyanfore's house in Chedepo Jarkaken. The road, like all the others, is a footpath. It crosses Neplen Creek at or adjacent to a point along that creek where the water really collects into a deep pool [**Wulo**]. We call this route—and the entire farming reservation through which it (the road) snakes—Tonken, for a dark place.

There is another route on that same side of town, the route that Mr. Victor Jah Noring and other Ponwaon people use. I am talking about the route that goes in the direction of Portornorgbae, a major creek and water source. We call that farming reservation Kujaysnumo. One of the devils the Chedepo people once served was Kayee Choloplay. That devil was in the Kujaysnumo farming reservation.

Then there is another road that passes by Mr. Wilson Martin Swen. It continues until it gets to Bodiaken, a popular hamlet for the family of Bowionpo. It continues to Mr. Isaac Gbasay Klay Doe's hamlet, which is known as Honklaeken. From there, it continues to Chenwnidolo, a famed foothill. In fact, we call that farming reservation Chenwniken.

The above are the farming reservations or 'Sonjigbae' that we have around Jarkaken. The Chenwniken reservation belongs to the mega family of Bowionpo. Tartymo reservation belongs to two mega families: Bowionpo and Magwulu. For Seayorken, it is a joint route. We also call Seayorken a 'Felsnu,' or resting route.

Seayorken takes a traveler to locations within the district lines of Chedepo District, within the confines of the district. A Felsnu, like Seayorken, does not venture to any of the clans in the districts around us, such as Gbeapo District, Killepo District, Potupo District, and so on. In fact, Seayorken Road is an epitome of what Chedepo people call 'Queje, ' a route that starts internally and ends internally. Queje means 'connected to self'. Like Felsnu, our Queje roads take us no further than Chedepo.

Conclusively, the paths that connect us to other external districts are our major throughfares. The ones that do not link us with adjacent clans are not as significant as those that do. If you take the route behind Mr. Dweh Kargbe Nyanfore's place, for example, it will take you to Chedepo Putuken. In other words, the road starts in Chedepo Jarkaken and ends in Chedepo Putuken. I am talking about the Tonken-area route. It is not a primary route.

The same is true for the road that goes through the borough of Karwea. Seayorken, as it is known. It is not the main Putuken road; instead, it branches off the main Putuken road. Seayorken road starts in Chedepo Jarkaken and ends in Chedepo Klaboken. It is not a primary route in Chedepo.

But if you take the route that leads to the Tartymo reservation, it will take you to the land of the Potupo people. Potupo is an adjacent district to Chedepo. Hence, it is a major road.

Also, if you take the route behind Mr. Wilson Martin Swen and Mr. Philip Amin's places (Chenwniken Road), however, it will take you to Killepo, an adjacent district. Thus, it is a major road.

Moreover, if you take the Dilamo (also known as Deorken, or Deormo) route, it will take you to a lot of external locations. Dilamo connects Chedepo to several major clans. This route connects us to the Killepo people, a nearby district. It also connects us to the Krahn people; it connects us to Grand Gedeh County, Liberia. Therefore, it is a very important route. And that's how our roads are laid out.

Obtained from the open web

18

Pennoken
Sapo National Park
Chedepo
Jarkaken
Putuken

Malu
Tweh
Pennoken
Gambo
Djavolo
Pynes
Tonkehn
Namo
Kileapo
Kanweaken
Tomwoken
Blaiken
Para
Lobo
Karié
Felhn
Our sleep point
Brown Village
Rock Crusher
Gbaquiah
Juwelbo
Yeebo Town
Lepoard
Swanmanken
Saygbeken
Jarkaken
Bawrekon
Putuken
Cheboken
Pah
Free
Cheboken
Geeken
Betuoken
Jaytoken
Pennoken
Production
Camp
Paluwah
Gbaweleken
Soloblo
Jarpuken
Mission
Sakliken
Warliken
Jorproken
Teah Village
Béréblo
Cheepoh
Fufue
River Gbe Camp
Hannié
Jarpuken
Nyouken
Pronoken
Fish Town
Karyillibo
Mission Town
Nékaounié
Joquiken
Sarbo Geeken
Town
Klibo
Mahino
Tugbaken
Fortiakpo
Gbarken
(Ponnoh City)
Feloken
Wessaitoken
Juluken #1
Gnato
Doewen
Gbaweleken
Geplaken
Toubo Sweaken
Chenwrinken
Glofaken
Cheboken
Jlatoken
Dougbo
Jlateken
(Tarlu City)
Sargloken
Karbuken
Grabo
Fété
Barforwin
Wedo
Sitor
Wissiken
Tienbo
Kronoken City
Siahé
Jargeloken
Getuke
Jeboken
Tiboto
Déblablé

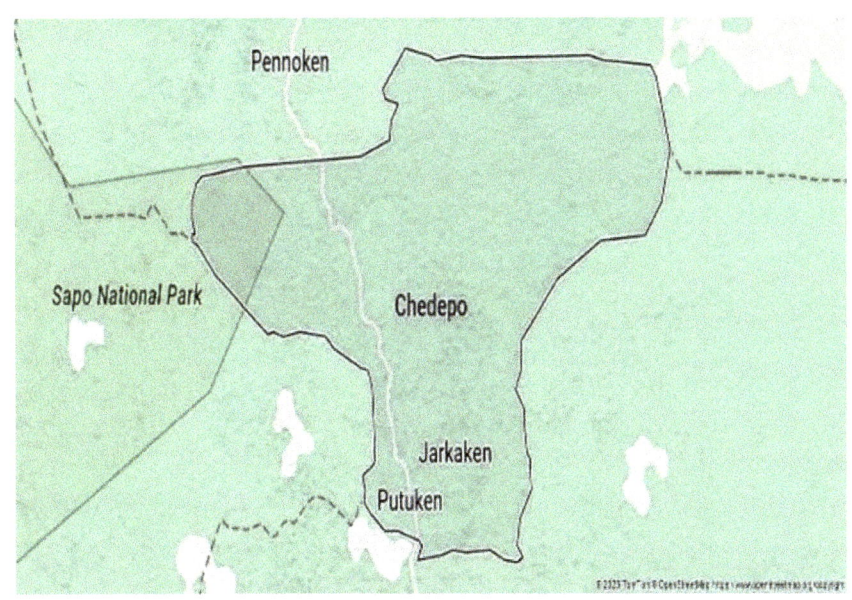

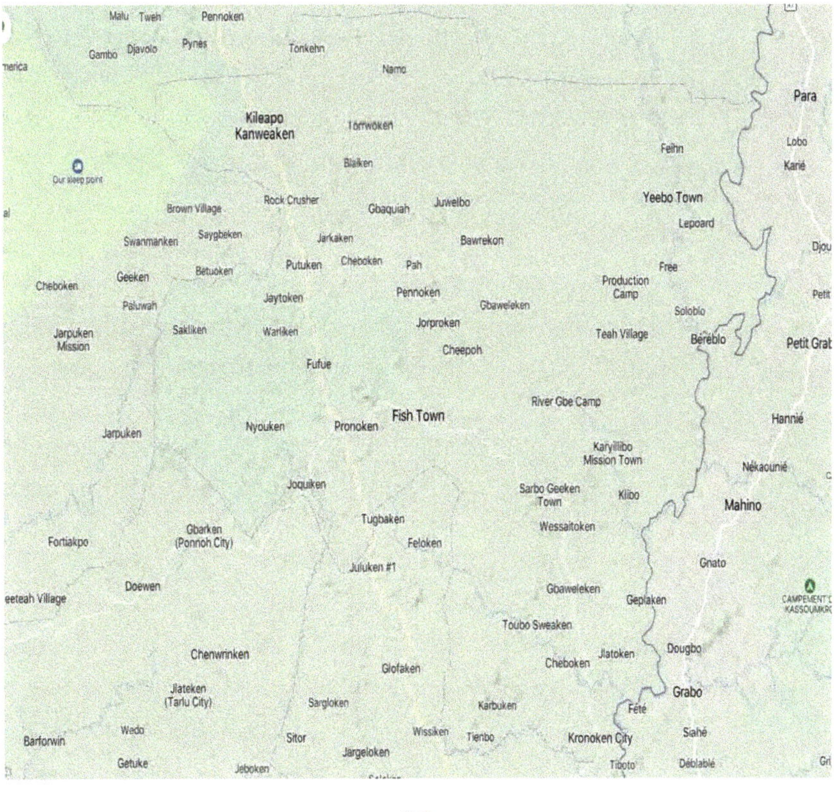

Chapter II:
The Grouping of Peers

Grebo is a Liberian tribe. It is located in River Gee County, and elsewhere in the southeastern region of the country. The people—also known as Grebos—have a unique system that groups peers in communities across their landscape. The method that Grebos use to group their peers differs from one village to another, but the idea is almost the same. People in a well-defined age bracket are categorized as a social class or a peer group. Then, a designated naming agent, usually the most senior elder in the community, assigns the peer group an identification in the form of a name (an epithet), which the group is known by until its last member ages and dies.

Then, like a free agent, the name is usually recycled (i.e., assigned to a new group). In other words, the names within Grebo's peer system are recurring or cyclical. They are routinely retrieved from prior peer groups whose members have aged and died out. It is worth mentioning that the naming agent, the town's elder, is at complete liberty to coin a name. There is no mandate to strictly use recurrent names. The name is not forced or imposed on a peer group. The peer group being named has a say in its naming. They do not suggest names. That is not their role. That is the responsibility of the naming agent.

But the social group to be named can refuse a name, and the agent is expected to find another name that the group deems fitting for their social class.

For example, in Chedepo, which is a variant of the Grebo tribe, within a social class, no member can be more than three years older than his peers. They call each social class *tonmo* (or *tubor*), and two or more social groups are called *tuwangbeh*.

Peer groups are placed into three subdivisions, each with its own traditional duty descriptions, expectations, and goals. The three sections in Chedepo's peer system are *Conjlopo*, the children's section, where the grouping of peers begins; *Kofa*, the young men's section, which traditionally trains and mentors the community's children while it provides free farming assistance to village title holders, such as the high priest; and *Gbor*, the elders' section, the most senior section that wields enormous authority, including the making and enforcing of traditional laws.

Conjlopo amass every three years and put together a new peer group that later seeks and usually gains a grown-up status from town elders. During the petitioning phase [they petition for a name for their peer group], all the kids are called Conjlopo, which is a Chedepo term that means "prone to anger." Although a new social class is comprised of kids who range from ages thirteen through fifteen, the kids' initial formations practically include children of all ages. To build up their roster, if you like, the children conduct many formations. These formations are traditionally designed to help foster cohesion; they help the kids improve their social skills. The formations also offer the children the chance to study the relations of other social classes within the tribe's system of grouping.

The children rarely, if ever, gathered during the daylight hours. Instead, they meet at the town center during moon-lit nights for many of their gatherings. There, at the town center, they learn and sing Conjlopo songs. They learn some adult traits, which they must perfect before petitioning the town elders for adult status. When the children gather, their formation is broken up into two main groups—one group, known as *Gblipo*, contains all the juniors, while the other group, *Dawu*, comprises the most senior of the children.

21

Gblipo includes children aged at least twelve and under, mostly males. Traditionally, the formation is intended for all males, but, at this level, it is too hard for the senior kids to properly regulate their formation. So, every ambulant child goes to the formations. Little girls, too, are found within Conjlopo's formations. But it really shouldn't matter who shows up for Gblipo anyway. It is going to be a long while before this subgroup can get a name (a pet name), which essentially signifies a promotion to adulthood. Some members in the Gblipo peer group will have to wait three or more years before reaching the age of maturity, the stage at which they can petition the town elders for their unique name. Thus, kids in this group are never really the focus during the outings of Conjlopo.

Not all Gblipo are enthusiastic participants during the gatherings. Their actual roles or contributions to the excursions depend on who you ask. One thing is clear, though: Gblipo serve as babysitters, looking after their much younger siblings who make it to the formations. Gblipo, together with their younger siblings, are arguably the noisiest whenever Conjlopo gather. Their involvement is considered a distraction for their seniors, the elder social group that is seeking an adult status. But cooperating with seniors is the last thing on Gblipo's mind. They are in this formation to hunt for the good stuff. Many Gblipo children go to Conjlopo's formation to eat. They are lured to the formations by the food the senior kids collect from their members who do not show up at formations.

Dawu is the second and most powerful of the kid groups. They are the seniors of Conjlopo. Traditionally, they make all the rules during their outings. The elder kids determine the placement of individuals within the two groups—Dawu and Gblipo. They are traditionally expected to regulate the formation, something they do not do very well.

The older children take their formations to the homes of other children, such as the ones who do not know their birthdays, and make their birth years. Many of the children, including those leading the personnel placement, do not know their own birthdays. This is so because many children were born to parents who did not track birth records for any number of reasons. The children, upon arriving at a child's place, request the child's information from available parents or their guardians. This is how they ensure the children get in the correct Conjlopo group. It is not unusual for the children to have some doubts or misgivings as they determine the ages of some of their peers.

In truth, when Conjlopo conducts group placement, it is rather perplexing or confusing. It is also quite chaotic; there is no order, it seems. To successfully place a child within a group, he is required to, at least at a minimum, know the year in which he was born. This is crucial information that Dawu must have. This is why they go from house to house to basically conduct year-of-birth investigations.

As stated earlier, not all senior family members can tell their children's ages. Some parents can only provide clues or hints to their child, such as naming a location of the family farm at the time of the child's birth. Other parents can only remember or mention an event or two that took place in or around the community at the time the child was born. And that will be all the information some children will know about the natal history—clues and hints. For example, a mother may say, "If you know the year in which we had our farm along Geeye Creek, that's the year we had you." Armed with this vague information, the child will go out to other family members and inquiries from them what year the family farm was along the creek. He continues the research until he attains the needed information from someone who knows the year.

23

Once the initial and time-consuming age determination—who's Dawu or who's Gblipo—is over, the children's formation is ready to move out. They go around the village, knocking on doors and picking up other children along their path while singing traditional Conjlopo's songs, such as these annoying lines:

Dowala'o Nagbe'o, ho Nagbe'o Blabloh'o, Nagbe'o, ho Nagbe'o

The song calls out random names: Dowala, Nagbe, and Blabloh.

Dawu members are responsible for keeping individual members in their place during their meetings. Dawu members make the rules that guide Conjlopo's outings. They force their subordinates to respect them. Dawu oversees the formation. They run the whole show. This makes sense because the pressure, traditionally, is on Dawu to assemble and form a peer group, which must soon display adult-like traits before it can get a name.

That is why the children from the two groups—Dawu and Gblipo—are not supposed to mix. Traditionally, they are not expected to assemble into one unified mass formation. Instead, the children must segregate every time they congregate. And where a child is placed in the formation is based exclusively on his age bracket. Members of Gblipo find every imaginable way to permeate Dawu's ranks. Whether intentionally or not, Gblipo seemingly works tirelessly against the team-building efforts of the older children.

And that is why, even though the children's outings are supposed to foster team unity, the personnel placement process ironically leads to routine fights, chaos, and confusion. But fights or not, members within the elder children group go to great lengths to avoid a mass formation throughout their meetings.

24

It is extremely humiliating when a member of Dawu (a kid from the older group) is placed into the ranks of Gblipo, the younger children. Although Dawu do not punish their own by throwing them into a subordinate group, it does happen to their members by mistake. New Dawu members who may be petite in form may be thrown in with Gblipo. Also, a Dawu member may find himself in a lower social class when his parents give erroneous birth information. But it is almost never done on purpose.

On the other hand, it is extremely prestigious when a Gblipo member—either accidentally or erroneously—makes it into the ranks of Dawu. To block erroneous infiltrations, the children section off their ranks using an imaginary line. Of course, a not-well-defined marker leads to a great deal of confusion that fuels cross-rank disorder, especially when a Gblipo crosses to Dawu's side. Thus, to prevent cross-rank confrontations, the elder children use a physical divide (boundary), like a stick (usually a mortar pestle or a bamboo) between the two groups of children. This actual boundary is held chest or waist high, keeping Dawu to their prestigious front while Gblipo are kept to their not-so-prestigious rear.

The kids build a campfire at the town center at the end of a formation. They dispatch a team of boys to quietly acquire some pieces of firewood from village huts. These children are not thieves; they are not stealing. They are actually preserving a long-held tradition that is known as *kpunken*, which means "to take quietly." It is a skill they will need to master before they can get adult status. It will come in handy when they get to the next level (discussed later). When caught in the act, it's often a cause for laughter. There are rules that guide this practice. The team is banned from having conversations during the mission. The boys cannot take more than two pieces of firewood from the back of one hut, and they must rotate so the same side of town is not visited repeatedly. If anyone comes

25

out of a hut due to a lack of noise discipline, the children must vacate the house.

Dawu members who do not attend formations must pay fines to their peers. The parents of absent children respect the children's tradition by paying the asking fines. The children do not levy domestic animals or money as fines. Instead, they collect food, which they eat at the end of a day's gathering. The fines include almost all local food types except the food types that require pots and other cooking utensils to prepare. They do not cook; they roast the fines over a campfire.

It is not uncommon to see an adult monitoring the children while simultaneously teaching the children some traditional Conjlopo songs. In fact, the most senior elder in the village, when ambulatory, may visit the children's get-together. The elder's visit is not a requirement, but it is one that means the world to the children because he is the only authority in the village who gives permanent pet names to peer groups. The children know that they must be on their best behavior whenever he is around them because the man's visit may be an assessment tour. He is the only man in the town who determines their readiness, the point at which they can be inducted into adulthood.

Dawu and Gblipo are not pushovers; they are rivals. Sometimes, the two groups flex their muscles for simple bragging rights. They test their strengths during the singing of the song of challenge, if you like. The singing of this song requires the groups to take sides— literally. As discussed above, they use a lightweight stick to form a divide. With Dawu on one side of the stick and Gblipo on the other, the kids pick up their barrier of choice and firmly hold it waist or chest-high. Then the song is commenced:

Dawu aa kpa nya le! (Dawu, take it forward!)

26

Chorus: zoo zoo ba yi zoo (Just sounds, no actual meaning.)
Gblipo aa kpa de le! (Gblipo, take it backward!)

Chorus: zoo zoo ba yi zoo (Just sounds, no actual meaning.)

The objective is for one group to apply an opposite force while the other charges forward or backward. It is not uncommon for some children to go home with bruised knees, elbows, or lips, especially when the peer group members in Dawu outnumber those in Gblipo at the formation. When more Dawu members flex their muscles a bit too much, it can sometimes lead to minor injuries. On the other hand, more Gblipo than Dawu only makes the strength test more challenging for Dawu. It is rare for Dawu to lose the strength test; Gblipo are the classic losers during this show of strength because they lack genuine group participation.

Sometimes, the two groups make a conscious decision to maintain civility during the song of might. This is especially a kind gesture for their much younger siblings, who stubbornly make it to formations, serving as meddlers. There is a downside to this alternative, though. Without the application of opposite forces, the kids must dramatize the lyrics. Doing what the lyrics say leads to a back-and-forth movement that nearly keeps the children in a few square meters. The kids must take a few steps forward at the sound of "Dawu, aa kpa le nya le!" Their counterparts take the same number of steps backward at the sound of "Gblipo, aa kpa de le!"

When the peer group of Dawu feels it has completed the team-building checklist after weeks of countless formations, the group alone—without Gblipo—goes to the oldest man in the village to request their peer group's name. At this point, the older kids see themselves as adults and want to graduate from Dawu to a named peer group (adulthood). But it is not how Dawu feels that matters; however, what matters most is how the oldest man feels about their readiness. It is either the oldest man's way or no way.

That was the case when my Dawu group in Chedepo Jarkaken petitioned old man Siahgbe in 1985 for our peer group's name. Naively embedded with Gblipo, we were very noisy when we arrived at his small mud hut, which, I still remember, was partially concealed by a patch of cocoa trees in Bokutoken, a borough in Chedepo Jarkaken.

Perhaps tricking us, the old man emerged from the cocoa side of his tiny, rounded hut (not built nowadays). He told us how noisy we had been, and he attributed the act to juvenile behavior. It was the last thing we wanted to hear. Nevertheless, we asked him for a name, and the old man gave us one without hesitation. "You are *Nyakinpotonmo!*"

It was one of the few names that had been repudiated from one generation to the next, and for good reason. We rejected it, too; Nyakinpo means "noisy birds." Thus, any peer group that accepts this name faces a lifetime of mockery from other peer groups. We pressed him for another name. But the elder Siahgbe wasn't convinced we were ready to be inducted into adulthood, so he gave us yet another name from the family of uncomfortable epithets: **Botuklenpotonmo**. Once again, we rejected it.

The old man cleverly inserted the term klen (a noisy device) in the name, essentially reinforcing the point made when he issued the first name. Siahgbe's unique way of saying no finally took hold, so we left.

Sapannetonmo Peer Group (Members are 1971-1973 Borns)

We returned to more team-building formations, and, a few days later, we returned to the old man again. This time, without the noisy Gblipo. The outcome was a triumphant one. The old man looked in all directions and said, "I have looked in all directions; I do not see any members of my peer group. I am the only one alive. All my friends have died out, so I want you to join me!" We knew exactly what he meant, so we agreed to be members of his **Sapannetonmo**. And, within the few months he lived following the naming ceremony, we called Siahgbe *"Baytonmo,"* Chedepo for comrade, friend, or buddy.

Obtaining a permanent name, such as Sapannetonmo, means Dawu members have reached maturity in Chedepo. They are now adults. Their former rivals, Gblipo, have now become the new Dawu, and therefore the new leaders of Conjlopo. The act of assigning Dawu members a name begins cross-generational promotion. In other words, a chain of promotions is triggered automatically at all levels within the peer system the moment a matured Dawu group receives its promotion to adulthood. Every peer group in the village gets a promotion that day; it is like a giant birthday for all the peer

29

groups. In fact, everyone—the oldest person in the village included—celebrates this birthday by simply adding one more named subordinating group to the total groups he or she outranks.

Kofa: Now that Dawu has a permanent name, this social class is no longer part of Conjlopo. It has graduated to the next and more prestigious section, which is known as Kofa. This new member joins three other social classes, each essentially representing a training phase. Members in each phase must meet all their training requirements in three years, the period during which the new Dawu gets a name.

Kofajlu (seated) are the youngest of all named social classes; Kofajesinyo (standing) are their seniors, caretakers.

But when Dawu members get their permanent name, they assume yet another temporary name in their new section. In addition to the nickname they have received from the elder, they are called **Kofajlu**, or the youngest of Kofa. Kofajlu is a status name, but the nickname they received from the elder is

30

permanent. Members of Kofajlu are typically twelve through fifteen years of age. Nyebajle ("young men") are the immediate seniors to Kofajlu. Members in this group are between sixteen and nineteen years of age. Nyomo ("blood"), twenty through twenty-three, is the next group. And the last of the groups in the Kofa section is Kofajesinyo, literally "the leaders of Kofa." Members of the Kofajesinyo range from ages twenty-four to twenty-seven.

Before doing its traditionally assigned duties—training and mentoring the new arrivals and helping some title holders on their farms—the social classes in the Kofa section must tackle some preliminaries. One of the things they do first, for example, is to elevate some personnel from the new arrivals. The tradition requires that all persons, regardless of age, must go through the initial entry process (the formations, naming, etc.). For this reason, some Kofajlu may contain older members who may be as old as those in Nyebajle, Nyomo, or even beyond. But most candidates for elevation typically fall within the Nyebajle and Nyomo groups. These two groups must look within the new arrivals for any members who may be qualified for higher placement. Those who may not have been around when their peer groups (now Nyebajle and Nyomo) were promoted may be among the new arrivals. Moreover, a recently confirmed year of birth may qualify a person for a higher placement within the peer system. Once the groups determined who must be elevated, they pulled them from the youngest social class.

The process of elevating a person from one group to another is called jeja or jah-ya, literally "climbing." There is no specific time requirement for personnel elevation, but it is best to remove the identified personnel from the ranks of Kofajlu as soon as possible. If the elevation is prolonged, the candidates will be treated like Kofajlu. This means that they will be treated in a less dignified, but culturally acceptable, manner.

31

Elevating a late arrival within Kofa is a very quick, but painful, process. The peer group leader takes the candidate and his colleagues to a remote area, away from human traffic. This occurs usually in the evening hours, but there are no time restrictions (ideal for daylight hours because of safety concerns). When done at night, it is advised to be done during a moon-lit night. The job of the peer group leader—who must be a Bocuwao family member for those in Jarkaken—is to count all members present. He must ensure that all the key families—Bocuwao, Magwulu, Dowao, Bowionpo, Ponwaon, and Kaytiao—that make up the village population are represented by at least one person. The person being elevated is not in the count. The event must be postponed when not all families are represented; the only exception is when a family originally doesn't have a member in the peer group, which may be the case for a small family like Kaytiao. However, when all available families are present, the group leader puts all personnel (but himself and the candidate) in two equal lines (roughly). Facing center, members in both lines open ranks and obtain double arm intervals between personnel. Even long before the lines are formed, each member must secure a switch. The leader makes his checks by walking in the middle and around the lines. He is making sure every member's switch is a tenmoine, a very flexible and soft plant from the palm family. This is the only switch that is culturally acceptable (and for a good reason, too).

Once every switch in line gets the leader's seal of approval, he positions the candidate at the beginning of the line. He emphasizes the rules one last time. The leader advises the one seeking promotion to speed through the lines when told. And once prompted, the candidate sprints through the lines at full speed, and the folks in line take their swings at his feet. So soft, the rope-like tenmoine naturally breaks on contact or frays, which—along with the speed of the runner—makes it quite unlikely (and reluctantly for some members) to take repeated strikes. If a person manages to strike a second time, the pain is expected to be lessened because of the fraying tendency of the tenmoine switch. But striking twice during elevation requires talent and an above-average striking speed.

Like many traditional practices, however, there are rules that govern the ceremonial elevation of latecomers. As mentioned, members must hit the person's feet only. No one is forced to take a swing, but all available members, except the leader (the overseer, the safety person), must physically line up and hold a switch. One family may have one person in line; another may have ten; it doesn't matter as long as the population of the town is represented. The candidate is automatically elevated the moment he is hit on an unauthorized bodily area, and all members must stop swinging the moment the person either falls accidentally or receives a wrong bodily strike. The leader (who is the safety officer) is empowered to initiate an investigation. When the reason for the midway stop is a wrong hit, the culprit must be identified before the gathering is over, and the person responsible for striking at the wrong bodily surface faces disciplinary actions. Racing through the switches is strictly reserved for ceremonial elevation; it is not used (or intended to be used) as a tool of punishment for the unruly members within Kofa.

After the promotions and subsequent elevations—if there had been any—are over, Kofa is fully charged to activate its duties. Again, from lowest to highest, here are the social classes that make up the Kofa Section: Kofajlu, Nyebajle, Nyomo, and Kofajesinyo. The preceding names are stage names. The social classes that are senior to the Kofa had these same names when their members were at these life stages within Kofa. The only name that is permanent is the one from the naming agent; the stage name is temporary for a social group. A social class outgrows a stage name every time Dawu gets a name.

33

The peer groups within Kofa have assigned roles. Their collective endeavor centers on training and mentoring their members, mainly the new Kofajlu, while they provide farming and other services to elders within the community who are title holders, such as the chief priest, *jegbadior,* the "chief of staff" equivalent for the town warriors, *jakwi*, a maintainer, and more.

Nyebajlo, with a container in hand, in a war dance costume

Although all Kofa members play vital roles during their activities, **Nyebajle** (plural), *the immediate seniors to Kofajlu,* seemingly get the least acknowledgment because, conventionally, they are assigned the least responsibilities. They only take care of themselves. They have no mandate to care for anyone else, besides showing up at Kofa's collective farming duties. The Nyebajle group has no specific assignments, none requiring them to cater to other members

34

within the Kofa section. They are an independent group, you can say; they do not have any defined obligations, such as those expected of the social classes above them.

This social group (Nyebajle) is not directly involved in the training of Kofajlu. In fact, for Nyebajle to participate in Gbawonwon, which is Kofa's version of wrestling, or "combatics," it often takes force for them to wrestle. Gbawonwon is a mandatory training requirement for Nyomo and Nyebajle. But the wrestling occurs only when one of the two groups—Nyebajle or Nyomo—challenges the other first. Nyebajle rarely initiates this training; in other words, they rarely challenge first.

Members of the Nyomo peer group in war dance costumes

When given the opportunity, Nyebajle will even run away from their immediate seniors (Nyomo). Frequently, Nyebajle will go to great lengths to dodge this painful but necessary endurance training. That is why the senior group (Nyomo) uses force to get them involved. Nyomo, the traditional challenger, marks an area in the road as a gate; this is a defying barrier the challenged should not cross, or risk wrestling the challenger. Any member who crosses the mark (which is called **tu** for a stick in Chedepo) has two choices. They can either counterchallenge a specific Nyomo member for a one-on-one

35

wrestling match or risk fighting any Nyomo member who gets to him first. Mind you, some members of Nyebajle do win some fights, but the older men usually win the most fights.

Anyhow, it is very rare to see anyone reminiscing about their Nyebajle days. And, considering the passive nature of a Nyebajlo's life, I am not surprised.

Besides the joint wrestling training that Nyomo is involved in as part of their role in training Nyebajle, this group (Nyomo) has two other key responsibilities. They are responsible for bringing the newest Kofa members (Kofajlu) to work. That is their primary duty. They are also charged with the responsibility of mentoring, teaching, and coaching the new members of Kofa. To accomplish these huge responsibilities or tasks, Kofa has a comrade (or Magniapo) system. In other words, subordinates are assigned to specific Nyomo members as mentors. These mentors within Nyomo must possess knowledge of Kofa's overall shared common interests and values because they are expected to enhance their subordinates (Kofajlu's) knowledge on a whole host of societal issues. They teach the new adult basic decencies and the functions of Kofa. It is the responsibility of Nyomo (and their immediate seniors, Kofajesinyo) to prepare and allow the new members of Kofa to develop and flourish within the peer system. Depending on the number of mentors available, one person may receive as many as four or more subordinates.

And once assigned, the subordinates collect their sleeping mats, blankets, and pillowcases and report to their mentors' huts, where they will sleep until the activities of Kofa are over. This may be a week, two weeks, or up to a month. Some may continue to the sleepover well after the activities of Kofa. The sleepovers give mentors and subordinates sufficient time to know each other; sleepovers also eliminate the need to go from hut to hut in the early morning hours, searching for Kofajlu

36

before farming work. Kofa's wake-up call comes from Jelatoh, a thirty-five-foot "talking drum" also known as Kofa Toku. The person who strikes this massive drum to wake up Kofa members gets his cue from the first sound of a rooster crowing.

It is almost impossible to talk about **Kofajesinyo** without talking about Kofajlu. The two are inseparable. Individual members within the Kofajesinyo social class have assigned nicknames, which are carefully picked words or word phrases. Many of the nicknames are local favorites, classics that are allotted to certain families. They are the first to be assigned to members, usually those on the ground (as opposed to those who may be in faraway communities or even abroad). When the classics run out, however, those without nicknames are justified in coining theirs. The names are usually tasteful and family-friendly. Every now and then, however, some coined names crossed the satire line and well into the dirty or foul category.

Kofajlu are the singers for Kofajesinyo. These young men begin their singing from sunrise to sunset, and they never seem to run out of songs. And why should they? Kofajlu converts the pet names of each senior of Kofa into clown-like songs. As stated above, every member of Kofajesinyo has a nickname, and the younger ones—coached by their seniors—turned each name into a song. So, they have a lot of songs to sing. The songs are as many as the number of personalities within the senior group. Sometimes, that amounts to hundreds or more songs for the juniors of Kofa to sing and dance. In fact, more songs are made up for senior Kofa personnel who may be in faraway locations, such as Monrovia (the national capital) or even overseas. This is what makes the Kofa season a fun time for villagers.

The season of Kofa brings farmland dwellers to town. Their activities, particularly the singing and dancing of the clown-like songs, attract men, women, and children to the town center. The dancing men are barely recognizable because they use white clay to paint their bodies from their heads to their toes. Each member wears a costume, which is known in Chedepo as a "chentiaye," a cloth wraparound that covers an individual from their waist to slightly below their knees. There are no drums during the singing and dancing, not even handclaps. The only instruments that help the juniors and their seniors are "kitaykwin" ("kitaykun," singular), hard leather bags stuffed with noisy junk. The synchronized sounds or rhythms from the rocking of the junky bags help the young ones and their seniors stay on beat.

Some key responsibilities of the seniors of Kofa are training and caring for all Kofa members, especially the Kofajlu. Generally speaking, the seniors of Kofa do this (caring) very well. The seniors—Kofajesinyo—go around the village shouting their signature word, "Sanuo!" ("palm butter"), perhaps their way of assuring villagers that the youngsters of Kofa entrusted to their care are, in fact, in good hands, nourishment-wise.

There is always plenty of rice and palm butter—a specialty of the Grebo tribe—to eat during Kofa's farming season, which precedes the formal induction of a new peer group. While eating, "I am tired, or full" is a forbidden phrase. The young men are not permitted to leave any food uneaten; that amounts to "spoiling" the title holders' food. If a Kofaju (singular) says, "I am tired" or "I am full," he receives a seemingly punishing handful of rice in his mouth. This doesn't mean the seniors of Kofa are heartless. They really do care about the children.

They usually pick one member from Kofajlu, usually the most disciplined kid, and give him the title of "Kofaa Jleyee," literally "the favorite of Kofa." His peers think he is a very lucky man, and they are probably right. Just like the seniors, Kofaa Jleyee carries a clown bag or kitaykun. He doesn't have one for himself. In other words, there is no bag made for him. Instead, he carries a bag for one of the senior members. Kofaa Jleyee also escapes a great deal of the humiliating acts that other members of Kofajlu typically endure. He is the first to eat; in fact, he eats with the seniors. After eating, he watches the rest of Kofajlu (his peers) as they eat in a continuous line around a giant pan, each scooping a handful and traveling in circular motion. He makes sure all members are eating and no one is throwing out food as they circle around the large pan of rice.

Gbor: When Kofajesinyo completes a three-year term, they graduate to the Gbor stage. They become *Gborjlu,* the first stage of the council of elders in the community, and arguably the most prestigious stage of all the peer groups.

The promotion from Kofajesinyo to Gborjlu is indeed the most dramatic of all. Every three years, potential elders from far and near converge in Chedepo towns to be inducted. The level of celebration is apt at this stage because the group will never have another ceremonial promotion going forward. Essentially, they will be reduced to quiet promotions in the future, which is why their subordinates are dancing a war dance; all groups beyond Gbor will sit, watch, and count the number of Gbor groups they have outranked.

The newest Gbor must be sponsored into the elder's council. Above, the couple who sponsored

The newest Gbor are celebrated—walked on a line of clothes ("lapas") and bathed in powder.

40

In preparation for the celebration, the newest members of the community elders use charcoal to paint their bodies, unlike their subordinates (Kofa), who use white clay (or powder—ha-ha—nowadays). Moreover, some Western influences are clearly visible in their dance. Nowadays, for example, not many dancers are seen with the traditional *"dabli"* costume—made from palm branches—that was once used for the war dance.

Instead, the dancers cleverly wrapped around their waists some flamboyant clothing.

("lapas") as a makeshift dabli. They are called *"Gbordale,"* for Gbor's clothing.

The youngest elders are the town's warriors. They are the soldiers, if you like, for the community. In fact, they are headed by a title holder called "jegbadior," the traditional chief of staff for the town's young forces. And yes, the men are armed during their induction ceremony. They carry traditional shotguns, loaded with BB cartridges, which they fire intermittently in midair. Other men—those without rifles—carry spears, machetes, or small tree branches, which they ceremonially toss up and catch in midair.

They make sounds of the battle; they yell intimidating war cries. The dance is orderly because people are told and do adhere to where they can fall in line.

Like Kofa, which comprises peer groups and different stages, Gbor includes many peer groups. "The first four peer groups on the elders' council—from the youngest peer group on the council up to the fourth peer group- are called *dinyomopo* ["blood eaters"]," according to old man Gbeh Chea Nyanley in Chedepo Jarkaken. These four groups of elders are the ones who eat the goats that the town receives as fines whenever a family crosses their corpse [their dead family member] over the town's perimeter lines, a serious violation in the village.

The ten peer groups above the "blood eaters" peer group, five through peer group fifteen, are "tested, seasoned, and experienced leaders." These ten peer groups, according to the old man, are known collectively as "Bolibo," literally "elders." Being a member in this category –the experienced elders— truly makes you an elder in the community.

Within the above group are more subdivisions, to be exact, two: *"u teba chimae bo"* and *"upa bablo bo."* From the tenth peer group to the most senior peer group is the board of elders, if you like. If you make it to this level, you are believed to have "entered the hall of famers"—*u pa bablo bo*—for the town's elders. Decisions of extreme importance to the town or even the region are made in the presence of these peer groups. The ninth peer group, whose members are knocking on the door of the hall of fame, marks yet another prestigious stage in the world of Chedepo elders. They are identified with this phrase: *u teba*

chimae bo, which loosely means "they are next in line to become hall of famers." There is still another category of elders. Elders within peer groups sixteen and up are called ***"dle korti blo."*** They are said to be draggers of walking sticks; in fact, the phrase loosely means "cane draggers." When a town crier wants to assemble all the elders at the town centers without any exceptions, he says, 'Everyone is summoned to the town center, even the cane draggers are not exempted."

Chapter III:
The Memorable Visitation

L to R: Winn Saylee (with cup), Gbayi Puwai, and Wleh Snoteh

Wleh Snoteh paid an early morning visit to his father, Winn Saylee. In truth, the old man was Wleh Snoteh's great uncle. And Snoteh visited him along with Gbayi Puwai, one of the sons of old man Gbayi Wliya. Their visit coincided with the presence of some of the old man's own children: Tinpan, Woday, Saylee Junior, and Sayjolo. The old man's wife, Kanbo Snoh, was at home during the stopover. Her brother, Kanbo Wiah, had arrived earlier and had been paying his own visit before the arrival of Snoteh, Puwai, and the other family members. They had a rather fascinating dialogue.

Snoteh is a comedian; he joins other siblings as natural comedians. Being funny does run in their entire family. Old man Wleh, their father, was a renowned comedian. In fact,

44

Wleh named his tiny farming outpost "Chianyeken," which means "an area of laughter." So, it's no surprise that the conversation captured below, dominated by Snoteh, the man from Chianyeken, is chock-full of humor.

"I will begin this conversation with a self-introduction. I am Snoteh, your speaker. And this morning, I am here to visit my father, old man Saylee. I also have with me, you, the young people. I will speak to you about what I know. And my message, as I said earlier, is for you, the young people. I am addressing my comments to all our young people, especially those who are overseas, because they do not understand our culture as well as we do in Jarkaken."

"Are you the only person visiting him?" Puwai asked.

"No. I will introduce all of you. I am going to tell our sons and daughters who are in America some of the things they do not know about our culture. I will speak to you about the little that I know. So, I am asking you to listen to me.

The man sitting next to me is Gbayi Puwai. His peer group is Tienpotonmo; our old man—the one we are visiting—his peer group is Sorpotonmo. Jacob, Wiah (who is sitting over there)—is a member of the Tienpotonmo peer group. Wiah and Puwai are members of the same peer group. They outranked thirteen peer groups, and each of the thirteen that they have outranked is are member of Gbor, the elders' council. Our old man outranked sixteen peer groups on the elder council.

The peer groups are many, but I will do my best and name the ones I know. I will name each peer group and call the names of its members. These will be people I saw with my own eyes. So, I will begin with the oldest peer group whose members I saw when I was a child, and continue to the youngest members of the elders' council today.

45

The oldest peer group whose members I saw with my own eyes was Wulopotonmo.

Our father, Teh, the father of Young and Wiah Teatay, was the only one I knew as a member of this peer group. I was a very young child when he died, but I was alert enough to know him and his peer group.

Next to this peer group was Sapannetonmo. I saw three members of this group. I saw Tabla Darkpe, whom Isaac Doe said deserved a slap in his ear. [The family laughed.] I saw Siahgbe, who was a member of the Dowao mega family, and I saw Quayee Swen, a member of our Bocuwao family. He was the father of David Karwolo Swen.

Next to Sapannetonmo are the members of the Jelepotonmo peer group. I saw two members: I saw Karpeh Dweh, and I saw Teaty Chea, the father of Chea Jarbo (John Chea).

The next peer group is Saypaytonmo. I saw many elders who belong to this peer group. I saw our father, Polee Winn; I saw Tylor Choloplay; I saw Maghtoh; I saw Wolo Nyenpan—that's four. They are the ones I remember now. Knorr Belleh, another elder, I am really not sure what peer group he belonged to; I think he was a member of Saypaytonmo."

"Knorr Belleh was a member of the Jelepotonmo peer group," Saylee said.

"Okay," Snoteh said. "Thank you. He said he was a member of Jelepotonmo. So, next to Saypaytonmo are the members of Duwontonmo. I saw old man Gbegbe—Tila Gbegbe, and I saw Finanyonoh Butty. Those are the two I remember in that peer group. They are followed by the Tarwontonmo peer group. I saw old man Tuwaju, and I also saw old man Wakar Jowa. There were many, but they are the two I remember now. The next peer group is Wamegntonmo. I saw old man Porto

Chefinne. My own grandmother, old lady Maghnor, was a member of this group (Wamegntonmo). Amos Jerbo—Choloplay, who used to live in Firestone, was a member of this group, too. And those are the folks I remember in the Wamegntonmo peer group.

Next to Wamegntonmo peer is Jelakpele'otonmo. Our father, Wedlyn Chea, was a

member of this group. Finanyonoh Jarbo was a member. Teaty Tibelay was a member. Also, one old man used to live in the hamlet of Chelateahken ... Beweh, he was a member of the Jelakpele'otonmo peer group. They are the elders I remember in that group.

Gbetekle'otonmo is the next peer group. Old Man Winkar was a member. I remember him very well because he was a messenger of the court. He was a member of the local government.

He traveled everywhere. Our son, Dormini Toe, was a member of this group. *[According to Gbeh Chea Nyanley, one of our forefathers, 'Tehfueh, and his wife, Jaytowel—a lady from the Ponwaon mega family—had a son, named Nyenaon or Jaytowel Nyenaon. Teh and Jaytowel also had Teh Gbeyee (Nyenaon's sister). It was this woman who married into the family of Teatypo. One of her children was our own son, Domini Toe [the father of Inspector, who his peers used to call 'Sepehtoh']. Teh Gbeyee also had Gbeyee Jarbo, the father of James Juty Jarbo and Alfred Klay Williams, [a onetime teacher at B. Nyemah Quayee Elementary, Jarkaken].'* The man who was in Geeken; he just passed away recently ... I just can't remember his name..."

"Billy Goat," Old Man Saylee said.

"Yes! Billy Goat and Kayee Swen were members of Gbetekle'otonmo," Snoteh said. "Today, this peer group (Gbetekle'otonmo) should have been the most senior on the elders' council in the entire land of Chedepo, but the group does not have a male member alive today. Old lady Paytee, the wife of Worjolo—a Ponwaon family man—is a member of this peer group. She is a native of Chedepo Geeken. Worjolo brought her to this town: Jarkaken. She is the mother of Karwea and Gbala. She is a member of Gbetekle'otonmo. She outranks twenty-three groups on the elders' council. It has never happened before, never. But she is a woman, so she has no name. She is not the oldest; the oldest must be a male.

Thus, Kayhepotonmo, which is the peer group next to Gbetekle'otonmo, is the most senior peer group in Chedepo. They outranked twenty-one groups on the elders' council. Old man Togbehjela in the town of Chedepo Putuken, also known as Malbert Jelee, a onetime pastor, is a member of this group (Kayhepotonmo). He outranks twenty-one groups on the elders' council, and he is the oldest in Chedepo today.

"So, if you calculate her age, she could be 100-plus years old," Tinpan said about old lady Paytee, the wife of Worjolo, who was old enough to be the oldest but wasn't because she was a female.

"Yes," Snoteh said. "Kunnehpotonmo is the next peer group. Nyantoh and

Choloplay is a member. They outranked twenty groups of elders.

Gbeyepotonmo is the next peer group. Sayonkon in Klaboken—listen to me. *[Sound of a woman's cry heard in the background briefly distracts some members in the audience, but the conversation continued. At one point, a woman is seen rolling left and right on the hard ground, but the men continued*

48

their chatting.] And in Geeken, there is an old man, Ditoh. These are the two men I remember in this peer group. They outranked nineteen groups of elders.

Flehpotonmo, in Jarkaken, are the most senior of the elders here. *[Wiah Toe is a member.]* They outranked eighteen groups of elders.

Petonmo is the next peer group. *[Sayee Teahfore is a member.]* They outranked seventeen groups of elders. These are our oldest living people.

Our father, who is sitting here with us [Winn Saylee], is next to Petonmo. His Sorpotonmo peer group outranked sixteen groups of elders. This is the same stage in life where his own father, old man Winn, was when he died [in 1974].

Pau'upotonmo is next. Albert Dweh and Samuel Doe are members of this group.

They outranked fifteen groups of elders.

Nonmonpotonmo is the next peer group. Augustine Noring and Barleh Gbeh (William Cholopray) are members. They outranked fourteen groups of elders.

Tienpotonmo is the next peer group. Puwai, Wliya's son, is a member. Lawrence

Winn is a member. They outranked thirteen groups of elders.

Debepotonmo is the next peer group. They outranked twelve groups of elders.

Newontonmo is the next peer group. Nyanley and Tolu are members of this peer group. They outranked eleven groups of elders.

Jelapotonmo is the next peer group. Bokuwo, Doteah, and Tuor Wesseh (who is in America) are members of this peer group. They outranked ten groups of elders. We say, "Upa ba blobo," and that means they are the youngest of the most senior of elders in the community. They have joined the ranks of the most senior elders in town. When you get to this stage in this land, you are old—you are the true definition of the word "old." Human beings do not grow horns. Basically, at this stage, your casket is in front of you, and you, in a way, are kicking it as you go about your daily duties. At this stage, you begin kicking your casket (as if you were kicking a ball) all the way to your soon-to-be final resting place. *[Family laughed.]* Upa ba blobo. Upa ba blobo. It sounds great. It is a great feeling to say you have entered the most senior elders' groups. But what comes after that? What lies beyond this stage? Looming death.

Snoteh, your speaker, has outranked nine peer groups. I am not a child. I am a member of the Paytetonmo peer group. At this stage, our people say, "A teba chemaebo." That means we are next in line to enter the most senior elders' stage (Bablo bo).

Next to us are the members of Sayportonmo. They outranked eight groups of elders.

Next to Sayportonmo are the members of Jleportonmo; they outranked seven groups of elders.

Next are the members of Nomurpotonmo; they outranked six groups of elders.

Sayjolo and Kpadeh's peer group, Wulopotonmo, is next. They outranked five groups of elders.

50

Next are the members of Sapannetonmo. [Komoh, Saybeh, Wliya, Kargbe Dweh, all these people are Sapannetonmo members. They outranked four groups of elders.

Then the peer group that follows is Duwontonmo.

"No. Jelepotonmo," Tinpan made a correction.

"Jelepotonmo. Tinpan is helping me now; that should tell you how old I am getting.

[Family laughed.] So, this group, Jelepotonmo, outranked three groups of elders. Who is next in line to Jelepotonmo?"

"Saypaytonmo."

"This is the peer group that has just joined the elders group; they outranked no one."

"No," Tinpan said, "they are not the group that has just joined the elders' ranks. Duwontonmo is the group that is next. Its members outranked one. The members of Tarwontonmo peer group are those who have just joined the elders' ranks; they outrank no one. They are the Gbor jlu, the youngest of Gbor, the town's council of elders."

"And next to the juniors of Gbor (youngest of the elders) are Kofajesinyo; below this group are Kofa'a Nyomon, then Kofa'a Nyebajle, and finally the newest of the Kofa section: Kofa Jlu. That is how our system of peers is structured. So, I will start from the top to the bottom—again:

- Wulopotono

- Sapannetono

- Jelepotonmo

51

- Saypaytonmo
- Duwontonmo
- Tarwontonmo
- Wamegntono
- Jelakpele'otmo
- Gbetekle'otonmo
- Kayhepotonmo
- Kunnehpotonmo
- Gbeyepotonmo
- Flehpotonmo
- Petonmo
- Sorpotonmo
- Pau'upotonmo
- Nonmonpotonmo
- Tienpotonmo
- Debepotonmo
- Newontonmo
- Jelapotonmo
- Paytetonmo
- Sayportonmo

- Jleportonmo

- Nomurpotonmo

- Wulopotonmo

- Sapannetonmo

- Jelepotonmo

- Saypaytonmo

- Duwontonmo

- Tarwontonmo

Tarwontonmo, this was old man Tuwaju's peer group that has come back into service. The old man we are here to visit knows a lot. He is old and frail. We visit him every now and then. If you have doubts about any of these topics we have been discussing, he will clarify them for you. We will get all the wisdom he has before he leaves us. [Family laughed.]"

"Old man Winn's death—please speak about that," Tinpan said.

"Concerning our father, Winn—I will explain the little I know. Our great father was Kargee Choloplay. In fact, all of us here should have Choloplay as our last name. Choloplay's wife was Swen Chie; she was a Killepo woman from the town of Kanweaken. She had Saylee. She had Sloboh. Saylee had Winn. Sloboh had Chea and Wleh. Winn had Saylee again. Chea and Wleh had us [Christian/Cynthia Chea family]. So, the old man we are visiting, Saylee, is the father now for all of us today [2009].

Chea has a son called Wesseh, who is older than old man Saylee, even though they are members of the same peer group.

53

But Wesseh, despite his long life, is not a chatty person. He doesn't know much about our history, about our people, about our culture; he cannot explain the way of life of our people to anyone. It doesn't mean that we do not visit him, but there is nothing he can explain to anyone.

Old man Winn, before his death (in 1974), I was a young boy. It happened in Puwaiken, where they took him when his health was failing. The day he died, we, the children, did as we had always done—played around him, checked on him, fetched things for him, and cared for him. What I remember most about him was his mustache. We call the type he wore tarchey. It was very long. He used to braid his mustache. He had two braids: one from the middle of his upper lip to the right side (or corner) of his mouth; the other went to the left side (or corner) of his mouth. That's how he did it; there were no razor blades in this area back then, so that was his personal solution. And you with this sususecum or magiki (camera) ... when you leave from here, tell the ones overseas, too.

Our father Winn, back then, if you had shown this camera to his face, attempting to steal his image, it would not have worked. And I will not tell you the reason; I will only tell you the day you get to this stage of my life. [Family laughed.]

The day the old man died—and I still remember this as if it had happened yesterday—he asked our mother Elizabeth (Snoh) for a piece of kola nut to eat. In a way, he knew when he was going to die. He wanted to die at the time of harvest. He was a jakwi, a traditional role. A lot of cooking is required whenever a jakwi dies, so he wanted the family to have food before his death. The family knew that, too. So, during the harvest of that year (1974), they built huge tents in the fields and stored the crops there. They only brought to town what the family needed for day-to-day consumption. This lasted for a long time. The thing is, the old man knew the time of harvest.

54

He was a seasoned farmer, so he knew that it was the time of harvest, even without seeing fresh produce being brought to town. One day, he asked Kpadeh and Sayjolo—they were little kids then, and they couldn't keep their chatty mouths shut [family laughed]—whether our parents were harvesting rice. They told the old man, 'Yes, our parents are harvesting now; we are eating fresh rice from the fields.'

After the conversation with the kids, the old man picked up his cane and walked to the section of our Dilamo reservation, where the family farms were located that year. The reason he knew the location so well is simple. He knew the area before all of us here were born. In fact, when I was a teenager, he used to take the main Dilamo road, pivot toward Chenwniken (toward Bowionpo's farming reservation), and pass by the foothill we call Murmagtogbe. That was the lane along which he set his gbeleyi (traps). There was no road between Weltehken and Murmagtogbe that the old man did not know. So, when he went out there with his cane that day, he saw the fields. Of course, it was the time of harvest. He saw the piles of rice our parents had stacked up in tents, and he must have said, 'Oh, so these children do not want me to die; therefore, they are hiding their harvest from me!'

It was the day after his visit to the fields that he asked Elizabeth for the kola nut.

When he received it, he took a bite of it and chewed it briefly. He did not even swallow the kola and passed away in his chair. I witnessed these things myself; these are not hearsay. I was young, of course, but I was the curious, alert type. I was totally aware of my surroundings when all these things took place. I saw them with my own eyes; I heard them with my own ears.

Many of the adults in the village left for the main town (Jarkaken) that day to help old man Wedlyn Chea, who, at the time, was building a new home. The old man stayed back with us in Puwaiken, our main farming outpost. So, it was us— mostly children— who were around him when he died. We weren't quite sure what death was back then. We did not know he was dead, in fact. We thought he was asleep. We thought he would wake up and interact with us again, as he used to do— sending us around to fetch things for him. We learned shortly thereafter that we had been looking at a corpse. Little did we know that that was it; he was dead. And so, that is what I know about old man Winn's death.

And Sayjolo—who is over there (now outranking five peer groups on the community's elders' council)—he and Kpadeh were born almost a week apart. *He misspoke. The two have twenty days between them. Kpadeh is January 1st, and his brother, Sayjolo, is January 21.* Ethel had Kpadeh, and Elizabeth had Sayjolo shortly thereafter, as I said, within a week. This was the period of Dr. Wiah Tai. Elizabeth laid Sayjolo here, and Ethel laid Kpadeh there. And they said, "Get Dr. Tai here to circumcise these kids." [Family laughed.]"

"Ah! Snoteh," Old lady Snoh said, "We were listening as you explained the family's past events, but now you are talking nonsense. [Family laughed.]"

"Sayjolo and Kpadeh," Snoteh continued—laughing, "who the young women in this town are chasing after today, back then, their privates looked like ground peas. [Family laughed.] But on a serious note," he regained his sanity, "that is what I know. If there is something left, someone else can explain it to you. I want you to know, however, that I do represent continuity for this family. When all these elders die out, I will be here to continue where they have left off. If any of you need to clarify a doubt you may have on any issue (whether it is about our people or our culture), do not hesitate to ask me. I will be very glad to help you. With that said, maybe the man sitting

56

next to me, Puwai, a member of the Tienpotonmo peer group (and our older brother), has something to say.

Even though I did not start this conversation with a chant of bati, I am ending it with one: El bati'o!"

"Bati!" his main audience said.

"You said 'maybe'", Puwai said, "I have something to say. Yes, I have something to say, but I have some limitations. First, special thanks to our father, the old man we are visiting today. And thanks to you, our little brothers and sisters, who have joined us on this visit. Our people used to send their children to schools of various types—they still do. These are special schools. Some children go to school to learn how to obtain palm wine. On the farms, others learn how to use an ax and cut down giant forest trees; they build elevated platforms or scaffoldings around these enormous trees for support and cut them down. These are just a few examples of the schools I am talking about. For me I do not know what you know, especially when it comes to our traditional system of grouping.

What I know is the forest ..." "Hunting," Snoteh added

"Hunter," Tinpan said, almost simultaneously with Snoteh.

"I went to school for hunting," Puwai said. "I am a practicing hunter. I remember my father used to sit us down after farmwork and tell us some of these things. In the evening, before bedtime, he told us stories. While you were naming the peer groups, I was counting quietly. I think you named thirty or twenty-nine groups. The stories you told us must be archived for us and later generations. As for me, since I joined the peer system, I know only one peer group: Tienpotonmo, my peer group. [Family laughed.] And so, that is where I will leave it. Thank you for what you have explained, and thanks to all of you who are gathered here with us."

"Your father, Wliya," Snoteh said, "the last moment I remember about him was during a period in our past when he was called upon for conflict resolution. In the village of Mubleken—actually, it was in the village of Weltehken, one of the largest settlements our people built on this reservation. When it fell, old man Knoh Toe was one of the last men to leave Weltehken.

Old man Neneh left Jarkaken one day (heading for Wotuken) and made a quick rest stop at Knoh Toe's house in Weltehken. Knoh Toe brought a kola for him, and the two men sat and chatted briefly before Neneh noticed that some branches of Toe's cocoa trees were nearly touching his wife Jallah's house. So, Neneh said, "Ah, Toe, maybe in the future our children will like to come back to these ruins and rebuild this historic settlement. Why are you planting cocoa trees here?" The conversation between the two men got heated, and they engaged in a fistfight. Neneh said Toe beat him, so when he got to Puwaiken, which is along the road to Wotuken, he made another rest stop. He reported to old man Wedlyn Chea. That time, this old man—Josiah—was still in Puwaiken.

Neneh complained to all of them about the fight at Weltehken. They told Neneh, "We will take the case to Wotuken, to Wliya, our father." That was the first of the many times I had seen them gathered to investigate cases among themselves. I have seen all these things; none of these youngsters can speak to these things. When they transferred the case to Wotuken, we, the teenagers, followed our parents there.

They investigated the two. Knoh Toe, they said, was wrong, and Neneh was right. Judgment for Neneh. They apologized to Neneh for Knoh Toe's behavior. And that is the one experience I had with your father, Wliya.

58

Our people respected one another. For example, they referred to old man Wliya as "our father." Yes, he was our father. However, while it is true old man Wliya was a member of a peer group that outranked old man Winn's peer group, in real life, old man Winn was older."

"Yes, he used to say that a lot," Puwai acknowledged.

"He was a member of Jelepotonmo," Snoteh said, "and old man Winn was a

member of Saypaytonmo.

"Really! Old man Winn was older?" old lady Snoh asked, surprisingly.

"Yes," old man Saylee joined the conversation. "Their situation is like that of Swen Martin today. They elevated Wliya to the Jelepotonmo peer group so the family of Bocuwao could have a member during their enlistment into the peer system. He was older because his peer group was older than Winn's peer group, but in real life, Winn was older than old man Wliya."

"The point is," Snoteh continued, "our people used to respect one another. They used to care for one another. We need to do the same; our family members overseas need to do the same. Respect one another. Wherever the other relatives are, we need to take time and visit them. I know our relatives overseas live too far apart from one another, but they still need to do these things. They need to do what our people used to do. Even though they were living in faraway communities such as Gbetohken, Puwaiken, Weltehken, or Wotuken, they still found time and visit one another. Our distance from others must not be the reason we do not see one another. They need to take time to gather and socialize. Caring for one another leads to stronger family ties; this is how family is enhanced.

Whenever we have questions, issues, or concerns, we come to this old man. We seek clarification from him. And this morning is no different. We have come to him to clear up some concerns for us. In this land, when our young people are joining the system of peers, starting with the section of Kofa, our people say a member of the Bocuwao family must be the first and last to enter. And that is the standard—first in, last in. This is something we want the old man to speak to. Tomorrow (December 30, 2009) is a big day; our children will join the peer system; we, the family of Bocuwao, will be first and last.

"Wleh Snoteh," old man Saylee said—smiling, "thank you. We live in this world by generations. One generation comes, lives out its turn, and dies. Another one comes and takes its place. One generation passes on a message to the other in the form of storytelling. And that is how people know who they are among others. All the mega families that occupy this land have roles to play in this land. Each family has important responsibilities. Our family has a vital role because this land itself belongs to us, the Bocuwao family. The people of Chedepo, a long time ago, presented it to us as a gift. They literally took soil from this land, placed it in a small clay pot, and presented it to the family of Bocuwao. It was passed on from one generation to another. Koon Gbalee is the reason you will not see the soil pot.

She was a bad-mannered woman in our family. Because of her stupidity and ineptness, we do not have the soil pot to show this and future generations of Bocuwao. She broke the clay pot that contained the soil. As I said, the clay pot survived many generations of Bocuwao until recently, when Gbalee ruined it. From time to time, we hung it up on the ceiling of our family's most senior person. We are keepers of this land, the symbolic sponsors of the country devil (the role of jakwi). So, these are the reasons we are the first to enter. We are known as *nyansunupo* (trailblazers, forerunners, pioneers). We are

60

leaders in this land. If the people desire peace—if they want this land to settle down— they look to us to make that happen.

And we do that by conducting a traditional ritual we call waisaya (petitioning) at *Deorblemgehn*, a location along the historic Dilamo road. We are the people who petition nature and our gods to restore harmony to this land. So, these are some of the reasons we are the first and last to enter."

"How do we own this land, old man?" Puwai asked. "Why did the people of Chedepo give this land to us as a gift? That is an enormous award. We appreciate it because it gives us power and prestige. It is a source of strength, just knowing that the entire land of Chedepo is a present to us from the people who dwell on it."

"Uh, pointing to the camera, you are recording this for all to see and hear, right? This land, as I said, is ours. We own it. It was Chedepo's gift to us. Why? The people of Chedepo fled this land a long time ago; our people abandoned the entire Chedepo land and escaped to the land of Jadeapo. But one person from our family stayed back. The Jadeapo man they ran to was ..."

"Why did they run?" Tinpan asked.

"War. The people ran because of war, which never happened. They ran because of rumors of war. Our people, long ago, fell victim to false claims that cannibalistic elements from the Krahn tribe were coming to Chedepo to beat, kill, and eat people.

Kloklo Wion, a Nyenawleken man from Putuken, stayed back, too. Wion had a palm wine tree; he gave people palm wine as they were running. He did not run. A Ponwaon family man and a member of our Bocuwao family stayed back; they were here with Kloklo Wion. And while they were in Jadeapo, there was a conflict between them and their host. It started on

61

the farm. The people of Jadeapo demanded Chedepo people go to the top of a hill; they told the Chedepo among them to cut the forest undergrowth going downhill. And Jadeapo would go upward so the two could meet in the middle."

"It has never happened before," Snoteh added.

"No," the old man agreed. "That is not the standard in this place. No one cuts vegetation facing downhill. But that was what Jadeapo wanted Chedepo to do. They knew what they were asking Chedepo to do was wrong, but they wanted the people of Chedepo to lose their dignity and self-esteem. The two people had a serious conflict over this issue, and it was the basis for Chedepo's subsequent return to their homeland, which they had fled due to speculations of war. The people who stayed back were concerned about the maltreatment of their fellow Chedepo people in the land of Jadeapo. They did something of a voodoo nature that lured the people of Chedepo back home.

When they prepared the voodoo, the Bocuwao man and the Ponwaon walked the perimeter line between the two peoples until they got to Kloklo Wion's palm wine tree. They put their voodoo around the tree, and every time a Chedepo person on the Jadeapo side tasted the palm wine, they remembered home. Moreover, they prepared juicy palm fruits, laden with voodoo, and took them across the perimeter. Every time a Chedepo person took a palm fruit from the container, they said something like, "Ah, this palm fruit from home is great; I am going home." That was how the first wave of Chedepo people came back home. They went there for fear of war and cannibalism, but a simple voodoo trick— from a Ponwaon man and a Bocuwao man—brought them back home. They did not just come back to Kaytoken (Geeken and Jarkaken area); they came back to Chedepo, period."

"So, when they came home, they meant the two men. Why did they give the land to the family of Bocuwao?" Tinpan asked.

"It was the Bocuwao man who took the voodoo-laden palm fruits to Jadeapo and

lured the people back home."

"So, in a way, the family of Bocuwao traveled to the land of Jadeapo and called their fellow Chedepo people back home."

"Yes. We brought them home."

"What did the Ponwaon man and his family get?"

"They put them in the high priest's hut! They get the high priest role in this land. That is a powerful role in this land, and it belongs to the family of Ponwaon for their service to the people of Chedepo."

"Thank you," Puwai attempted to join the Tinpan-Saylee exchanges. "Old man. I want to understand something else..."

"But Ponwaon alone does not have the high priest role. The family of Bowionpo has that role, too." Tinpan said.

"Yes. And it is not every member of Bowionpo that can be a high priest. The presence of this thing—a video camera— makes explaining these things a bit challenging because some of these things are sensitive in nature. Anyway, Ponwaon originally was the only family that had the high priest role, and it was only in Nyenawleken. Before the high priesthood could get to the land of Kaytoken, the people had to make a painful sacrifice to their gods in the form of human blood. A man from the Chenchipo section of the mega family of Bowionpo made that painful sacrifice to the gods of the land of Kaytoken. It was then that the high priesthood was brought to Kaytoken.

A courageous man from Chenchipo—oh, my people [the old man pointed to the camera reluctantly]. [Family laughed.] Wiah, who was just sitting here a moment ago, is a member of the Chenchipo branch of Bowionpo. A man from this branch of Bowionpo sacrificed his own child a long, long time ago so that the high priesthood could come to the land of Kaytoken. So, that is why our people gave it to Bowionpo, and only a Chenchipo man can be a high priest in that family."

"Recently," Snoteh entered into discourse, "Dokpeh Toe, the jegbadior [chief of staff of the town warriors], ran from this land. Before the induction of the new borjlou (warriors), the town needed a replacement. They said a jegbadior had to be present before the ceremony could happen. I heard a voice or two saying, "If the family of Dowao does not have a replacement for Dokpeh Toe, we can put a Kaytiao person in his place." So, whose role is it—Dowao and Kaytiao? Do they share it?"

"That role belongs to both families," the old man (Saylee) said. "That brings me back to what I said earlier, my reluctance over the presence of a recording device. We have two types of jegbadior in this land; they are strictly along family lines. The families of Bocuwao, Magwulu, Dowao, and Bowionpo are known collectively as Munnor. The families of Kaytiao and Ponwaon are not part of the Munnor. Those two families— Kaytiao and Ponwaon—are collectively called Ponwaon Daisu.

The families that constitute Ponwaon Daisu have their own jegbadior; the families that constitute Munnor also have their own jegbadior. But there can be only one jegbadior at a time, either from the Munnor section or the Ponwaon Daisu section. Historically, the Ponwaon Daisu are the last to get to this land. We decided not to treat them like outsiders anymore, so we gave them the jegbadior role. The high priest in this land has a hut, which we built.

Around it is a fence we call sakpa. Kaytiao people are not allowed in it; that is the only discrimination against the family of Kaytiao that I know in this town. We gave them independence to be just like us, except that they are not allowed in the high priest's fence."

"We have Bocuwao people in Tienpo, and we have Bocuwao in the land of Chedepo. How did that happen? In other words, how are we related to people that far away?" Puwai asked the old man a question.

"There are Bocuwao people in Tienpo; that is true. They are Bocuwao, but we call them Bilaye. There are not a lot of people. But in terms of origin, the Bocuwao in Chedepo originally came from Tienpo. [Family laughed.] We were Bilaye before we were Bocuwao. Our relationship is strong. They come here when we have a death in the family or for social events. We do the same. We are more than just sisters and brothers."

"The relationship is strong," Puwai added. "Even in Monrovia, where I live, whenever we have something going on, like a tragedy or a social event, we see them among us. Tarley Toe is a Bilaye family member in Monrovia. He and his family join us to do many things, like fundraisers and cookouts."

"Bilaye may be a small family, but they are not pushovers. They are very influential in Tienpo. When they say something will happen to someone, you better believe it will happen. They joke about receiving portions in Tienpo "that are so small for Bocuwao, and even smaller for Bilaye."

"I always thought some Bocuwao people left Chedepo and traveled to Tienpo to settle."

"No. We left Tienpo and came to Chedepo. They are our fathers. We came here in droves and left a few behind in Tienpo. That's what happened. But right now, if a Bocuwao person says, "I am going to Geeken to settle," we will say, "Have a safe trip." Because we know that you will come back. Try it. Go to Nyenawleken to settle. You will come back."

"So, there are no Bocuwao people in this area besides Tienpo and Jarkaken?" "Teh-Nagbe is in Potupo," Tinpan said.

"Yes, Nagbe is in Potupo. He grew up there and never came home. He was here as a small child. His father was Teahswen. And what I am about to tell you—turn that thing [camera] off ..."

The old man ordered the video recording to be turned off. It was ended abruptly. And the conversation did not continue—at least not on video—because the old man weighed the sensitive nature of what he was about to say and decided not to say it on camera.

Chapter IV:
Echoes of Sorrow

No death is without a cause. Every death happens because something has triggered it. A cause of death is associated with every deceased person. A natural cause of death, such as death by a disease contracted from our contaminated environment, is one of the reasons many people lose their lives.

But in most of rural Liberia, however, there are no medical examiners to perform autopsies, the scientific method most urban areas use to determine the causes of their deceased people. This is especially true for the people who live in and around Chedepo Jarkaken, my hometown. So, there is no way for the local people to logically know the causes of some of their deceased. Hence, this lack of science, if you like, makes room for the locals to belief that there must be a human culprit for every life lost in and around their community.

Granted, there are plenty of instances where there are proven perpetrators, but the assumption in this northeastern corner of Liberia is that most of their dead people are homicidal in nature. They did not just die; they are dead because someone killed them.

Almost no death happens naturally there, it seems. Any family affected by the loss of a loved one hardly accepts the possibility that it might simply be a natural tragedy. In fact, even in situations where natural death is obvious—say, a fallen tree takes the lives of adjacent farmers during a powerful thunderstorm—many rural Liberians will not settle for a mere natural cause. Someone caused the wind to grow fierce, and thus was responsible for the tree to fall. In short, someone bewitched the victims.

This brings to mind the death of Mr. Thomas Nyenyonoh Jbeju Nagbe, a Bocuwao family man. It was in the year 1982 when his tragic death transpired on his farm, located on Bocuwao's Dilamo farming reservation. By the way, it is important to lay out a disclaimer as firmly and as forcefully as I possibly can. If I do not do this, stating this disclaimer, readers might erroneously be led to believe that the farmer's death was due to a natural cause. Maybe it was, or was it? The short answer is: I have no clue. I don't know; I will never know, period. I do not know whether the death of Mr. Nagbe, who was popularly called "Nyenyonoh Jbeju," his Grebo tribal name, was natural or not. I will leave that with my readers to make their own assessments and, eventually, their own decisions, after reading this chapter on the tragic story. My goal is to tell the story, without making any concerted efforts to sway you or anyone in any way. Any decision(s) one makes on, say, his cause of death or the culpability (blame) of anyone, will be entirely theirs.

Now that we've gotten that out of the way, the incident transpired on his farm, where he was fencing a very large field, a routine but tedious task that involves tightly lining up thousands of wooden pieces, each about three or four feet long, either around the entire farm or along a section of it to keep animals out.

One day, Nyenyonoh Jbeju was found unconscious on his farm. And soon, the emergency crew pronounced him dead. The emergency people reported that a piece of wood was found across his body, and that initially left the impression that, perhaps, he had slipped and fallen to his dismay while transferring the wood. Moreover, this was the wet season, and Liberia (especially the eastern region) is heavily vegetated; thus, it is not uncommon for the region to receive as much as eighty inches of rain per annual. So, the wetness could have explained a slip and fall.

68

But the scene, based on the people's subsequent investigation, appeared to have been staged. The investigators said the piece of wood was too light; it was not heavy. They came to the conclusion because it was evidently light, and they said it was a split piece of wood from a local tree known as 'tutwaye.' This tree is naturally lightweight. And the fact that it was a split piece from this tree type, the piece of wood had to be extraordinarily light. They said a piece of wood—especially the size discussed above—could not have weighed more than a pound or two. And, moreover, Nyenyonoh Jbeju was not a small man either, they reasoned. He was a large, towering man. So, right off the cuff, the investigators said the scene had to be staged by the man's killer(s), an attempt to deceive the public.

Shortly after the death of Nyenyonoh Jbeju, the people in the town of Chedepo Jarkaken got the word that, indeed, a crime was committed on the victim's farm. We heard that someone had taken the life of the farmer.

The initial suspicion of the investigators was confirmed—somehow—that the scene at his death had been staged, and his death was definitely not an accident; they claimed. In fact, this was not just a speculation. They had the names of the suspected perpetrators.

They had the names of not one, not two, not three, but four elderly men. All the accused men were members of the Bocuwao family. These men, they said, had teamed up—allegedly—and killed the farmer, Nyenyonoh Jbeju.

We were shocked when the townspeople revealed the names of the four elderly men. We were saddened, too, about the news because the alleged perpetrators were people we knew well. They were household names: Wedlyn Wleh, Tebateh Neneh, Wlebo Jah, and Nyanley Chea. These were prominent

69

Bocuwao elders. They were men we looked up to for guidance. And all of them, I believe, had to be near or over sixty years old when they were charged with the death of Nyenyonoh Jbeju, himself a member of our greater Bocuwao family.

In truth, I did not know all the men personally because I was quite young—ten years old, to be exact—when these events happened in the town. But I knew two of them very well: old man Wedlyn Wleh ('Matalley') and old man Tebateh Neneh ('Pop Grey'). I knew these two men because we lived near one another on the Dilamo reservation. Old man Jah used to live in the village of Gbetohken, several miles to the north of our Wodaiken hamlet. I did not know him that well since we did not frequent there as much as we did old man Wleh's Chianyeken village. Unlike Gbetohken, old man Wleh's hamlet had to be two or three miles from our Wodaiken hamlet. For Pop Grey, we knew him and his kids very well. They used to pass through our Wodaiken hamlet to get to his village, which was close to Wiah Nyonoh Nowinnie's Wotuken village. For old man Nyanley

Chea, I definitely did not know him. Unlike the other three elders, Nyanley Chea was a town dweller. He lived in Jarkaken proper, and we lived in the village. This is important because we did not visit the town frequently at this time in my life. We traveled to the main town only for situation-driven reasons. And we rarely had strong enough or good enough reasons to travel to the town. Only our parents and older siblings came to town frequently. They always ensured another adult stayed back to watch us.

I was quite young when these things happened, so I may not know a great deal of the fine details. But I can assure you that I do remember some of the obvious details surrounding what, to this day, represents a huge scar on our greater Bocuwao family's image. This was a very sad period in our family. Yes, I was a young child, but I felt it.

The men were accused of witchcraft; they were guilty of bewitching the young man, who was a family nurse. In fact, many down dwellers called him a doctor; he was well known because he treated a lot of people. He also circumcised a lot of babies and young people, so he was not exactly a stranger despite spending much of his adult life in the easternmost county of Maryland, Liberia.

Then we heard that the men had confessed to the act, though not until allegedly undergone torture by the townspeople. They were reportedly manhandled by the townsmen. No, I do not have any proof that torture did happen. However, I know that the people who are typically accused of this type of crime are abused—physically beaten—and are forced to plead guilty. The four men were allegedly beaten when the townsmen collected them.

Though accused of the crime, there was no evidence directly linking them to the death of the farmer, who was their extended nephew. Again, this was not totally out of the ordinary. This was not unusual in Chedepo Jarkaken and its environs during this time.

Routinely, people were often beaten and even killed based merely on allegations or unproven charges. Some unjustly endured lasting shame and stigma. As regrettable as that may sound, it was the norm, especially in 1982 and the years prior.

I am not insinuating that the men were not guilty. I am not saying that at all. I am not saying that they were guilty either. In fact, it is possible that they were guilty; that they did all the acts alleged. There are reasons, too, that—when employed—could lead a reasonable person to say the men did not do the crime, or (at a minimum) that their confessions should not have been

71

accepted as genuine since they were allegedly obtained through coercion; through an outright intimidation. All I am saying is that when the men were blamed for the death of their family member, the townspeople picked them up and reportedly tortured them, something that was quite common as a way to compel or induce the confessions of the accused.

(In fact, in my later years, for example, I saw the townspeople put some of their accused on the ceiling of a village hut, built a smoky fire below them, and had them confess to certain allegations under such conditions. This is not hearsay—I have seen this happen numerous times, with my two eyeballs during the daylight hours. The townsmen brought the accused down from the smoky hut ceiling only after they—the accused—had "admitted" to the alleged crimes.)

In the case of the farmer's death, there was no scientific evidence—or any expectation of such evidence—that placed the men on the crime scene (the farm) or a murder weapon that linked the men to the man's death. The men did it because someone—maybe a witch doctor—said they did it. And the burden of proof was on the suspects, not on the townsmen who made the accusatory claims. The townspeople demanded confessions. Anything less than outright confessions was not acceptable. That was the norm during this period of time in Chedepo Jarkaken.

Anyway, the men did not live to talk about this ordeal; they were put to death.

Somehow convinced that they were the killers of Nyenyonoh Jbeju, the townspeople took the men to the outskirts of the town. Correction: the townsmen did not take all the men to the outskirts of the town. Again, I was only ten years old when these tragedies transpired. I had started school at Kaytoken Junior High School two years prior, in 1980, so I was quite aware of

72

my surroundings, even though the fine details still elude me, even to this day.

I still remember the horrible scenes to this date. In truth, I do not know exactly which of the men died where in the town, but the townspeople placed their corpses at random locations around the town, in broad daylight. And people were roaming the town as if they were tourists, viewing the men's lifeless bodies, which were placed—absent any form of afterlife dignity or courtesy—at their locations.

There was a victim (a corpse) at the foothill of 'Wowatogbehdolo,' on the side of the hill that was closer to old man Joe Teahfore Sayee's house. The victim was just a few hundred meters behind a nearby creek: Sawleh Creek. And the corpse was along what may now be a disappearing timber road. (In fact, I did not see much of the road when I visited the town in October 2018.) Anyway, at the time, you could see the corpse from Sawleh Creek.

There was another corpse at or near Mentannwon; this was a popular hangout spot for the town's men. They used to meet under this once giant mentann tree during this era. In fact, the corpse at Wowatogbehdolo and the one at Metannwon were no more than three hundred meters apart.

Then there was another corpse along Tartyken Road. It was laid over a rocky area, not too far from the home of teacher George Kwi Karmon. This latest corpse had to be at least five hundred meters from any of the previous two corpses.

The last one, however, was far removed from the first three. Without doubt, it was in the town proper. I remember it was placed not too far from the Rev. Luke Cojolo and Mr. David K. Swen's houses. At the time, the land between Rev. Cojolo's place and Geeken Road (a cross-town road) was nothing but 'wawa' trees; these trees were child-friendly. We frequented them because they were dense. They had barely any undergrowth. So, we frequented the area to play in the cool and shaded clearance provided by the local wawa trees. Moreover, their fruits—also called 'wawa'—are local delicacies. Wawa trees—along with 'tencoco' plants—were everywhere in Jarkaken during this period. I remember this latest corpse was directly behind teacher David K. Swen's house. It was across the Geeken-bound road, and near the point where the road had an obvious curve.

The house of Henry Tley Tuwleh Swen ("Biju-biju") used to be across this road, exactly at or near this curvy spot. He, by the way, is old man Wlebo Jah's son.

The townspeople gave the accused chulu, supposedly a telltale juice squeezed out of the balk of a sasswood tree. The locals used it widely, and its results were equally accepted as the ultimate decider of guilt or innocence, especially in a situation where a person was accused of bewitching another. To be vindicated, the accused had to puke or vomit the fluid. Surprisingly, this [puking the fluid] was true for some of the accused people. There are numerous people I know who puked the contents of chulu. But some of the accused, like the Bocuwao men, did not puke the fluid; thus, they perished.

In my opinion, however, this [the chulu fluid] was grossly a flaw, which had been around for many centuries as the yardstick for determining guilt or innocence. Again, this is entirely my opinion. That is just my opinion. Others may have plenty of reasons why chulu is fair. And they may be right—or even convincing—because this [chulu] has been around for many, many generations. We know victims who perished, and we know people who survived the test. So, it is just a matter of who can argue it best.

74

I am not in the camp that says it is fair, though—not yet and maybe never. I believe that the people who had tolerance for the juice (and therefore drank more of it) succumbed to it. They drank a lot of it and died because they retained copious amounts of the stuff in their system (without puking it). When they died, they were declared guilty. Death was the ultimate "proof" that, indeed, they were guilty. Thus, they deserved their destiny. Really!

When the four Bocuwao men died, I remember being told not to cry openly for them, especially for Popa Wleh, the father of Mr. Gibson Bokuwo (Bokuton) Kpekeley Chea, aka "G. Bocu." Old man Wleh was a member of our household. We called him Popa, which was what we were calling most of our uncles and fathers. For distinction, he was called Matalley, mainly by people who were senior to us. We, the children, never called him Matalley. We always called him Popa, or Popa Wleh in his absence, whenever we had to describe which Popa we were talking about. Anyway, after the men were buried on the same day of their death, we went to the village and wept openly for them. By the way, while our people were crying indoors, many people, including young people, were going around the town (including in our neighborhood), singing, dancing, and chanting. I was one of the children who went with the chanting crowd for mere entertainment, but the sadness hit me when I went home to the mourners. Ironically, our parents were crying quietly in the house. On the outside, however, the crowd had coined a song, a catchy one-liner on which they tagged the names of the chulu victims:

Teba Teh Neneh na chulu, chulu porlo, umm-or, enuelewan!
Wedlyn Wleh na chulu, chulu porlo, umm-or, enuelewan!

Wlebo Jah na chulu, chulu porlo, umm-or, enuelewan!
Nyanley Chea na chulu, chulu porlo, umm-or, enuelewan!

75

Translation: "[Name] drank chulu, chulu killed him, oh yes, it did its job!"

In some instances, the accused had no tolerance for chulu, so they vomited it upon consumption. They were assumed to be innocent of the deeds for which they were charged. So, they were set free.

Note that not guilty subjects usually, not always, celebrated their vindication, an act during which they reclaimed their good characters, which the ordeal may have smeared or damaged. The locals refer to this celebration as 'kaypopoel', for "the joy of vindication." Members of the community join the vindicated person—who may dress in white and rub white clay on their body—in an act of solidarity. They take victory laps around the town for several weeks or even months. The duration of this celebration depends on the momentum and stamina of the vindicated person. When the vindicated is satisfied that the world (his or hers) is aware that he or she is not guilty (based on credible, available evidence), the victory laps end.

Those deemed guilty, however, do not live to tell their stories. They do not throw up or puke the fluid. Instead, it collects inside their stomachs, overwhelms them, and kills them—violently at times, reportedly. Once again, whether this is a fair determining factor is like the ever-present chicken-and-egg inquiry: which came first?

Chapter V:
On Relations

Families gathered in Colorado to celebrate a 60th birthday bash for Ma Sue Winn.

Family. It was Tinpan [Roland T. Winn] who wanted to know more about the families who live on the Dilamo reservation. Tinpan specifically wanted to know more about the family of Magwulu, which is believed, historically, to be the newest to arrive in the Dilamo reservation. The newest of the three families in the Dilamo reservation, Magwulu, is wedged between the villages of Bocuwao and Dowao families, so Roland was curious why they were in the middle of the two families, who (unlike Magwulu) are generally believed and accepted to be native in the region. "How did the family of Magwulu end up over there?" Roland asked.

77

At first, the old man, Gbeh Chea Nyanley, was reluctant to talk about this story, the one about Magwulu. He considered it an intricate or complicated story, and talking about it was comparable to walking a very fine line. Anyway, he decided to answer Tinpan's question. He emphasized that, historically, our family [The Bocuwao Family] has been small, and that our numbers were (or are) sometimes augmented by people we welcome into our villages.

My own father, Winn Saylee, made a similar point to us over the years. In one conversation he had with Gbayi Puwai, the son of Gbayi Wliya—Winnville, Jarkaken, on December 29, 2009, the old man discussed the subject of relations in depth. Some members of his audience were stunned when he discussed Bocuwao's original ties with Bilaye, a family in the clan of Tienpo, which is far removed from Chedepo.

"We have Bocuwao people in Tienpo," Puwai said, "and we have Bocuwao in the land of Chedepo. How did that happen? In other words, how are we related to people that far away?"

"There are Bocuwao people in Tienpo; that is true." The old man said, "They are Bocuwao, but we call them Bilaye. There are not a lot of people. But in terms of origin, the Bocuwao people in Chedepo originally came from Tienpo."

The family laughed.

"We were Bilaye before we were Bocuwao," the old man said.

Long, long ago, we, the family of Bocuwao, left Tienpo for Chedepo. It is hard to find true originals anywhere because humans, by their nature, are travelers. Other families, it is fair to assume, came to Chedepo from elsewhere, too. But at least the people of Bocuwao know where they came from. It is not a joke;

the families in Tienpo and the ones in Jarkaken embrace one another.

So, how did the latest family, Magwulu, join Dowao and Bocuwao? Roland wanted to know from our uncle. The old man [Gbeh Chea Nyanley] was being really careful. In fact, he displayed a reluctance to dive deeper into the topic. While the story is true (and generally occurs in the lives of every generation of people), Uncle Newton was a bit timid about telling us.

My approach to this is a regret—because stories die out when narrators hold out (or refuse to share). When a narrator is concerned that some people in his or her audience might apply the stories in the wrong context, that narrator may fear being blamed for any potential consequence. That was his fear:

"We do not explain some of these things [stories] because some chatty mouths may use the information in the wrong context, and when someone asks tomorrow, 'Where did you get that kind of information?' The answer might be, 'My father, Nyanley, told me,'" he offered a firmed prelude.

The information below is invaluable. It exemplifies our collective humanity, in my opinion. It puts us, the family of Bocuwao, in a positive light, especially when we consider the caliber of the citizenry who came from such relations.

I am a living example of what is dreaded here. What do I mean? I came to the United States in 1994. I have two children here. They are Americans, unambiguously. Moreover, I was born in Puwaiken, just outside Jarkaken. However, I applied for naturalization a few years ago in the United States and was approved. So, I am naturalized; I am an American citizen, just like my two children, Komoh (born October 2010) and Jarbo (born December 2011). I have decided to dwell here for the rest of my life, and the United States of America is generous enough to welcome me and millions of people from around the world.

In Jarkaken, my Aunty, Nagbe Jowa, is married to a man with Ghanaian roots, a Fante tribal man named Kofi. He decided many decades ago to settle down in our town. The town embraced him. He is a Bocuwao family member today, with Bocuwao children. The townsmen have unconditionally embraced the gentleman and other people, like Mr. Philip Ami, an Ivorian-turned Dowao family member, with similar stories. These are positive stories.

As one with a liberal arts degree, I relish our common humanity. In fact, I want to thank Uncle Newton (old man Gbeh Chea Nyanley)—along with other members of our family—for their willingness to pass to us (and to our offspring) some vital pieces of information, mainly on relations, a topic that has always been difficult to untangle. I share my uncle's concerns, though. With great conviction, however, I believe no one will transform these precious anecdotes into divisive family stories. And in the unlikely scenario that that becomes the dreaded reality, my uncle is cleared of any blame.

Again, Uncle Newton was responding to Tinpan, who asked how the family of Magwulu "ended up over there," by which he was alluding to the Dilamo (Deorken) reservation, just outside Jarkaken proper. After firmly rendering a disclaimer, the uncle provided a lengthy response. He said the family of Magwulu went to the reservation in 1931 through a Magwulu man, a renowned citizen of Klosoken, who married a daughter of Bocuwao. Before explaining how exactly he (and therefore Magwulu) got "over there," Uncle talked about Bocuwao's fore relatives, particularly, the family tree of Madam Nyenaon Jaylee. She was the Bocuwao lady who married the Magwulu man.

"One of our forefathers was Poli Tehfueh, and his father was Sanma. Sanma was a migrant from the clan or district of Gbeapo. He was a Tarwiao family member. Sanma was experiencing hardship in Jaykwiken, his home of origin. So, he decided to leave his hometown in search of a permanent settlement. He was not a thief. He was not a witch. He was not running because he had bewitched someone in his hometown; that was not his reason for leaving his town. He did not offend anyone. Sanma was a good man. He was just tired of his native land, and he wanted to try life elsewhere."

He told his folks in Gbeapo Jaykwiken that he had decided on Chedepo," Uncle Newton continued the story. "And he chose the hilltop community of Klosoken, where he was hoping to turn his life around. They told him in Gbeapo, 'If you want to dwell in the town of Klosoken, go to the family of Bocuwao.' That was the reason he went to the home of Wiah Chie, a renowned forefather of Bocuwao who was the family's oldest man at the time Sanma arrived in Klosoken. He told our father, 'I have come to stay. I have come to be a member of the Bocuwao family.' Our father, Wiah Chie, welcomed him without any preconditions."

Uncle highlighted to us that the migrant was a good man who had added to the headcounts of our greater Bocuwao family, an increase that gives the family respected citizenry, including extraordinary leaders, not just within Jarkaken but in the land of Chedepo and beyond.

"He [Sanma] did not run from a war. No one chased him out of Jaykwiken. He did not bewitch anyone. He did what people do all the time. This is something that has been happening for generations, even today. It is happening now across all the families in our areas and beyond—people can just get up and choose to relocate to a different place to settle. By choosing

81

Bocuwao, Sanma's children are authentically Bocuwao, and his children's children add up to a town's population today."

He gave us an example of another Bocuwao man who did what Sanma did— traveled in search of a permanent settlement elsewhere. The next Bocuwao man, Sloboh, was a guest of his own father, Saylee Winn.

"Another man came to us and added to our population," he said. "His name was Sloboh. When he came to Klosoken, he went to my father, Winn. Like Sanma, Sloboh told Winn he wanted to join the family of Bocuwao. And Winn welcomed him. Sloboh was the father of Weleor Dweh, who we know as Elijah Dweh Sloboh. Sloboh also had Kanmu, and these are Bocuwao members. The movement of people, from one place to another, is public knowledge within all the families in this town and beyond."

"Tinyan," he gave us yet another example, "was a Jegbadior [a local title] in the family of Dowao a very long time ago. One day, he upped and left Chedepo. He said he was tired of being a Jegbadior, so he fled the clan of Chedepo and went to the clan of Potupo. The people of Chedepo were still living on the foothill of Kan, which is not too far from the town of Klaboken. That is how the family of Dowao has a branch today in Potupo. It started with one man's annoyance with his assigned task. Obviously, our family is not exempted; no family is. We can even extend this to the people of Chedepo. We are not that many after all (in terms of our numbers), especially when compared to other clans in land areas comparable to ours. But the strangers we welcome to Chedepo complete us. It is not a bad story to tell. It is a good thing to be friendly. It is a good thing to demonstrate our hospitality towards other people, mainly those who come from faraway places, with the intention to call this land home. It confirms our appreciation for humanity."

He continued, "And so, Sanma was our forefather. He was Wiah Chie's adopted son [and, therefore, a member of the Wiah Chie subdivision of the Bocuwao family]. Wiah Chie got him a wife. And he, Sanma, became the father of Poli Tehfueh [Teh, the Elder].

Tehfueh and his wife, Jaytowel—a lady from the Ponwaon mega family—had Nyenaon. Teh and Jaytowel also had Teh Gbeyee; it was this woman who got married into the family of Teatypo. One of her children was our own son, Domini Toe [the father of Inspector, who his peers used to call "Sepehtoh"]. Teh Gbeyee also had Gbeyee Jarbo [the father of James Juty Jarbo and Alfred Klay Williams, a onetime teacher at B. Nyemah Quayee Elementary, Jarkaken]."

We were glued to our seats as he impressively untangled what was clearly the complex family tree of Nyenaon Jaylee, the Bocuwao family woman who got married within the Magwulu family.

"Jaytowel Nyenaon's oldest son was Teba Teh (or Nyenaon Teh), the father of Neneh, Jayblee Nyonoley, and Masan Nyonoh, who died recently. Masan Nyonoh was the mother of Quenneh and others. Nyenaon Teh also had Gbalee, who was married in the family of Ponwaon. She was the mother of Togbeh Nowinnie [John N. Choloplay, a tailor whose house was across the street from John Paytee Jarbo Chea's house]. Gbalee also had Saiyounu, who sounds like a waterfall when he is talking," he added a satirical comment.

"Nyenaon's second son was Sayee. He was the father of Sayee Teahfore [Joe T. Sayee]. Nyenaon Sayee also had a son with his father's name, Jaytowel Nyenaon [Brown Nyenaon Sayee]. Then Sayee had Paytee Pah [William P. Sayee, he was a high-ranking immigration officer (along with COL. William G. Cholopray). He, William P. Sayee (Paytee Pah), spent

83

much of his adult life in Toe Town, a border town in Grand Gedeh County, Liberia. Say had Sayee Chie (a female), and he had Sili Towa (another female). Moreover, Sayee had Farley, who Sayee Teahfore has again [Sayee Teahfore has a son he named Farley]. The original Farley was a soldier in the Liberian Army. He died in Lofa County, Liberia. Sayee also had a daughter called Porpur ["Heyi Porpur"]. She was married in the town of Chedepo Geeken. Her husband's name was Komoh."

Uncle didn't stop there. He said Sayee had two wives, so he continued with more of Sayee's children.

"Sayee had Nyankpe, the father of Thomas Nagbe, who we knew as Nyenyonoh Jbeju. "Jbeju" is his nickname; it means "man" in Chedepo (i.e., Grebo). Again, that is not his actual Bocuwao family name or given name. His given Bocuwao name is Darckorty; again, Sayee Teahfore has given his name to one of his sons: Mendrake Obi Darckorty Sayee. Anyway, the original Darckorty was a medical doctor. It was this man, Thomas Darckorty "Nyenyonoh Jbeju" Nagbe, who died tragically on his farm in the early 1980s when they [the townspeople] killed all those men. [See full story in *The Echoes of Sorrow.)* Specifically, the men, who were accused as the perpetrators, drank **chulu**, which is fluid (water), mixed with juices from the pounded bark of the sassy wood tree, a traditional Southeastern Liberian way to proof guilt or innocence. The men were all Bocuwao family members: Wedlyn Wleh, Wlebo Jah, Teba Teh Neneh, and Nyanley Chea. Nyankpe also had Teahswen [Winn Saylee has him again; Gbeh Chea Nyanley has him, too.], who was an overseer in the Firestone area. Teahswen's son, Jayblee Teh, is here [the speaker was in Fishtown, Potupo]—in Potupo Jaytoken. Also, Nyankpe had Magsnoh; then he had Sankon, who died without leaving any children.

84

"I have talked mostly about our father Nyenaon's male children. So, I will discuss his female children. One of his daughters was Saewiah. She was engaged and married to Jegbadior Tinyan in the Dowao family. She was the mother of Saykpa, the father of Kaika, who is a peer group member of Komoh [Wilfred Winn]. Nyenaon had Nyentar. She got married in Khorbo. His daughter was in Charles Saylee's village. He had a daughter who was married in the town of Seaborken, in the clan of Killepo. Her grandchild is married to Kannor Swen (Sam Quayee, son of Welmo Quayee, from the Teatypo family of Bowionpo in Jarkaken). Nyenaon had Nyenaon Jaylee, who was married to Kolobah [Chief] Welleh. She and Kolobah Welleh had Jaylee Pah; they had Poyee Ju; then they had Komoh, who was Borlo Teh's father. Nyenaon also had a daughter [he could not remember her name]; she was married in the town of Klaboken. Her children include Matthew. Those were Nyenaon's female children."

Then we got to the Magwulu story—how the family "ended up over there," on the

Dilamo reservation.

"Welleh, a Magwulu man who was also known as Kolobah [Chief] Welleh, got married to a Bocuwao family girl. He was married to Nyenaon's daughter. Our father, Nyenaon (as the previous passages have shown), had several children. Jaytowel Nyenaon added to our greater Bocuwao family. He had nine children—five females and four males. His first daughter was **Nyenaon Jaylee**. She got married within the mega family of

Magwulu. The man she married was Kolobah Welleh. He was a paramount chief in Klosoken. It was his name that the family of Magwulu gave to Mr. Jeffery Welleh Toe, [the father of Welleh Snoh.] Kolobah Welleh and Jaylee had Jaylee Pah, and they had Poyee Ju, the father of my friend, Deaju. Those

85

were the children of Kolobah Welleh and Nyenaon Jaylee before the death of the Paramount Chief."

Bocuwao received a bride price for Nyenaon Jaylee, so she was a Magwulu family woman. Therefore, after her husband died, she had to remain in that family. She had to select another Magwulu family member to marry.

"Magwulu asked Nyenaon Jaylee to look within the family and pick another man to marry. She complied. She opted for another Paramount Chief named Gbagba Toe, the father of Charles Wah. She wanted to marry another king [the audience laughs]. Jaylee and Gbagba Toe had Kanmu, the father of Borlo Teh. Jaylee and Gbagba Toe also had Chenapoh, whose daughter Victor Noring's father, Nowinnie, married."

He talked about a significant occurrence in Klosoken, which was so detrimental, it

amounted to changing the lifestyle of Jaylee's second husband.

In 1928, the people of Chedepo requested Christianity, which was the only way schools came to the rural areas. They wanted mission schools for the Chedepo region. The request for Christianity and the written form of education transpired during the reign of Chief Gbagba Toe. The people of Chedepo sent two people to Harper, Maryland County, Liberia, to meet with Vice President Allen N. Yancy [1881-1941], whom the people in Klosoken called 'Mennee Yanseh,' ["Civilized Yancy"]. He was the Vice President for President Charles Dunbar Burgess King (1875-1961). He complied and sent to the Chedepo people a white missionary, a woman from Missouri, United States. Her name was Carson. In Klosoken, they built a hut for her on the outskirts of the town because they feared the collision of local and Western religious values. So, her church—or 'the mission town'—was built just beyond where my brother's house is now located in Jarkaken [the part of town Uncle is referencing is now referred to as *Winnville,* and it is less than two miles from the historic 'mission town']. We call the area—the mission town area— Soklotogbe-dolo [Cassava Hill]. That was the location of her house. Today, breadfruit trees are at the location."

The missionaries were reluctant to go to what is now referred to as River Gee, Liberia. They did not want to go too far from the ocean. So, ironically, the local people were the ones who used to go to Harper, Maryland (and other coastal areas) to request that missionaries go into their remote locations. In other words, instead of the missionaries going out in the forest, where many indigenous people were living, in order to spread their Christian religion, the locals were the ones looking for them. It is worth mentioning that the people really wanted schools in their areas, and, during that time, to get a school, you had to embrace Christianity. You couldn't have one without the other in the remote forest areas. That was the reason the people of Chedepo met and decided to send two people to Harper—one from the Kaytoken section and the other from the Nyenawleken section—to petition for schools and Christianity.

"Our people [in Kaytoken] sent Jayee Pah [son of Kolobah Welleh and Nyenaon Jaylee] and Tuweli, a man from Chedepo Putuken. These two men went to 'Mennee Yanseh' to request a missionary, and they got a woman. It was a challenge to have white people come into the forest. Anyway, that was how they got Mrs. Carson. When she arrived, people realized that her church, the Assemblies of God, was not a fan of alcohol or liquid. One day, Gbagba Toe, the second husband of Bocuwao's daughter, Nyenaon Jaylee, went to his palm wine tree and brought home some palm wine. He was reportedly drunk; he claimed he was drunk. With the palm wine in his hand and purportedly drunk, the Paramount Chief managed to

87

get to Mrs. Carson's church, which was far removed from the main town. Gbagba Toe went inside the church with his palm wine while the woman was preaching to her congregation."

The people of Chedepo were embarrassed; obviously, the missionary was embarrassed; even Gbagba Toe, the paramount chief, was embarrassed after he sobered the following day and had realized the magnitude of what he had unconsciously done.

"She was angry. 'The people who went for me are not respecting me and my religious values,' she reportedly said. So angry, she left Chedepo and went back to Harper. She told her people that we, the people of Chedepo, did not respect her and the religion she represented. It was an embarrassment for the people of Chedepo, granted that the people of Chedepo did not beat the woman, like the people of Tienpo did when they beat and pumped their assigned missionary. The people of Chedepo did no worse than the people of Webbo, who killed theirs, made pepper soup of the corpse, and ate it. Yet, the palm wine occurrence in Klosoken caused the people so dearly. Ms. Carson, the missionary, left our mission town at Soklotogbedolo (the foothill near today's Winnville) and went back to Harper, Maryland County."

The paramount chief, who was supposed to exemplify peace and the law, was, in fact, the one who violated the church values and embarrassed the people of Chedepo. The people in Klosoken were also extremely angry. They took swift action the next day, after the Chief had slept off the palm wine.

"The next day, they used sounds from a dug-out drum to summon him to the traditional town center. When he reported, they told him he was no longer the paramount chief. They fired him, and they named a replacement. Gbagba Toe's replacement was Kolobah Quayee Chiliteah. After he was terminated, Gbagba Toe was extremely ashamed. It was during that state of mind that he decided not to remain in the town of Klosoken. He wanted to get out of the town of Klosoken. Therefore, he went to the Bocuwao family, his father-in-law. He went to the oldest person in the family at the time. His name was Panteah, the son of Jorpoh Chea Fueh. Jorpoh Chea Fueh had Jorpoh Chea Jaklay. And Jaklay had Jaklay Dweh. Jorpoh Chea Fueh also had Sli Waiah Toe, who turned around and had his father again, Jorpoh Chea, who was the most recent one you know as 'Jakwi Jorpoh Chea.' But that is beside the point."He redirected the story to Jorpoh Chea Panteah and Gbagba Toe.

"He went to Panteah because he, Panteah, was just above the Nesimehn creek area. That is the location of Blalorken. That area was Panteah's area. He used to set traps in that area. So, Gbagba Toe went to Panteah and said, 'My in-law, our farming reservation is too small. It is not big (or spread out) like your Deorken reservation. Your reservation continues until it gets to the Krahns [the people of Killepo Torwloken were not over there, either].

We, the Magwulu family, have **Quejay** ["connected to"], because our frontiers are only connected to other Chedepo areas. We connect to ourselves, not to other external clans.'"

The area from Cheanorgbae to the foothill of Kaytoken is Magwulu's area. This was the location the shamed chief was describing to our great father, Elder Panteah, in the 1930s.

"Gbagba Toe told the family of Bocuwao that he was not a chief anymore, and because of the unceremonious nature of his sacking, he wanted a place to hide out. And the family of Bocuwao told Panteah, 'Take him. He is our in-law, and he is an honorary gentleman.' That was the reason Jorpoh Chea Panteah took him to that area. He took Gbagba Toe to the foothill we call **Wlehpotogbe**, behind **Menor**, another

89

foothill, and told him to settle there. And he went there in 1931, cultivated the place, and built a temporary shelter there. He moved into the tent and remained in it while he constructed a hut on the land. And that was how Gbagba Toe—and subsequently the family of Magwulu— 'ended up over there.' We, the family of Bocuwao, are the owners of the Dilamo reservation. We are here with Dowao. It is important to know that no one from the family of Magwulu, prior to 1931, was in the Dilamo region. Not one. Instead, this place is for Bocuwao and Dowao. That is a fact. Bocuwao and Dowao own the Dilamo reservation. If anyone tells you otherwise, it is a diabolical lie."

I couldn't agree more because Uncle Newton knows the issues; his narratives are

supported by evidence.

He told us that our son-in-law, Gbagba Toe, got his job back.

"Subsequently, the people of Klosoken sent people to Harper and appealed to Mennee Yanseh to send the woman back. Their request was honored, and Carson came back to Klosoken. They told Carson that Gbagba Toe had served his long suspension; that they had decided not to make the punitive action lasting or permanent. He was not losing his job permanently. He was a good chief before the unfortunate incident; the town saw reasons to forgive him. Hence, they were ready to reinstate him as their paramount chief. They called him back from the Dilamo reservation (back to the town of Klosoken) and offered him his job. And that is the reason behind Gbagba Toe naming the spot our father gave him as *'Blalor'* or *'Blalorken,'* Chedepo for "Go get him." The name of Gbagba Toe's village means 'Go get Toe, so he can resume his job' in Klosoken as the paramount chief."

90

After looking over my initial 26-page drafts, which covered the now infamous gazebo historical conversation, Uncle Newton reassured me—and readers of the stories— about his trustworthiness as a narrator. In truth, I had the opportunity to do what many writers rarely have the chance to do—having the narrator of the stories I wrote edit my drafts, which Sayjela, my brother, printed in Greenville, Sinoe County; drove further east to Fish Town, River Gee; and delivered them to his father. I wanted to ensure that the transcripts of the stories were as accurate as his narratives. And, yes, I did ask if he wanted to retract any of the anecdotes. It was this inquiry that prompted the response below:

"Dundunne," he called me. Uncle is one of the few relatives who still call me by that childhood epithet. "This is something I probably didn't tell you when you visited me the last time. I am not a liar," he said. "What I tell you is the truth. I know you have a great interest in our past. I have seen that you have written down our last historical conversation; people will get the chance to read your works. I want to assure you that I am telling you the things that I know to be true. As a teacher [He was a classroom teacher for decades.], I understand the importance of saying 'I do not know' if you do not know something. If you, as a teacher, teach a lie to a student, you are teaching a lie to a generation of people. You will corrupt the minds of a generation. So, I want you to know that my narratives are true," he said.

Then he went back to Gbagba Toe.

The family of Magwulu went to the Dilamo reservation in the year 1931. You have demonstrated that knowledge in your recent write-ups because I told you. What took Magwulu there has to do with the relations between our two mega families— Magwulu and Bocuwao. We carry out intermarriages. Gbagba Toe was our son-in-law. He was a good man. As a paramount

91

chief, he took care of his people. People liked him. People enjoyed his reign. Moreover, he had lots of children. He was the father of Charles Wah, the father of Madaline Jaklay.

But he did something in Klosoken that was unbecoming of a king, and, as I said earlier, it was detrimental to the point where he was sacked. Gbagba Toe was elected as a Paramount Chief, but when he shamed the people of Chedepo, he was removed unceremoniously. They removed him without following any standard processes. They did not involve the government at all.

They fired him. They said, 'You are not a king anymore. If we see you playing king, you will be in serious trouble. If we see you among a group of children, then that will mean you are still playing king.' So, he found himself in an embarrassing situation. Imagine you are a king. You walk around the community with a gown and are being admired by residents. And then, suddenly, you are jobless and find yourself beneath the people you once led. This was the reason that led him to the family of Bocuwao. He cultivated the place our father, Panteah, gave him for his escape. He had his son, Tweh (who is in your father's generation), and other children in the village of Blalorken. He went to his in-laws to escape, and then the family of Magwulu followed him. Today, they have remained there. Someone might ask tomorrow. 'Who gave him the spot to settle?' Now you know that it was Jorpoh Chea Fueh's son, Panteah. He was our family head in the 1930s. That is the information that was passed on to us, and I am glad to tell you, too, because I know you want to know our history."

He went to Gbayee Tebae.

"The man we call Gbayee Tebae has done us [the family of Bocuwao] a big favor. He went behind them [Magwulu] and settled, which keeps them in the general area that Panteah gave

Gbagba Toe. Now, Ponwaon is over there. Paul Dweh and others are over there, so it is a huge area now. It is what they call Dowarwan. That is what I want to correct."

Now that Magwulu is in the Dilamo, what is the family's role? "Historically, they do not own the reservation with us. When we petition the

wishes of our people at Deorblemgehn, we do not wait for Magwulu. We don't even ask

them to come. In truth, they do not have to be there either. Once Dowao and Bocuwao are there, the ritual is observed. The road is for Bocuwao. So, we are the ones who do the petitioning. Dowao, do not petition when we meet for the ritual. We proceed with the ritual once we get the chicken or the goat; those are the animals we typically sacrifice. Magwulu, do not petition with us. And, even though the family members of Dowao have the right to be there, they do not conduct the petition. They are required to be there as spectators. This is what our people told us. This is what we have seen."

And when we petition near Chichi (near those reefs)," uncle continued the story, "there is a small road that goes up the hill. It continues above the tiny creek we call **Chutunorgbae.** Our people planted a tree there. It is called **tlalala**. They clear under it, prepare the food (the sacrifice) there, and it is where they eat the sacrificed animals.

Before they eat, they will call on the spirits of their long-departed relatives, "Let's eat!" They would say. They take a portion of the food (a scoop of rice with red oil over it) and put it on a circular leaf, which is known as **blatawonfone** for their departed people's spirits. This act—feeding the spirits—is called 'Monma.' Your grandfather, Saylee Winn, every time women brought food during farming work, he always ensured the spirits of our long departed had their share, too. How

93

hungry we were had no bearing on this ritual. In fact, they ate first before us. He consistently took the first scoop of rice, drenched in palm butter soup, and placed (sometimes tossed) it under a Tlalala tree. He used to call the spirits to come and eat. Whether they answered him or not, I do not know," he said. Then he added, "But he did that because it has always been the tradition. His father taught him, and the fathers before them passed that on, too."

The paths that connect us to other external districts are our major throughfares. The ones that do not link us to adjacent clans are not as significant as those that do. If you take the route behind Kargbe Nyanfore's place, for example, it will take you to Chedepo Putuken, the Tonken area route. So, that is not a primary route. If you take the route behind Swen Martin and Philip Amin's place (Chenwniken), however, it will take you to Killepo. Thus, it is a major road. Moreover, if you take the Dilamo (Deorken, Deormo) route, it connects Chedepo to several major clans. The Dilamo route connects us to the Killepo people. It also connects us to the Krahn people. Therefore, it is a very important route. If you take the route that leads to the Tartymo reservation, it will take you to the land of the Potupo people. Hence, it is a major road.

Chapter XI:
Bocuwao Family: Their Road, Their Hamlets, Their Relations

The village of Wodaiken, a tiny

Farming Outpost Oldman Winn Saylee was established in 1975

Saylee Sayjolo braced the early-morning dew along the Jarkaken-Wodaiken route and conducted an impromptu interview with his father, Winn Saylee (Saylee).

The conversation took place on January 19, 2004, in the village of Wodaiken, a tiny farming outpost the old man established in 1975 in the Dilamo farming reservation, located outside Jarkaken, the main town. The old man embraced the opportunity; he responded to a myriad of questions with hardly any interruptions for ninety minutes. He discussed serious topics, including a lengthy family tree, historical events, and his beloved Dilamo region.

"I am Saylee, your speaker."

In his usually calmed and collected tone, the old man started the conversation, staring in the direction of Sayjolo's cassette recorder. It was an old radio that had been around the family for a few years. Besides using it to play music and listen to *Focus on Africa,* a program on the British Broadcasting Corporation (BBC), the radio was, for the first time, being used to create a historical recording. It was an impromptu conversation; the old man had no prior knowledge about the interview. But he was happy, nevertheless, for the chance to narrate on record many of the familiar tales he repeatedly told friends and family members.

"We are in Wodaiken Village," he picked up where he had stopped. "Before I moved to this foothill to settle down, I used to live in the village of Puwaiken. It is the old hamlet we passed through before getting to his foothill, Kantogbe. I was there [in Puwaiken] with my parents and many members of our greater Bocuwao family. But as the saying goes, 'There's a time for everything.' And so, I decided many years ago to leave Puwaiken. I assured friends and relatives in Puwaiken that my decision to leave was not prompted by something anyone had done or said to me. I left of my own free will. I chose to leave the hamlet without any external pressure or force. It was a decision I made voluntarily. No one did anything wrong to me; no one did anything wrong to any member of my family. In fact, I like the old Hamlet. So, I wanted them to know I was not abandoning Puwaiken, or 'Puwai,' for short. I named this hamlet 'Wodaiken' exactly for this reason—to highlight to present and future generations that I did not abandon the old hamlet. The name comes from this phrase, 'E wodai; E se

96

chela,' which means, 'I have relocated; I did not abandon Puwai.' I just moved to a place I can call my own, a personal spot. Relocation is not the same as abandonment. So, we are here in Wodaiken. My son, Sayjolo (Saylee Sayjolo), is here with me. He brought a radio from Chedepo Jarkaken this morning to record my voice. Sayjolo's mother, [Elizabeth] Snoh [Winn], is here. [Benda] Kaylor [Winn], our daughter, is here, too. In fact, there are many here."

After briefly setting the scene, the old man went back to the old hamlet.

"Puwaiken is probably two miles from where we are sitting [Wodaiken village], but it takes a while to get there from here because the road is very muddy. During the rainy season, nearly every trip to Puwaiken or from Puwaiken is a challenge because a very large section of the road, about half the path between the two outposts—Wodaiken and Puwaiken—is underwater. The water and mud are there because of the merging of two small creeks: Geeye and Talwloh. The creeks flow side by side and, generally, in the same direction. Between the creeks is a large and fertile land median.

The creeks overflow their banks during the rainy season and bring their waters together on the land median many times during the wet season. This process repeats every year. In other words, the creeks have been bringing their waters together on their shared median for a long, long time.

But the land between the creeks was not always muddy. In fact, it used to be a dried land corridor a few decades ago. Back then, the median had forest protection. The roots under the forest had a net-like blanket over the entire median, which made the land stable and prevented the erosion of the soil. But today, however, we make farms on the median. We cut down all the trees on the median, and we leave the land without any forest

97

protection. It is our own doing. There is no functioning root system there anymore to hold back the soil. And that is why the entire median has become a mess. The road condition gets worse every rainy season," he said, laughing.

"Surprisingly," he said, "we are accustomed to the muddy route, which may be as much as two feet deep in most areas of the median. This kind of sludge does not stop us from carrying on our normal activities. I used to place a chain of wood along the route, which was my attempt to create a temporary, hardened passage between the creeks.

Sometimes it worked fine for a long time; other times, it worked only briefly, especially when the rain came too much during that season. The wooden pieces used to get under the swamp by as much as a foot or two, but somehow, travelers still traced the wooden pieces along the path and continued their trips to and from Puwaiken. When the sun comes, we get some relief from the mud. The heat waves can dry up much of the sludge over the median. And that makes travel normal, until the rainy months come back."

His audience was glued to their seats as he talked about Wodaiken and its surroundings. He relished the occasion. The day was just getting started; they could see the morning rays of the sun as they rose slowly over the horizon overlooking Puwaiken. Until a few years earlier, this was a lone-hut farming settlement. But the "1982 harvest," another familiar story he frequently told, which led to the development of the hamlet. The hut ceiling caved in under the weight of the rice stored above; hence, the family built two huts and redistributed the yields within them. But by the time of the recording, the hamlet had five huts.

"I will discuss many topics," the old man said. "First, I will talk about old age— getting or growing old. Many people in our

98

family did not get to live long at all, and that is worth talking about. I am old now; I am an old man. I am seventy-two years old, which means I have been in this world for a long time. Second, I will talk about relations, mainly how all of us in the greater Puwaiken area are related to one another. Third, I will discuss the main road, which links the villages and farms of our greater Bocuwao family. In fact, I want to talk about the road first," he changed the order of the discussion. "This small foot trail we use every day has been here for many years, many generations. We, the family of Bocuwao, built it. It is the primary route to this huge reservation, which we call our 'Sonjigba,' or our farming reservation. We use this route to travel from Jarkaken to where we are now, and well, even beyond this point. This route links us to our farms. It connects us to our small and large hamlets. We call this route 'Dilamosnu' or 'Deorkensnu' because it is located on the Dilamo reservation. Dilamo means "this is the way," and we use the terms with a bit of arrogance, a chest-pounding way of saying our location is superior to neighboring locations. That this is the place to visit, this is the place to live, and this is the place to simply be. We say it with the impression that no other place compares to our reservation. We use Dilamo in that sense. It sounds a bit awkward in Chedepo—a variant of the Grebo tribal language—to say Dilamo in a conversation, so we call this reservation Deormo (or Deorken) for short. [Other family members define Dilamo as a breadbasket, a place where mouths go to feed.]"

"So, this farming road starts in Jarkaken proper?" a faint voice asked.

"Actually, yes. It starts in Jarkaken. But the exact starting point is on the outskirts of the town. It begins from Tarwulu, which is a foothill just outside the main town. A traveler from Jarkaken will first see Kloso, a once-inhabited foothill. This foothill is about three-quarters of a mile outside the town.

99

From Kloso, the next foothill is Tarwulu. This is the official beginning or start point of the Dilamo road. In truth, Tarwulu is a tiny mount; it is technically not even a foothill, especially when compared to Kloso, which is more vertical and steeper. It is on this mount that the first Bocuwao hamlet was established a long time ago. That first settlement, as I said, belongs to us because it was one of our forefathers who first settled the area. His name was Teh. He was the first to build and live on the foothill of Tarwulu. The tiny village he established at Tarwulu was called Chutu or Chutuken. In due course, however, the settlement transformed into a sizable community, particularly after fired destroyed Klosoken, which was a nearby community, as I said earlier."

He discussed in detail the formation of the route, which runs across the vast reservation, naming villages and their original settlers (or pioneers).

"Our people left Tarwulu or Chutu until they got to Joyl, the foothill immediately after Chichi, which is the northern section of the Gee River. Jayee Teh, another forefather of ours, was the first to establish a hamlet over the peak of the Joyl foothill. He called his settlement Joyl. So, from Jarkaken, Joyl is the second Bocuwao hamlet. It is the first from the first Teh's Tarwulu (Chutuken) settlement."

All eyes were on the old man as he discussed the route. The interviewer, Sayjolo, briefly checked his recorder and moved closer to the old man, who was clearly relishing the moment. The old man moved quickly to the third settlement and its pioneer. It would have been his birthplace; he once told the family. However, his parents relocated elsewhere on the reservation due to personal tragedies—the death of their initial children.

"Then," the old man continued, "another forefather settled not too far from Jayee Teh's Joyl. We call this third forefather Tehfueh, or Teh, the Elder. He went about two miles beyond Jayee Teh's Joyl, and he started a settlement, which he named Welteh, or Weltehken. This third hamlet was, on record, the largest Bocuwao settlement on the reservation. It was practically a town. Now, the first three settlements I have talked about so far were built by men who, by mere chance, were named Teh. The pioneer at the third settlement is Tehfueh. His wife was Karfor Paytee. And that is all I know about him. In truth, the settlement of Welteh has two founders. It was rebuilt. Our people left Tehfueh's settlement a long time ago. They abandoned the hamlet. Later, the family of Bocuwao returned to its ruins and rebuilt the famed town. The man who rebuilt Weltehken was Magsnoh Nyangbe. Today, Welteh is no longer occupied. The last of its former inhabitants left the site most recently. But Welteh was a respected community. It was our healing center. That is why we advise our people—present and future Bocuwao family members—to avoid planting cocoa or any cash crops over the ruins of Weltehken. We can always rebuild it. It was Kaytoken's therapeutic center. For example, every time the people of Klosoken took their sick to Weltehken, they almost always recovered."

He went back on the road, near its beginning, to talk about certain historical landmarks.

"If you cross Belwulo—the creek you see after you leave the foothill of Chutu (Tarwulu)—and go up the tiny hill that follows, just before you get to Chichi Creek, you will come to a small shrine on the right side of the road. If you look straight ahead from the shrine, you will see a patch of baboon plants (known locally as "kukanyi") about 150 meters on the left side of the road. From the baboon plants is another 150 meters before you get to Chichi Creek. Therefore, the shrine is at least

101

300 meters before Chichi. The location of the shrine is called Deorblemgehn, a term that loosely translates into 'under Deor's tent.' We, the members of the Bocuwao family, are regulars at the shrine, but we are not the only family that uses the shrine. Other families, to include the Dowao and Magwulu families, frequent this traditional shrine, too. Near the shrine is a burial site. It is exclusively for the family of Bocuwao. We call the burial site Wailaya, which translates into 'a resting place.'"

He had a lot to say about the shrine because of its family relevance. The old man said his paternal grandfather, Kaji Choloplay Saylee [the old man's namesake], was buried at the shrine.

"But not every deceased Bocuwao family member is buried at this resting site," he continued the story. "The burial site is reserved for Bocuwao's great hunters, people who—during their hunting careers—racked up very impressive kills. Getting a burial spot at the location is not just based on the number of kills the hunter had amassed, which is also an important element, but it is based primarily on the types of animals the hunter had killed. The hunters who accumulate large career kills, such as buffalo or wild bulls, are buried at the resting site, which is not too far from the shrine at Deorblemgehn. You cannot see the burial site from the shrine, which is along the main Dilamo road, because the entire place is a very dense forest. To give you a clue, the burial ground is in the thick jungles that surround the entire basin created by Belwulo, Chichi, and Chutunorgbae creeks.

To get to the resting site, the locals follow a trail that forms directly across from the shrine at Deorblemgehn. This road is on the left side of the main Dilamo road when the traveler is facing Chichi, which is actually the northernmost section of the Gee River. When traveling from the direction of Jarkaken, the

102

road is at least 300 meters before the traveler gets to Chichi. It is a long trail; it doesn't end at the adjacent burial ground.

Instead, the people use it, not just to get to the resting site, but most importantly to farm the fertile land basin formed by Belwulo, Chichi, and Chutunorgbae creeks. The family also buries its 'sayleejlu' [its most respected or honored members] on the special burial ground. Bocuwao's most senior elder, the oldest man in the entire family, is taken there, too, for burial."

"We know the location of the shrine, but we don't know exactly what the family does there. Please explain the functions of the shrine to us," Sayjolo said.

"Thank you. Several traditional events or activities transpire at the shrine. The family of Bocuwao facilitates the activities at the shrine. And, in some cases, the family leads the events. Even though the family of Bocuwao leads all activities at this roadside shrine, not every member of the family can lead these sacred activities. We, the descendants of Wiah Chie—also known as Wiah Chie Po, a subdivision of the Bocuwao family—are the traditional leaders during the activities at the shrine. Our cousins, the Nyansunupo—the Nyansunupo branch of our family—do not lead these roadside rituals because their traditional role is in the town proper. They are the ones who give orders to wildlife wandering in the town proper to leave immediately; that is what they are assigned to do by our tradition. They tell intruding or out-of-place wildlife to get out of the town and go back to the adjacent forest. Thus, since it is their job to get wildlife out of town, they do not have any additional authority to go to the wild, where they have sent the animals, and tell them to do anything else. And that is where we, the Wiah Chie Po, come in. We tell all wildlife to settle down and be quiet. We are the people who petition nature and our gods for palm trees to produce enough palm wine, for hunters and those who set traps to kill or catch

103

prey, and for our women to conceive so we can multiply. These are just examples of the types of activities that take place at Deorblemgehn. Our activities at Deorblemgehn are not restricted to the Jarkaken community. We, the Wiah Chie Po, also petition the wishes of the entire land of Kayto, which comprises the towns of Jarkaken, Geeken, and their respective environs."

He returned to the road—how the family of Bocuwao started it, and named more Bocuwao hamlets, as well as the family's forefathers or the pioneers who established those settlements.

"There are many tiny settlements on this reservation. In fact, I am going back on the road to talk about more of our settlements and the men or pioneers who built them. If you pass this spot [Wodaiken village] where we are, you will get to the settlement we call Wotuken. It is an important Bocuwao hamlet. The man we call Wiah Nyonoh Nowinnie was the original pioneer at Wotuken. Note that Wodaiken, our current location, is about halfway between the villages of Weltehken and Wotuken.

Then there is the hamlet we call Puwaiken, the old hamlet I left before settling down here at Wodaiken. Puwaiken actually sits on a foothill we call Portogbe. In other words, the location was not always called Puwaiken. It was Portogbe until the family built the hamlet over that foothill. In fact, Puwaiken, the name, was coined by a man we call Wedlyn Chea, the son of Kaji Choloplay Sloboh.

Long ago, one of our forefathers, Gbayi Wliya, went to Portogbe to make a farm. At the time, it was heavily forested. It was a vast expanse, densely covered with original forest, as in never been cultivated, or no known prior cultivator. It remained a vast forest for a very long time because the location,

104

as I said earlier, was too far for the farmers in the village of Weltehken or the village of Wotuken to commute there and cultivate the area.

So, it was not only a dense forest but quite an isolated area, too. So, when Gbayi Wliya decided to make his farm at the location, it was a big deal for many people, particularly the family members who were traveling the road between the two large hamlets [Weltehken and Wotuken].

For years, the families had been complaining about that segment of the road. The Wotu-Welteh road had no rest stops. What they had in mind was not just temporary roadside rest stops; instead, they wanted rest stops in the form of tiny farming outposts or settlements, places where they could put down their loads and relax a little before moving on to their intended destinations. This was a serious concern for many family members, and more so for the area's women travelers. That was why Gbayi Wliya, having a farm at the midway point of the large hamlets, was greeted with considerable relief. They hoped and prayed for Gbayi Wliya to establish an outpost at the end of the farming year, which they could use as a rest stop between Wotuken and Weltehken."

"So, Gbayi Wliya was the first to farm the area; he must be the owner of the area,"

a faint voice is heard on the audio tape saying.

"Well, it is complicated. It is true that Gbayi Wliya was the first to start a farm there. He quickly brushed a huge section of the forest undergrowth at the foothill of Portogbe. Then all of a sudden, he upped and left the Portogbe area. Wliya departed suddenly and unexpectedly, with prior notice or explanation for the family members in the area. To the surprise of many family members, Wliya halted his farming activities at Portogbe. The people started worrying and complaining again.

105

Disappointed and upset, some family members were directly confronting Gbayi Wliya, peppering him with questions. Whenever the locals approached Wliya with questions about the farm he had abandoned over the foothill of Portogbe, he had many responses, but one memorable response stood out: 'Bo swen bi waea pu che, e'e dbala gbalolo.' In other words, Wliya said, 'Even if it takes me ten years, I will cut down the forest and continue the farm.' To this day, it remains Gbayi Wliya's most quoted response.

The uncultivated forest—with barely any undergrowth—sat there for a very long time. It was an eyesore, a blemish for the family of Bocuwao, who are known and regarded as strong or hardworking farmers. In fact, Dilamo is sometimes defined as a place to come and eat." So, Gbayi Wliya leaving an incomplete farm was an embarrassment for the family.

Like many of the family members who were peppering Gbayi Wliya with questions about the farm he left at Portogbe, Wedlyn Chea, a distant cousin of Gbayi Wliya, went to his cousin and asked about his abandoned farm. 'When will you go back to the foothill of Portogbe and continue your unfinished farm?' Gbayi Wliya's response was unchanged. He told his cousin that he was in no rush; even if the wait continued up to ten years, he was not bothered, he said.

Frustrated about Gbayi Wliya inaction and bothered by the inquiries from other family members, coupled with the possible public denunciation of their larger Bocuwao family, Wedlyn Chea went to Portogbe, cut down the trees on the farm, and completed the farm. At the end of that farming year, Wedlyn Chea built an outpost at the foothill of Portogbe. He coined a name for his settlement. He called his hamlet Puwaiken, which he defined as 'Area Ten.' This was a direct reflection of what Gbayi Wliya used to tell annoying and inquisitive family members. When Gbayi Wliya heard the name of the new Bocuwao settlement, he was reportedly thrilled about it. He liked the name of his cousin's outpost; in fact, Gbayi Wliya named one of his own children Puwai [Uncle Philip P. Noring], perhaps as an appreciation. The entire foothill is not renamed; it is still known as Portogbe. The section of the foothill on which Wedlyn Chea built his settlement is Puwaiken."

He moved on to another location—his:

"I said earlier that I used to live in the village of Puwaiken. I relocated here, so I call this place Wodaiken, which is Chedepo for 'move over' or, more appropriately, 'relocate.' I just want to move to my own place; I did not leave Puwaiken because of any frictions with others. I did not abandon Puwai. In fact, I did not want to go too far from Puwaiken. So, I just crossed the water—two small creeks: Talwloh and Geeye—and settled down here. During the heat of the Charles Taylor war, when fighters from various warring factions were crisscrossing Jarkaken and its satellite hamlets—including those in the Dilamo farming reservation—I went further out in the direction of Wotuken, to Wlehpotogbe, a foothill. I built another settlement there. I call that one Pobodaiken, which means 'to go further.' It is my second Hamlet."

He discussed a few tiny hamlets, many of which, he said, were established by folks who, like him, once lived in the hamlet of Puwaiken.

"There's a Bocuwao village we call Gbetohken. Quayee Swen was the pioneer at Gbetohken. He was the first to settle the area. Quayee Swen was a Bocuwao man, but he went to that place [the location of Gbetohken] with the man we call Nyekan Kosolo, a much older gentleman he respected. He [Kosolo] was not a Bocuwao family member. He was a member of the Dowao mega family. But the two were friends, and, as I said earlier, Quayee Swen had a great deal of respect for his older friend. In fact, at some point during their stay at the new area, Quayee Swen—the father of Karwolo [David K. Swen]—gave ownership rights of his Gbetohken outpost to his older, respected friend: Nyekan Kosolo. Quayee Swen was a young man when he did that; he thought he was doing the right thing. But Gbetohken is not for Nyekan Kosolo. It is for Quayee Swen. It is a fact. It is public knowledge. And so, it means that the settlement of Gbetohken is for us, the family of Bocuwao. In fact, when our daughters who marry into other families [Newarnyono] sing, they say, 'A kon Gbetohchechaen; a kon Gbetohfueh.' In other words, 'We have Small Gbetoh; we have Big Gbetoh.' Big Gbetoh is Quayee Swen's first settlement. He later moved to the outskirts of that first settlement and built there, too. The second settlement he built is what our daughters refer to as 'Small Gbetoh.'"

"So, Gbetohken is not for the Dowao family," his wife commented.

"No," the old man said, "Quayee Swen is the owner of both hamlets—big and small Gbetohs. Moreover, the Bocuwao man we call Wean—Kwiyeyee Wean—left Gbetohken and crossed the water [northern Geeye Creek] before settling down. Sayee Wean, as we also call him, named his settlement Dbawloken, which loosely means 'to be patient.' It is one of many hamlets formed between Weltehken and Wotuken. Also, when you leave the settlement of Weltehken, coming toward our location, Wodai, the first village you will see is Mubleken. Mubleken means 'Go home,' or more appropriately, 'Go to your home!' The Bocuwao man we call Chea Quelley is the owner of Mubleken. He was the first to settle the spot. No one evicted Quelley. That was just the name he chose for his village. For some reason, Chea Quelley was fond of evicting terms. He had a dog, for example, which he called 'Kpalehmo,' meaning 'Go with it,' or literally, 'Get out of here with it!' And when you leave Chea Quelley's hamlet, you will come to a fork. A left turn will take you to Puwaiken. If you make a right turn, you will see Salayken (or Salay for short), which means 'Leave me alone.' Togbe Barfeh was the original pioneer there. He owned it, but Barfeh did not tell anyone when he was moving to the area. Whenever family members asked about the activities at the site, he used to tell the folks to leave him alone. Thus, the name Salayken. The man we call Dowu Choloplay was the first to settle the hamlet of Nikonteken, a small outpost outside Salayken. Dowu Choloplay's hut was built on disputed land, that's why he called his hamlet Nikonteken, or 'That's the reason why.'"

"These are all Bocuwao settlements," Kaylor said.

"Yes. This entire road we have built, along which we have lined our hamlets, belongs to the Bocuwao family. Of course, it is true that we are here with the Dowao and Magwulu families. We do things together with these families. But there are still more villages to name," he said, smiling.

"There is a small hamlet not too far from our location. It is just outside Puwaiken.

We call it Chianyeken, which means 'an area of laughter.' Wedlyn Wleh—brother of Wedlyn Chea—was the pioneer at Chianyeken. The hamlet has a nickname. It is known as Nyefinken, literally 'an area of farts.' The assumption has always been that Wleh himself coined the tactless one-word pet name. Besides, he was a comedian. He used to joke about anything. He made people laugh.

Sayjolo was familiar with the origin of the fouled name. He later explained:

109

"Local historians traced its origin to Old Lady Magnor; she was the mother-in-law of Wedlyn Wleh. She was the mother of Danyonoh, Wleh's first wife [Wleh had two wives.]. Like many Bocuwao families, Wedlyn Wleh used to live in Puwaiken, the hamlet of Wedlyn Chea, his older brother. And like others, he left, too. Wleh's departure was reportedly not under peaceful conditions. He did not just leave Puwaiken because the time was right. He left his brother's village allegedly because of a conflict between them. He reportedly told his brother, 'I will leave your village and build my own hamlet elsewhere.' His brother reportedly responded, 'Kpa blade nyenfin'o mu!' which loosely translates into these angry outbursts: "Okay, take your farting ass and go!" And that is the basis for the 'Nyefinken' nickname. When Wleh settled on the spot behind Dbanorgbae Creek, Old Lady Magnor, the mother-in-law, used to pay visits to her daughter and her grandchildren. The route to Wleh's hamlet passes through his brother's village. Unless you take the route that passes through Chenwniken—a farming reservation for the Bowionpo mega people— you must get to Puwaiken before making it to Wleh's hamlet. Anyway," Sayjolo continued, "the old lady used to stop at Wedlyn Chea's village first before getting to Wleh's place. And every time she was leaving Chea's village, she used to say, 'E mi'e Wleh mo kle Nyefinken,' And that loosely translates into 'I am going to Wleh in his Nyefinken village.' She started it; she popularized it. Moreover, Gibson Kpekeley Bokuwo ['Bokuton'] Chea, the elder son of Wleh, and his other siblings used to hear it from their grandmother. They, too—especially Bokuwo—started to use the hamlet's foul nickname frequently. To this day, Bokuwo is known in the main town as the self-proclaimed 'Nyefinken Township Commissioner,' which is not a thing. But they are all comedians.

They come from a long line of comedians, including their grandmother, their father, their uncle [Wedlyn Chea], and their own mother." The old man returned to the settlements.

"Thank you. Again, many of the tiny settlements I have been naming have their origins in Puwaiken. In other words, the original pioneers at many of these scattered farming settlements were prior settlers of the greater Puwaiken area. And these are the things I want all of you to know.

One Bocuwao man, Panteah, has a farming outpost that is not too far from Wotuken. He called it Fleteahken; it means 'to diminish, lessen, or weaken the problems, concerns, or opinions of others.' Then there's another Bocuwao man, Tebae, who has a farming outpost, too. For Tebae, he left the village of Wotuken [Wiah Nyonoh Nowinnie's village], penetrated the vast forest over there, and ended up several miles behind Blaliken [Blalorken], which is a large farming settlement for the Magwulu family. He was quite young when he decided to have his own farming outpost, so he considered his entire experience experimental, a trial. Tebae chose the name Nyesanken, which roughly means 'a youthful area.' Nyonoley was another Bocuwao man who built a farming settlement as well. He called the tiny community he built Humm, or Hummken. Note that Nyonoley's Hummken and Panteah's Fleteahken have the same or similar meaning. They take mocking tones.

Like Fleteah, Humm is a subtle disrespect. It degrades, belittles, or puts down someone or his or her efforts. I don't know how much is left on the cassette, but there are still many more tiny hamlets to name. Because of space, I just want to put strong emphasis on the main road along which we have settled; it is a very important road. We, the people of Bocuwao, own it. We call it Dilamo. However, it sounds a little awkward in the Chedepo language to say, 'E mi Dilamo,' or 'I am going to Dilamo.' So, we use the word Deorken in the place of Dilamo:

111

'E mi Deorken,' or 'I am going to Deorken.' This is smoother on the tongue and easily comprehensible. So, these are some of the things I want to talk about before I move on to relations—how we are related to one another in the larger Puwaiken area."

"Huh, Saylo," Sayjolo said.

"Yes, thank you," the old man said. "Kwiyeyee Saylo, the brother of Kwiyeyee Wean, has a settlement. He named it Normowloken—an area of kindheartedness; that is what that term means.

"Papay," Sayjolo called.

"Yes."

"All the topics you have been talking about—the road and all the hamlets our family members have built along it—are fascinating things to hear and talk about," Sayjolo said. "We appreciate you for making all this vast historical information available to us.

You want to move on to other issues of importance, like relations. We will get to other subjects; however, I still have a few settlement-related questions for you. We hear a lot about Wiah Chie, one of our forefathers, and his Sindoloken hamlet; however, we do not see this settlement as we do other historical ruins in this region. So, where is Sindolo? Is it along the Dilamo road? And if it is not on this side of Jarkaken, can you tell us or describe where it is as accurately as possible?"

"Oh, thank you, Sayjolo, for those good questions. I am glad you asked about that hamlet. Wiah Chie, the Bocuwao man we call Wiah Chie, built a settlement on the top of Sindolo foothill. Thus, we, the family of Bocuwao, are the owners of the foothill of Sindolo. To answer your questions, Sindoloken is not in this region. It is not one of the hamlets on our Dilamo reservation. So where is it? There is a foothill we call Nyenawle. It was once settled by the people in Nyenawleken. Adjacent to the foothill of Nyenawle is the foothill we call Polo. Sindolo is between the foothills of Polo and Nyenawle.

It was on that Sindolo foothill that Wiah Chie, a prominent historical figure in our family, had his settlement a long, long time ago. The foothill of Sindolo and the foothill of Kayto are directly across from each other. They look face-to-face at each other, if you like. During the period our forefather Wiah Chie was at his Sindoloken village, another important historical figure used to live across from him, on the foothill of Kayto. The man who lived next to Wiah Chie was not a Bocuwao man. In fact, he was a member of the Magwulu family. This Magwulu man was called Blisa. He was the pioneer at Kaytoken village; he built or established the settlement of Kayto. They lived as neighbors for a long time. After some time, however, Wiah Chie (and many other families who lived in the settlements around the foothill of Kayto) moved to Blisa.

They joined him and lived in the village of Kaytoken. Blisa's hamlet grew into a town; it became a very large and populous community. In fact, all the mega families in today's Jarkaken and Geeken trace their ancestral connections to the people who lived in Blisa's Kaytoken township. Therefore, the people in the communities of Jarkaken and Geeken are known collectively as 'Kaytokwen,' for 'the people of Kaytoken,' he said, smiling.

"There's something else I want to tell you. Long ago, while these families were living in Blisa's Kaytoken, some salespeople from the north brought what, by all accounts, was fascinating merchandise to the town. It was a toy— a very beautiful toy—that the children in the town had hugely fallen in love with. The people in Kaytoken coined a local name for it. They called the popular toy Kusnohgbe. The traders, I must

113

add, were good people. They allowed the children of Kaytoken to play with the toy while they were trying to sell it to the people in Kaytoken. Everyone in the town loved it. But they complained that its price tag was too much for the average person in the village to afford.

They wanted a cow in exchange for the toy. That price was extremely expensive, the people said. The salespeople stayed in the town for a while, but there were no buyers. "Who will purchase Kusnohgbe, the toy?" That was the question during the merchants' presence in the town. This was the topic of discussion, the issue of the day. The salespeople valued their merchandise so much that they didn't want to sell it for anything less than a cow. They told the residents, as they did the villagers before Kaytokwen, Kusnohgbe would leave town with them if it had no buyer(s). They were going to take the toy with them; it didn't matter to them how much the entire community, particularly the children, had come to love the toy. Kusnohgbe, they said, would leave town with them. The people became more anxious as days came and went. "Our children love this toy; we must buy it so they can continue playing with it," they said.

"Who were these people—the salespeople?"

"They were togbiakwen [northerners]; they were black people. Our father Wiah Chie was a man of means. He had plenty of livestock: cattle, bulls, steers, oxen, and bullocks. He had sheep, goats, chickens, ducks, and so on. These were the things that defined wealth in those days, so he was clearly a man of means. The people of Kaytoken cried out to their residents of means to help secure the toy they had come to love so much: "Our children love this toy," they said, "but the traders will take it with them if no one in our community purchases it. We are appealing to you to purchase this toy so our children can continue playing with it." Wiah Chie heard

114

the people's appeal and told them he was going to purchase the toy. And he did. He gave the northerners their asking price of a cow, and the children at Kaytoken continued to play with Kusnohgbe, their newfound favorite. And that is how Wiah Chie became the purchaser of Kusnohgbe, the toy. Moreover, for this purchase, the entire land of Kaytoken—defined today as the greater Jarkaken and Geeken areas—gave the family of Bocuwao an exceptional, everlasting praise: 'Jay bloforpo (felpo), kwi mininedeh u ton neh,' and that is loosely translated as 'The pioneers who purchased what the civilized have played with.' And that is the origin of this popular phrase; it started long ago in the now-ruined Kaytoken town many, many years ago."

"This is a very popular phrase, as you have eloquently stated. It is truly historic. Other families in this area try to lay claim to this phrase, that it came about because of actions they had taken in their past. The way you have expertly explained its basis, with remarkable clarity and confidence, gives us a sense that we are truly the owners of this phrase. For the record, can you explain whether there are people or families in this community who share this acclamation with the family of Bocuwao? What other groups of people either share this praise with us or have a similar phrase of their own?"

"No other families share it with us. This is a unique commendation; it exists because of the historic purchase of our forefather, Wiah Chie, the pioneer at Sindoloken. No other families have a similar phrase of their own."

"So, the family of Bocuwao is the sole owner."

"Yes. We, the members of the Bocuwao family, own this praise phrase. The only family in this community that is trying so hard to lay claim to it is the family of Magwulu. I have no knowledge of any other family trying to own it. At the beginning of this conversation, I told you my name, that my name is Saylee, your speaker. I also told you my age, that I am seventy-two years old this year.

On one occasion, I did argue this with the Magwulu man we call Toe Wiah. You, the young people, know him as 'Geegba Wiah.' My conversation with Toe Wiah, which later turned into a full-blown argument, happened in the gathering of other elders. He said they were 'Tarpeh Magwulu, kwi mininedeh u ton neh.' And I told him that that version of the praise—with 'Tarpeh Magwulu' in it—does not exist in this land. The family of Magwulu does not own a praise phrase like ours. In fact, the only Magwulu connection to this phrase (if you can even call it a connection at all) is its origin. The origin of the phrase is traced to the village of Kaytoken, which was founded by Blisa, a Magwulu pioneer. But the people of Kaytoken did not coin it for Magwulu. I gave him a chance to explain how their family obtained the phrase. He said their family got in trouble with the town and was forced to pay a huge fine. And despite the size of their fine, they settled the trouble within a single day. The people around us booed him.

You know, when you break the law, as in their case, you are forced to pay a fine. There is no begging involved. You must pay the fine. Whether you pay it immediately or not doesn't indicate that you are a well-to-do person; nor does it mean that you deserve any praise. If you must borrow the fine, then that's what you must do. And you are not praised for a lifetime for paying a fine, notwithstanding the speed with which you paid it. You can take influential people with you to borrow from well-to-do people, if that is what you decide. It really doesn't matter. For us, the members of the Bocuwao family, the town of Kaytoken appealed to us (through our father, Wiah Chie). We honored their request and purchased Kusnohgbe. Paying a fine doesn't make anyone special. So, Toe Wiah and other elements from their Magwulu family are the only ones

116

claiming to be 'Tarpeh Magwulu, kwi mininedeh u ton neh.' But they are not that at all; such a title does not exist for Magwulu. It is made up."

"Kusnohgbe, which you have talked about, describe it. How did it look?"

"Kusnohgbe is what you English speakers refer to as "doll baby.""

"What is the origin of the name Kusnohgbe?"

"Kusnohgbe is a feminine name. The toy was beautiful; it had the likeness of a

female. That's how it got the name."

"How big was the toy?"

"It had the appearance of an infant. It was fragile. It looked like a human being, with similar hands, fingers, feet, toes, and so on. This Kusnohgbe doll—I am sure by now you remember the location of Sindoloken, right? Wiah Chie, the man who bought the town's favorite toy, had a son. His name was Kopeh Nowinnie. It is this name, Kopeh Nowinnie, that has evolved into the present-day Wiah Nyonoh Nowinnie, the namesake of the person who founded Wotuken Village, where I was born [in 1930]. Anyway, Wiah Chie's son, Kopeh Nowinnie, was born in Sindoloken, but he died in neighboring Kaytoken. The death of Kopeh Nowinnie took a stressful toll on the father, as any parent can imagine. He was overwhelmed with emotions. In fact, Wiah Chie took Kusnohgbe— the fragile (breakable) doll the town was still relishing—and shattered it on his son's grave, perhaps to mark the grave and as a sign of respect. If you cross Neplen, a major creek along the original Jarkaken-Klaboken footpath, you will see a traditional grave marker. A 'Tailalie tu' (a tree) is planted near the grave. To this

117

day, tiny pieces of the broken toy are still visible around the tree, if you look very carefully."

"So, he destroyed the toy at the same location where the child was buried?"

"Yes, he was devastated; that was his way of honoring the memories of his son."

"We understand everything you have said about Wiah Chie's Sindolo. Today, you are the father in this area. You will still talk about many, many things. I think we need to switch to relations now. Your biological father, how many of his forefathers can you name? And if those forefathers had children, how many can you name?"

"Thank you. Our people used to talk, but we did not ask them as many questions as you are doing today. As for me, I did ask my father a few questions, and this is what he told me: The oldest person on our family tree that I know about is Cheafueh (or Chea the Elder). I refer to him as our first forefather. Cheafueh had a son, and he named him Wesseh. I refer to Wesseh, the son of Cheafueh, as our second forefather. Wesseh, too, had a son, and he named him Chea. I refer to him as our third forefather. Then Chea, the grandson of Chea the Elder, had a son and named him Wesseh; he is our fourth forefather. So those are four forefathers and their offspring that I can talk about with relative ease.

I will elaborate on Wesseh, the fourth forefather. Wesseh had two children: he had Kargee Choloplay, and he had Nyanley, whom we also call 'Gbeh Chea Nyanley.'

Kargee Choloplay had two children. He had Saylee; he also had Sloboh. Kargee Choloplay's wife was born in the town of Killepo Kanweaken. Her name was Swen Chie. She was a member of the Dewlebo family in Killepo Kanweaken. She was the mother of Saylee and Sloboh. And of the two children, Saylee was older.

He talked about Saylee's Children:

Saylee had a total of fourteen children: he had Wesseh (Toboseh); he had Kargee [Jowa] Choloplay; he had Jowa Doe; and then he had Polee Winn, my father. Toboseh died without leaving any children; he did not marry. Jowa Doe and Choloplay did not marry either; they were older men when they died. All three brothers did not leave any children. Polee Winn, Saylee's lastborn in the male birth order, was the only surviving male. And he was the only male who had children. Polee Winn is our father today. And Saylee, my paternal grandfather, also had female children. He had Saylee Welayor; he had Saylee Gbasay; he had Saylee Wedlyn; he had Saylee Teaty (married in the town of Klaboken, the mother of Wayto Sloh, whose daughter, Kubay, often comes to us); he had Saylee Chie; and he had Saylee Sinamen (Menmen), who many of you have seen. She got married in the town of Killepo Kanweaken. All these children I named were from Saylee's first relationship. He had a second wife [Tuwobo Gbalee]. He and the other woman had the following children: [Gbalee] Duhl, [Sagiah] Kayjeley, [Sagiah] Wiah, and Queenyanoh. And those were the children of Saylee, who was Kargee Choloplay's older son."

He moved to Sloboh:

"Sloboh, the younger brother of Saylee, had three children—two males and a female. Sloboh's children were Wedlyn Chea, Wedlyn Wleh, and Saytowon. Saytowon got married in this local area, but she did not leave any children. Sloboh's wife, Wedlyn, was a member of the Tuway'o family from the Nyenawleken section of Chedepo. And that's how the relationships are here in this greater Puwaiken area.

119

Wedlyn Chea is the father of Wesseh, my cousin, who is also a member of the Sorpotonmo peer group. His English name is Joe Chea. The following are Chea's other children: Sloboh, Wonley, Tweh, and Gbelei. Chea also had Mongie. We all know her as Cynthia Chea. And Mongie's mother is Gbornyonoh ('Ma Nyonoh'). She comes from this town. Gbornyanoh's father was Kaity Chulu, and her mother was Jaybloh. She is not from this town. She was a Potupo lady, from the town of Gbakebeya.

Wedlyn Wleh's wife was Darnyonoh. She was a hometown woman, from the Ponwaon family. She was the mother of Bokuwo, whom you call "Bokuton." His real name is Kpekeley. The reason for Bokuwo [landfill] is that all the children before his birth did not survive. His parents lost several children before him. Therefore, when he was born, his parents said he, presumably, was going to join the lost ones; that he, too, was just another waste. And that is how his unique nickname came to be. Darnyonoh and Wedlyn Wleh also had Snoteh, Jlopoh, Teaty, Weleoh, Kaylor, Duhl, Juwelay, and Sayonkon.

Wedlyn Wleh had another wife. He had a second wife. Her name was Pinnyonoh. She was the mother of Wannie, Teponley, Jebleh, Beweh, and Tebateh. Like Darnyanoh, Pinnyanoh was a hometown woman, from the Magwulu family."

He talks about Gbeh Chea Nyanley and his descendants:

"Gbeh Chea Nyanley had one child. Chea was his name, and he (Chea) had Wesseh (Toboseh). Wesseh had two children he had Gbeh and Choloplay. Gbeh had one child; his name was Chea. Choloplay's children were Saylee and Sloboh. Chea's children

include Quelley, Nyanley, and Gbeh.

Gbeh (Darsey) and Nyanley are Gbeh Chea Nyanley's children. The two were half-brothers; they had separate mothers. Darsey Gbeh's children include Knoh Toe, Dowu Choloplay, Sloboh, Wesseh (Toboseh), Qwenynonoh, Wolowon, Barfeh, and Tarwiah. I want to say something about the name Dowu Choloplay. His actual given name was Kargee Choloplay. But members of his peer group gave him the nickname "Dowu" because he was a large man, and Dowu implies 'huge' or 'massive.' That is how the name Dowu remains in this family. Originally, it is not a Bocuwao name.

Darsey Gbeh's wife was Jayee. She was the mother of Knoh Toe, Choloplay, Tarwiah, Qwen (Qwenynonoh), Wesseh (Toboseh), and Sloboh.

Darsey Gbeh had a second wife. Her name was Togbe. She was the mother of Barfeh (whose village is known as Salayken), and she was the mother of Wolo (Wolowon).

Dowu Choloplay's children include Tefinneh, Kpekelay, Wesseh, and Sloboh.

Knoh Toe's children include Tumon, Kantey, Wesseh, Gbaka, Khalifa (Wannie),

Dakpaye, Tu, Jebleh, Nyanogbeh, Paytee, and Jallah ("Tayklaygbe").

Sloboh's children include Seoh, Gbeh, and Komoteh.

Komoteh had Choloplay and Minawin. and

Seoh had Jayee, Polebo, Dbawolo, and Karpolo ("Saiday").

Barfeh's children include Kaynyonoh, Weleoh, Worchili, Klawanley, Chea Quelley, and Jowa Doe.

Nyanley's children include Chea, Jaylee, and Worlei.

121

Quelley's children include Kpateah (*whose children are Jaylee, Tiawolo, and Chie*), Doboh, Monjie, Nyankpe, Tiawolo, Tankin, Bloteh, Sloboh, Chea, and Sanma. That's how we are related here.

And that's how we are related in this area. We are brothers; we are sisters—all of us are related one way or another in this greater Puwaiken area. That's how we have come to live together. Joe Chea and I are the elders here today. As I said earlier, we are members of the same peer group, but he is older in real life."

"We understand everything you have explained, Sayjolo said. "I am sure this cassette has captured all that you have said. The man we call Saylee, your paternal grandfather, is the one this next question is about. What was he known for? I am assuming that even though everyone was a subsistence farmer; yet, everyone had something they did on the side, like producing palm wine or setting traps in the wild. Was there anything he did for which the public knew and recognized him?"

"The man you referred to, Saylee, knew how to produce palm wine; he was a trap setter, too. His traps caught very large animals. In fact, my father [Winn] used to do those same things. My father was essentially what we often refer to as 'like father, like son.' But Saylee was a renowned woodcarver, a profession we call 'settee' in Chedepo. He used to fashion wooden utensils; they looked like modern-day bowls. He also fashioned unique dishes. He used to fashion large wooden pans, completed with small, rounded bowl attachments. The pans were used during group eating, and the attachments were used to store meat, fish, or whatever was in the soup for that day. He also fashioned traditional chairs; if you sit in one of his chairs, you will forget about any comfortable chair you have ever sat in.

Sloboh, Saylee's younger brother—Wedlyn Wleh's father— took on a different profession. He was a speaker in the community. He was a spokesperson, a profession we call 'wuluhug' in Chedepo. Sloboh was a very short man, but during his time, they simply called him 'Orjay barti ortonmor,' which translates into 'he stands tall at the sight of barti.' Barti is a large wooden staff that regulates the rotations of speakers. They joked that the short man (Sloboh) grew taller every time an issue came up. He knew the issues of the day. He always had the wooden staff ('barti tu') in his hand; he was quite a chatty person."

"I have heard from other sources that Toku, the large dug-out drum for the peer groups within the Kofa [the young adults] section, was carved by Sloboh. Is that a true story?"

"Yes. That drum ... Sloboh was alive when it was carved out; they carved it. The truth, however, is that he, Sloboh, was not the primary person during the drum work. The man we call Nyekan Kosolo from the Dowao family was the main person during the drum work. The drum, you called it toku (dug-out drum). Well, that is not its actual name. We call it 'Jelatoh,' and the name comes from the foothill on which they cut the huge tree used for the drum work. The tree they used to build the drum is known locally as 'portu.' Jelatoh, the foothill, and the foothill we call Blotoh are connected. These hills are on the Dilamo reservation, on our side of the town. I had my farm on one side of Jelatoh in 1984, the year Saylee Junior was born. It is on the left side when you leave Weltehken and before you get to Tenor, a creek."

"Your father, Winn, what kind of work did he do for the public?"

"Winn was a woodcarver [settee], too. And yes, he had a public role. The job he had is known as jakwi, a maintainer of

123

traditions. Anyway, let me say something about this job. It is reserved solely for the family of Bocuwao. In the land of Kloso, a man from our family is the only one who can serve as a jakwi. Again, only the descendants of Wiah Chie can serve as jakwi, not just any Bocuwao family member. And the consistency is there throughout our history; it has always been the descendants of Wiah Chie. We had Jakwi Kpekeley; we had Jakwi Chea; we had Jakwi Nyanley; Gbeh Chea was a Jakwi; we had Jakwi Cheafueh [Chea, the Elder], and we had Wesseh Chea as a Jakwi. All these people I am naming once held this post, and they are direct descendants of our great father, Wiah Chie, who was the pioneer at the village of Sindoloken. Also, Tebateh was a jakwi. Tebateh was the father of Ninneh [old man Grey, the father of Jackson Gray]. It was Tebateh who died in the town of Chutuken before my father, Polee Winn, became jakwi. Most recently, we had Nyanley Chea as a jakwi. Then we had another Chea, Jorpo Chea; he was a jakwi. Then yesterday [speaking in relative terms], we had Jakwi Jeklay, who is the current one [January 19, 2004]."

"Did your father get the job before your birth, or did he get it after your birth?"

"He had me before he was selected for the job. After Tebateh, the jakwi of Chutuken village, died, the people of Chutuken wanted to replace him. They traveled to Weltehken, where my father was living at the time, and captured him for the post in Chutuken. Remember that a jakwi selection is typically a surprise to the person who is being picked or selected; there is almost never prior notification. My father served in that role in Chutuken until that hamlet started to fall apart. Many residents from the town of Chutuken relocated to neighboring hamlets, particularly Chedepo Jarkaken, where we are today. The fall of Chutuken led to an increase in Jarkaken's population and land area, too. Moreover, after the town of

Klosoken accidentally caught fire [in 1931], its residents—like those who vacated Chutuken—went in droves to Jarkaken.

Quayee Swen, a member of the Nyan Sunu Po branch of our Bocuwao family, was Jarkaken's jakwi when Chutuken fell. [Quayee Swen was the pioneer at Gbetoh village]. As I said earlier, by tradition and throughout our history, Nyan Sunu Po members of our Bocuwao family are not favored for the job; it is traditionally reserved for the Wiah Chie Po members of Bocuwao. So, when my father entered Jarkaken for a permanent stay [in 1942, eleven years after fire destroyed the town of Klosoken], without following the usual process for Jakwi selection, Quayee Swen unilaterally turned over the job to my father.

First, he prepared a special meal for the town of Jarkaken. When the men of Jarkaken gathered, he transferred the post over to my father, saying, 'This job has always been for you, the Wiah Chie's offspring. It has always been your traditional role in our family and in towns across our region. So, we must continue to honor our custom. Winn, you have been doing this job anyway [at Chutuken]. And so, here it is. You can have it."

"Okay, before we move on to another topic, I want you to talk about your mother—the woman who gave birth to you. Please call her name and the names of her parents. If you can, please talk about her children and about the place where she was born."

"As I said earlier, my name is Saylee. I am Winn Saylee. My mother is Teaty. She hailed from the town of Gbeapo Podloken. She was engaged there and brought to Jarkaken. I am her first child. But technically, I am not her first child because she had two children in Weltehken before I was born. She had [Sagiah] Kayjeley and Saylee Gbasay before I was born. After these two children died in the village of Weltehken, my parents [Winn and Teaty] moved to the hamlet of Wotuken, where I was born. Then, three other siblings followed me: Sagiah Kayjeley [Paul K. Winn, Sr], Bocuwao Welley [Lawrence W. Winn], and Gbeh Chea Nyanley [Newton N. Winn]. So, the four of us are her [Teaty's] children.

Kayjeley, the one who is next to me [Josiah Saylee Winn], had two wives. His first wife was Towah [Elsie]. Towah's father was Naetoh, from the Dowao family here in Jarkaken. Her mother was Gbarjlee [Susan Sayonkon]. Towah and Kayjeley had several children: they had Nyonorju ["Eairl"/Sister Sophia]; they had Winn [Randolph / "Kpikpi"]; they had Beweh [Perry/ "Peltee"]; they had Klaynyonoh [Eliza]; they had Chulu [Johnson]; they had Saylee Sinamen [Vesta]; and they had Juty [Baby]. Kayjeley also had a second wife. Her name was Char [Ma Esther]. She was a Nyenawleken woman from the town of Klaboken. Char and Kayjeley had the following children: Parteh/ "Sagiah Kayjaley" [Paul K. Winn, Jr.], Choloplay [Julius/ "Kofee"], Towah [Small Elsie], Quelley [Eugene], and Petelnyonoh [Jemama]. Kayjeley had two other children; their mother was a Mano tribal woman. They had Gbalee [Naomi]; the original Gbalee— Tuwobo Gbalee—was the namesake of old man Winn's stepmother. Kayjeley also had Jaydweh [Meme Girl].

Bocuwao Welley, the one who is next to Kayjeley, has a child of his own. His name is Sagiah Kayjeley.

Gbeh Chea Nyanley, my mother's lastborn, has the following children: Teba Teh [Leartes], Nouwenou, Sayjela [Johnson], Teaty, Towah, Decontee, Jlaylei, Nyonoley [Bobby], Teahswen [Rooney], and Tarwiah.

My mother, Teaty—the one who hailed from Podloken— her mother's name was Wlayee. My maternal grandmother

126

was Wlayee. She was born in Potupo, in the town of Gbakebeya. My maternal grandfather is Nyankpe. Nyankpe and Magh Saylee were brothers. Nyankpe was older, but the younger Magh Saylee was well known in and around their community. He was popular. Magh Saylee had the following children: he had Masan, he had Wlala, and then he had Nowinnie. Nyankpe, my maternal grandfather, had only one male child. His name was Tarchie. But Nyankpe had several female children: he had Nyankpe Teaty (my mother); he had Nyankpe Kaylor; he had Nyankpe Jaydoweh; and he had Nyankpe Tanbo. And that's how Magh Saylee and Nyankpe are related. Even though I go by the name Saylee, it is not the Magh Saylee name that I go by. I want to make that clear."

"I was about to ask you."

"My name is derived from my father's side. My father is Winn (Polee Winn).

Winn's father is Saylee. It is my paternal grandfather's name that I have, not the Gbeapo's

Saylee."

"All right. Your father had two wives. Who was the other wife? I want you to call her name. Where was she born? If she had children, what are the names of her children?"

"My father, Winn, had another wife. She was born in Chedepo Klaboken. Her name was Kaygba. She was a member of the Tuway'o family. She had the following children: Teaswen, Sagiah Wiah, Nagbe Jowa, and Saylee Wedlyn. So, my mother had four children; the other woman had four children, too. We are eight from one father. He left all of us alive when he died. Teaswen has no children. He has since passed away. The man who is next to me in birth order,

127

Kayjeley, is not alive. He passed, too. Two have left us, so we are six today. [Wiah was alive during this conversation.]"

"Tell us, how old were you when you got married? Were you in any of the Kofa peer groups [ages fifteen through twenty-five] or Gbor peer groups [twenty-six and up]?"

"I was a member of the most senior Kofa peer group. We were six months away from promotion to the Gbor stage when I got married. I got married in the year 1956. In fact, I got married on September 19, 1956. Coincidently, my wife gave birth to our first child, Agatha Gbasay Winn, on September 19, 1957."

"I want you to call the name of the woman you got married to."

"Bolju—Bai Toe Bolju. She was born in Killepo Kanweaken. She was a Waile'o family member. I engaged with her there and brought her to Jarkaken. Her father was Bai Toe Toplay. Toplay died while Boju was still a small child. So, she never knew her biological father. She knew Jahowl, the uncle who raised her. Bolju's mother was Cheta Kpalee. Boju had the following children: Gbasay [Agatha], Darty [Sandy], Suhsuh [Susannah], Kpadeh [Satara], Komoh [Wilfred], Tinpan [Roland], Wlotoh [Lavocture], Doe [James], Jahowl [Fredrick], and Saylee [Josiah Jr]."

"You have a second wife." "I have a second wife." "Her name?"

"Her name is Snoh. She is a hometown woman. She was born here in Jarkaken.

Her family is Bowionpo, from the Chenchipo branch of that family. Her father was Kanbo, and her mother was Borto. The following are her children: Sayjolo [Mantee], Taynue

[Chester], Targiour [Nelson], Nouwen [Lucia], Kaylor [Benda], Polebo [Hilary], Woday [Eric], Konnenee ['Butyes, Emmanuel,' KBE], Teahswen [Derris, aka 'Small D'], Magnynoh [Big Girl], Snoteh [Christian], and Benubo [Winford]."

"What we are recording today will go a long way. It will take a long time before this cassette comes to an end. That means it is recording all the things you are talking about. Your great-great-great-grandchildren will have the chance, one day, to listen to your voice. Did you go to school?"

"Hmm ... I went to school. But things were hard back then. I had no support or

supporter, so I stopped in the fifth grade."

"You have not returned to school since?"

"I have not returned to school since then. I entered school in the year 1950; I left school in 1955."

"Okay, after the brief school attendance, you returned home. What job did you

do?"

"Upon return, I began performing subsistence farming. Farming lasted several

years before I started working for the government."

"All the children you have—who you have successfully sent to school—how were you able to support them financially?"

"I have always believed in farming. Every farming year, my wives and I did our best to help our children. Getting outside help was always difficult, perhaps even nonexistent. We relied

129

on our farms to support our children's education. Also, when it came to all my brothers' education, it was hard to find anyone to help. Some of my brothers were in school too: Welley and Kayjeley. In fact, it is ironic but true to say that I left school because of school. I needed to support my brothers in school, so I turned to farming.:

"Within the family of Bocuwao, I want you to name those who are our renowned blacksmiths (or teba) that you know. The ones we have or had in the past."

"We have many blacksmiths. Here are some: Tebateh Fueh (Tebateh, the Elder) was a blacksmith. He was the father of old man Neneh. Tebateh the Elder knew the issues of the day. He was a jakwi as well. We had Jayee Teh; he was a blacksmith. We had Wayee Dweh; he was a blacksmith. Those are the blacksmiths that I know."

"Who are (or were) our great hunters? I am talking about the ones who dominated the field of hunting in this family, or at least the ones who were well known."

"Hunters? We have a lot of hunters. If I count with my hands, I will need more fingers to complete the tally. Tebateh was a hunter. Magsnoh Nyangbe was a hunter. Sayee Teahfore was a hunter. Sloboh was a hunter. Wedlyn Wleh was a hunter. Ah, as I said, I can go on for a long time (and we, the descendants of Wiah Chie, are smart). Knoh Toe was a hunter. Quelley was a hunter, and so on."

"Let's discuss your children's names. Some of the names you gave your children are not traditional Bocuwao family names. Typically, the Bocuwao family uses repeated or recurring names of long-lost kindred, which is not the case for many of your children. You have Wlotoh, Kpadeh, Sayjolo, Tinpan, and Targiour, just to name a few. These names ... we do not hear about them in our history. We don't know of any of these being recurrent or repeated from previous relatives. So, I want you to talk about them individually, if you can.

"Yes, these names ..."

"Please give a short explanation for each name; I think the cassette is nearing completion."

"Okay. The name Sayjolo ..."

"Let's begin with the name Kpadeh."

"**Kpadeh**—this name has its origin in the town of Chedepo Bletiken; it is a Bletiken name. Kpadeh, as a child, brought his own name.

Sayjolo—this name came about during turbulent times in our family. Every time an issue came up, we found ourselves in a state of uncertainty. We worried. We endured episodes of painful thinking. We felt so helpless and overwhelmed—even depressed. In a nutshell, Sayjolo is the catastrophic thinking [depression] we experienced during tough times in our family. It is not originally a Bocuwao name.

Tinpan—this name is similar to Sayjolo. Tinpan is the stressful feeling you get when you are in trouble; Tinpan means 'being squeezed or wedged between dilemmas.'

Wlotoh—one time in the history of this area, our people were getting hurt and even killed violently by falling trees due to very strong tropical storms. That is how his name came about. Our father, Wedlyn Chea, the man who was the founder of Puwaiken village, gave him the name Wlotoh. He said the family of Bocuwao was, in fact, engaged in a war with nature. He used terms like Diatoh and Wlotoh (urban warfare) to describe the storm's

131

violence. Chea said we were in a 'domestic war' with nature itself.

Targiour—my own father, Winn, gave him that name. Winn said the name means

'Winn is a spectator in his world.'"

"Winn had no one. He watched his peers from the sideline live full and abundant lives," Sayjolo added.

"Yes, that was the reason behind the name Targiour. You know by now that Winn lost three of his older brothers while they were young men. These losses deeply impacted Winn's life; in fact, he never truly recovered from them. Moreover, he was never shy to make it known to the world that, while he had managed, for the most part, to live a somewhat normal life on the outside, he was nevertheless a miserable, unhappy, and depressed man on the inside.

The name Welley is another reminder of Winn's unhappiness. Yes, my father was the one who coined the name Welley. But it—the name Welley—is more than just capturing Winn's personal losses. It is a reflection on the losses of the entire family of Bocuwao. The same reasons that gave rise to the name Welley led to the name Targiour, but Welley expands the reasons to a much larger scale. It is not just Welley; it is consistently pronounced with a qualifier: **'Bocuwao Welley.'** Of course, Bocuwao is the name of our mega family. And every time an issue came up in the family of Bocuwao, every time the family of Bocuwao was in trouble with the town of Jarkaken (or Chutuken), the people looked to Winn for a solution.

They depended on him to solve it for the entire family. His attitude had always been that people looked to him to solve the family problems because all the men who would have solved

132

them were deceased. So, Welley means 'the people of Bocuwao have died out; Winn is the only one suffering on their behalf.'

Konnenee—this is not a Bocuwao name either. My cousin Sayee Kupulu (a sister of Sayee Wean) coined that name. She said, 'Kupulu, you have your own issues. Everyone has his or her issues, not just Kupulu.'

Wodai (Woday)—originates from my relocation from the hamlet of Puwaiken.

When I moved here (to this farming settlement of Wodaiken), the first male who was born in this village was Woday (Eric). I gave him the name Woday to highlight to past, present, and future generations of Bocuwao that I did not abandon Puwaiken. I want this to reflect in Bocuwao's history that Saylee did not abandon the famed hamlet—that I did not abandon all the many friends and relatives who called the hamlet home when I decided to 'relocate.' I always say, *'E wodai; E se chela.'* Basically, 'I relocated; I did not abandon Puwai.'"

"Thank you for discussing the names. What year did you leave Puwaiken village for Wodaiken village?"

"I came to this place in the year 1975."

"What is the original name of this foothill on which Wodaiken is situated?", a faint

voice said.

"This foothill on which we sit now is Kantogbe, or Buffalo Hill. It became Kantogbe after one of our forefathers, Quelley Chea Quelley, killed a huge buffalo (or ken) here. In the Bible, God told Adam after the creation period to name things. And whatever name Adam gave an animal, that was that animal's

133

name. The same is true here. I am sure this place had a name before Quelley killed the buffalo. After that event, however, Quelley changed whatever the original name was for this location to reflect his triumph. Now, after relocating from Puwaiken to Kantogbe, I did a name change, too. But I want to make something clear. I only changed the name of the side of the foothill on which I built my huts. The rest of the foothill is still Kantogbe."

"Papay," his wife called.

"Yes."

"Old man Wedlyn Wleh said that this foothill, before Quelley's kill, was known as

Kagba," she said.

"Okay."

"Here in Wodaiken, what is your water source?" a faint voice said.

"We drink from the Geeye Creek. I should say we used to drink from the Geeye. We have since switched to well water. We drank from the Geeye for many decades before switching to well water. We do not drink from the Geeye anymore because we believe it is not sanitary. Our neighbors to our immediate north do laundry in the water and deposit waste in the creek. (We do laundry in the creek and send our dirty water downstream, too. So, there's absolutely no fault with our neighbors.)

However, we sometimes saw solid waste floating down to our section of the creek, perhaps from our neighbors' laundry water waste. Look, we have the folks in Salayken to our north, we have the folks in Normowloken to our north, and we also have the folks in Dbawloken (the Gbetohken area) to our north. These people are pouring their laundry water into the creek (or are directly doing laundry in the creek) and sending dirty water downstream. So that was the reason we decided to stop drinking from the creek."

"Please explain the subgroups within the family of Bocuwao," a faint voice said. "Okay. Bocuwao is historically a small family. But that is changing now. Our

numbers are growing. We have our origin in the land of Tienpo, where our people are

called Bi-laye. We were Bilaye before we were Bocuwao. There are two subdivisions in our family. We are Wiah Chie Po (or Wiah Chie Po Jlu). The other subgroup in our family is Nyan Sunu Po. They are our cousins. We and the Nyan Sunu Po are cousins ("*Gbeyejlujlu*,"). We are children of brothers. We go by the name of our father, Wiah Chie, who history tells us was the pioneer at the settlement of Sindoloken."

"Does the family of Bocuwao—and this is something I have been pondering, and I do not hear folks talk about it either— have witch doctors? Has there ever been a witch doctor to the best of your recollection?", Sayjolo asked.

"We had a witch doctor. He lived long, long ago; in fact, he is several forefathers

back on our family tree. That is why you don't hear about him. The man we call Kargee Choloply and Nyanley were half-brothers. Nyanley—we also call him Gbeh Chea Nyanley—was a witch doctor. I called him earlier, but I forgot to mention that he was our only witch doctor. We have not had any since his time."

135

"The pet name for your peer group is Sorpotomo." "I am a member of Sorpo."

"How many Sorpotonmo members from Bocuwao do you know, and what are their names?"

"That is a sad question. That really makes me sad; I am quite emotional right now.

We were ten, but only three of us are alive today. The first seven I will name have departed this earth. They are Nowinnie Kofa, Tom Pah, Kwiyeyee Saylo, Jowa Doe, Welley Wesseh, and Karpolo [he inadvertently left out peer group member number seven]. The next three are alive now as I am talking (January 19, 2004): Nowinnie Weateah, Wliyor Wesseh, and myself (Winn Saylee)."

"Thank you. In Puwaiken, which you left, who were the other original pioneers at that now-uninhabited hamlet? Can you name the men who lived there at the peak residential area of that famed hamlet— men who had homes there? Name some of them, if naming all would be challenging."

"Well, this is an extension of your previous inquiry, which made me particularly emotional. This latest question of yours is a moving one, too. But I must answer it.

Wedlyn Chea was the founder of Puwaiken; of course, he was one of the inhabitants. Wedlyn Wleh was another; he and Wedlyn Chea were brothers from one mother and one father. My friend Jowa Doe was there; Welley Wesseh was there; the man we call Welteh was there; Dowu Choloplay was there; Knoh Toe was there; and Chea Quelley was there too, even though he left for Wotuken to settle later. All the above-named men are dead; I, the one counting out these names with my fingers—along with Wliyor Wesseh—am the only one here today. I am here with the offspring of all these departed men."

"Here in the village of Wodaiken, which you founded and where we are based today, do you have a hut here?"

"Thank you. I founded Wodaiken. I also have several children. The short answer is no; I do not have a hut here anymore. I am living in Jarkaken proper now. Every time I come here; I am here for a visit. The children I come here to visit periodically are Sayjolo and Kpadeh. They are the two I have left here to continue what I'd done for several decades here. Again, I am in the main town; I do not do anything anymore. I rely on these two to find food for me to eat."

"In my recollection, as a small child and even during our young adult period, you had some livestock—goats, chickens... You are no longer a homeowner here, but do you still have livestock here?"

"Yes. They are still here. These are some of the reasons that continue to entice me to this village. I come here periodically to see them, too."

"Your children who live far away, including overseas, will listen to this cassette. Do you have a message for them ... something they can hear and cherish?"

"Yes. I have a message. The first message is for all who will play this audiotape and listen to it. I want to express my greetings to all of you. Next, to those overseas: Lawrence

W. Winn, the man we call Welley, is their father. They must show him their utmost respect. I want them to see eye to eye with one another. Let them put their lives together. None of them should do anything with the potential to bring shame and embarrassment to our family. We are known and regarded widely as a group of people who live responsible lives. We are vigilant, maintaining our watchful eyes all around us. And wherever they may be, it is apparent that I am no longer their

137

immediate caretaker. But I want them to listen to me. They shouldn't touch anything that is not theirs without permission to do so from the owner. They need to take action only on sound judgment, not just doing something because someone else is doing it. Before copying anyone, that performance must be constructive. So, on behalf of the family here, I am expressing my heartfelt greetings to them. We need assistance. What we want, and this is especially for their father, Welley, is a house in Monrovia. No, I am not suggesting that all of us will leave this place and go to Monrovia; that is not what I am talking about. Look at me. I am old and in poor health. Am I going to leave this place and go to Monrovia to live? No. However, if they build a house in Monrovia, our children can live in it and continue their education in the city. If they build more homes and choose to rent them to the public, that is something I will support as well. This message is not for Welley alone. Of course, Welley needs to build his own house, too. He has been over there for a long time. Susannah, Komoh—in fact, all of them—need to get together; they need to work as one. Taynue, Wlotoh—all of them need to build their own homes, too. The children we have are too many. If we have homes in Monrovia, some of them can relocate there. The idea is to make life a little easier for our children, whether in Monrovia or even here in Jarkaken. So, I send my greetings to all of them!"

"I have something to say, too," the wife said. "To all our children and other relatives overseas, our family has always relied on farming as the main source of support. Yes, your father had a government job; it helped, too. But farming made it possible for many of you to get educational support. We need the same support system to continue for the rest of your little siblings. They are far too many here, perhaps more than when you, the older ones, were coming up. All of them are entering school, and that is a challenge for us. I agree with your father's housing proposal for you. Some of these children need to get

138

out of here. I know how much you are helping; please do not think that I do not understand. For example, the family members who now live in Monrovia rely entirely on you. Even Tinpan and the others who have left us, and we do not even know where they are [Buduburam, Ghana]. They, the ones overseas, know where Tinpan and the others are and how they are surviving in those places. You, the ones overseas, are the people providing all their needs, whether schooling, food, clothing, and rent for the places they are staying. I know all that. I am very grateful to you for all that you are doing. It is because of you that they are living in those places. I have nothing to contribute to their day-to-day lives. So, I am very thankful to God and to you. Here in Jarkaken, people admire the spirit of unity within our family. 'Saylee's children care about one another' is what you hear when you go out to visit with friends and relatives.

I am asking you to continue that spirit of unity. No one should go off course. Use consensus to get things done. Susannah, please continue to give them your advice. You are the oldest of our overseas children. Your father is not well. We are taking him from place to place (out of one clinic into another), but we are seeing very little improvement in his health. He continues to be in poor health. He cannot go to the farm anymore. You need to focus on the ones who really need you in Monrovia. We need intermittent assistance from you.

This will help us help your father. Thank you, and greetings to all of you."

"What was your water source in Puwaiken village while you were there?" a faint

voice said.

"Dbanorgbae and Talwloh creeks were our water sources. But let me say something about Puwai's water problems. The lack of water in Puwaiken, not conflict, was largely responsible for the fall of that hamlet. And even this reason for Puwai's fall is rather ironic because, as I said, there are three creeks near the village: Dbanorgbae, Geeye, and Talwloh. Dbanorgbae, for several decades, was our drinking water. It is a small rock-bedded stream. We drank it; our neighbors to our side, in Quelley's Mubleken, used to drink it, too. This small but important creek was also between us and Chenwniken, a farming reservation that belongs to the family of Bowionpo. But of all Puwaiken's water sources, Dbanorgbae was the very first to fall because something quite mysterious, even to this day, happened. The mystery forced Puwaiken and Mubleken, where Quelley, Togbe Barfeh, and others were at the time, to turn abruptly from Dbanorgbae. What was the mysterious occurrence? A giant footprint. Our women saw a huge footprint by the creek one early morning when they went there to fetch water. It was so long; it was about the length of my entire arm."

"Was it a person's footprint?"

"It was clearly a human footprint. Dbanorgbae Creek was not always between Puwaiken and Wedlyn Wleh's village. That village, Wleh's village, was not always there. At the time of the mysterious footprint, Wleh was still living in Puwaiken. Hence, the Dbanorgbae Creek was basically between Puwaiken and the other farming reservation we call Chenwniken. It belongs to the mega family of Bowionpo. When we saw the mysterious footprint, we knew that it was an unnatural phenomenon. We knew with conviction that someone was trying to hurt us. Someone, perhaps sympathetic to Bowionpo, was trying to bewitch us because the people in Chenwniken were accusing our people of either farming on or near their declared land area. That was the reason we turned from Dbanorgbae to Talwloh Creek (between Puwaiken and Wodaiken) for all our water needs. Then, like other people who

140

decided to build their settlements out of Puwaiken, Wedlyn Wleh, a courageous member of our family, went across Dbanorgbae Creek, perhaps to seal it from the Chenwniken people. Wleh was the only one to go in that direction. No one followed him across Dbanorgbae to settle. By turning in that direction and building his Chianyeken settlement across Dbanorgbae Creek, which was literally a stone's throw away from our huts, Wedlyn Wleh was considered an instigator in Chenwniken. The people in Chianyeken saw Wleh as a flamethrower. His move renewed a long-held, though subtle, farmland conflict between the two families: Bowionpo and Bocuwao. Maybe the mysterious arm-length footprint was a prank, but we took it seriously because of the tension that existed between the reservations at the time.

We were confident that what we saw at the creek was not a child's play. We considered it a deliberate effort through witchcraft to do us harm in Puwaiken. That was what we believed; hence, we told our women to stop fetching water from Dbanorgbae. We declared it impure and tainted.

We put it off limits to Puwai and Muble's residents."

"The way Talwloh's water looks, was it like that while you were drinking it?", the

wife said.

"No. It was not like that. It was not always like that. Not long after we switched from Dbanorgbae to Talwloh, we encountered another problem. We had to leave Talwloh, too. This one was clearly our own doing. Our own careless farming activities—cutting all the forest around Talwloh—left the creek without protection. Lots of trees fell and decayed in that water. What we see now is the result of all of that. We ruined the water."

"During the period of Bell Timber Company (BTC), I think heavy timber

equipment was used to crisscross it, too. Didn't that help to ruin the water also?"

"Yes, the companies brought heavy pieces of logging equipment. First, it was BTC; then it was PTP (Prime Timber Products). The last of the companies was LIPCO (the Liberian Produce Company). This last company did the absolute worst damage to Talwloh. So, the truth is, we do not drink from the creek anymore because of the carelessness of our farmers in conjunction with the recklessness of the timber companies."

"The question about the water source, who asked that question?", Sayjolo asked. "Snoteh," a faint voice said.

"We also call him Kulu or Jugbeye. Yes, that's Jugbeye! Papay, the pioneers who settled at Mubleken, Salayken, Wodaiken, and other places around here, all left Puwaiken before establishing their settlements. Did they move out of Puwaiken due to any conflict?"

"In Puwaiken—while we were there—there was no major conflict. No one left Puwaiken because of any conflict. I had explained earlier the main reason why we left Puwaiken; its water sources were either tainted or polluted. Even in Mubleken, which, like Puwaiken, was vacated, there was no water there. The two communities used to drink from a tiny spring, which has long dried out. Human beings love water; that's one of the reasons why. Barfeh left Mubleken and moved to Salayken, which is along the creek we call Geeye. , I crossed the water— Talwloh and Geeye creeks—and settled along Geeye. We drink Geeye. Talwloh is dirty, so we moved to places where we could obtain water to drink. Anyway, I want to highlight this: Deorblemgehn is a roadside shrine located here in the Dilamo region. We the people in this region

142

of Jarkaken—known collectively as Deorkwen—go there to perform our traditional rituals. On one stormy day, strong winds piled up trees on the original site. The place was deformed because of the violent winds. Moreover, the footpath we used for generations was practically erased. It was hugely altered by timber roads. As a result, we discontinued the footpath and began using one of the timber roads. I, your speaker, cleared a spot adjacent to the ruined spot and planted a tree there. The local name for the tree I planted is Chinyan, which was the same tree we had at the original shrine. I did it so we could have a place to continue our tradition."

"Old man Nyenaon said he planted that tree at the new location," the wife, Snoh, said.

"Nyenaon did not plant it. I planted it. I planted it in 1984. We still performed our activities after the storm damaged the shrine. I am not saying that I planted the tree before we started performing our rituals. I planted that tree as an alternative after the powerful storms destroyed what we had at the old spot."

"Today is the 19th of January 2004," Sayjolo said and ended the interview.

Chapter XII:
Home, Sweet Home: No Place is Better than Home

I took a trip to Liberia in November 2018, which—to this day—is one of the most eventful of all the trips I have made back home; granted, that was only my third visit since 1994, the year I came to the United States. To this day, it remains the most memorable of all my visits.

I made a hasty decision on lodging. I elected to stay at the home of a close cousin, Agatha Bornyonnoh Sayee, as opposed to lodging at my immediate family's "Big House," a two-house compound I built for them in Caldwell, just outside Monrovia, Liberia.

Though referred to as big, it is important to note that neither of the two houses in the compound is necessarily bigger than any of the other family houses in the greater Monrovia area. But together the Caldwell houses contain a total of eight bedrooms. There are three bedrooms in the smaller house, and the larger one has five bedrooms. Thus, it is, indeed, a spacious complex. Moreover, the main reason the term "big" may be a fit for the compound is that the houses were the first on the scene, if you like, when the family desperately needed a place of their own in that sprawling city.

The idea of building a house in Monrovia had been on my mind for a very long time, probably from the day I entered the United States. But the means did not come until I enlisted in the United States Army in 2001. In 2004, my father, Josiah S. Winn, Sr., provided the momentum when Mantee Sayjolo Winn, his son, helped him to record a lengthy video message

144

for all his US-based children and other relatives. They managed to send the recording to me that same year (2004).

"We need assistance," one of the messages said. "What we want, and this is especially for their father, [Lawrence] Welley [Winn], is a house in Monrovia. No, I am not suggesting that all of us will leave this place [Chedepo Jarkaken, River Gee] and go to Monrovia; that is not what I am talking about. Look at me. I am old [72] and in poor health. Am I going to leave this place and go to Monrovia to live? No. However, if they build a house in Monrovia, our children can live in it and continue their education in the city. If they build more homes and choose to rent them to the public, that is something I will support as well. This message is not for Welley alone. Of course, Welley needs to build his own house, too. He has been over there for a long time. Susannah [S. Winn], Wilfred] Komoh [Winn]—in fact, all of them—need to get together; they need to work as one. [Chester] Taynue [Winn], [Lavocture] Wlotoh [Winn]—all of them need to build their own homes, too. The children we have are too many. If we have homes in Monrovia, some of them can relocate there. The idea is to make life a little easier for our children, whether in Monrovia or even here in Jarkaken."

My goal, initially, was to build a single house for them; however, once I started sending the resources for the construction of the house, Roland Tinpan Winn, who led the operation (along with other family members), decided that a five-bedroom house—though appreciated—would not have been big enough for the family of families. So, without telling me, they decided to make the house, well, big. Hence, they added a smaller house: a three-bedroom house, which they call the "Boys' Quarter." I did not know anything about the house throughout the construction period.

145

"I repeatedly warned them—in the strongest terms possible—not to tell him [about the added house]," Roland explained the story to our mothers in 2005, the year I first visited them. It was my first time ever in Monrovia. "It was not in his plan to build two houses, but we are too many here. Once he said 'Build a house,' I thought it was an opportunity to increase the living space."

Anyway, I found out about the smaller house when it was time for the family to do the roofing work. They had to tell me, or I would have provided just enough roofing materials for one house. My reaction to the presence of a second house was mixed, a bittersweet one, if you like. I felt that including me in the deliberations and decisions to add another house would have been a better course of action. In other words, leaving me out of the decision-making, sort of, was one of the many inconveniences I highlighted to them. Besides, I was very grateful, particularly for the management skills they had employed. Upon completion, the compound was big enough for all of them.

But a few years later, my younger brother, Lavocture W. Winn, and my oldest sister, Susannah S. Winn, adhered to our father's message. They built their own houses elsewhere in the city. And when their homes were completed, many family members began to trickle out of the Caldwell houses and into the new houses.

My brief visit to Monrovia, Liberia:

"It will always be the big house. It is the headquarters," Roland told me on

November 2, 2018, was the day I went to the Caldwell houses for a kola or welcome ceremony.

146

In November 2018, family members gathered at the Caldwell houses outside Monrovia and presented a kola nut to me, a traditional Grebo welcome ceremony.

So, it was this Big House that the family expected me to lodge in when I visited them in November 2018. But, in retrospect, I was a bit naïve. I did not even consider the detrimental effects such a decision—leaving the United States and staying away from the Winn family—would have had on family members. Yet, I agreed hastily to stay at a location that was far away from them. It was a hard lesson-learned for me. My action was painful to them.

I had clearly "ruffled many feathers," as the saying goes. I tried to repair the damage because some family members had, in fact, developed theories—reasons they thought had triggered my decision to stay at Bornyonnoh's place. Of course, their reasons were not rooted in the facts, but I knew they came from a place of agony.

147

Hilary Polebo Winn, my brother, told me to my face—which is something I appreciate—that, indeed, I "hurt" the family's collective feeling. "We are hurt," he told me while the family assembled at his place for one of their rotational meetings. I could see the pain he was talking about at the family gathering. And suddenly, I wanted to develop the ability to formulate perfect sentences in my rebuttal to Hilary's powerful and emotional comments. I wanted to find perfect words to tell them how deeply sorry I was—words that would have made it clear that I understood the pain my action had caused them.

I had no one to blame, not even Bornyonnoh, but myself. For the record, Agatha Bornyonnoh Sayee requested to host me as a way to express her gratitude for the several years her support I gave her (and her family as well). She almost died in the city of Côte d'Ivoire. Thank God, she was able to respond positively to treatment, which included a surgery in the commercial city of Abidjan. She recovered. And after her illness, I paid her way to leave Côte d'Ivoire and go to Monrovia, Liberia, to be with her immediate family members. (She had been alone in Abidjan for many of the Liberian warring and post-warring years.) And so, this was her reason for wanting to appreciate me by demonstrating her family's hospitality towards me. And I spontaneously agreed.

In truth, I think it was very painful for my immediate family members because the

decision to stay at Bornyonnoh's place was not a collective one. My immediate family was left out from the onset. It was shocking to them, if not vexing, that I—a Winn—was back home from abroad (the United States) but was not in the family house.

They were not against Bornyonnoh either. They had nothing against her. In fact, many of them managed to make frequent trips to her house while I was there. They clearly did not blame her for anything. They were not happy because they were left out of the decision-making process.

Bornyonnoh was present at the meeting place, where the family confronted me.

And I am glad she was there.

Given the opportunity to respond, I simply apologized to my immediate family members for my action. Then I sat down.

Thankfully, Johnson Sayjela Winn, my brother, was the next orator. He got up and changed the subject from what had actually been a double whammy.

Micky Jaydweh Winn, Uncle Paul Kayjeley Winn's daughter—the younger sister of Naomi Gbalee Winn—was the first to create a powerful scene at the meeting place.

149

It was my first time to meet her, assuming my recollection had served me well. I knew about her. Gbalee used to talk about her in Jarkaken. The opportunity to meet her did not come until 2018. By this time, she was an adult. Anyway, Jaydweh was beyond angry that day. She was not happy. She was quite furious at the Dixville home, where we gathered. The Winn family, she said, had "forgotten" her, and she wanted to know if she wasn't a member of the family anymore. She was stomping, taking a few steps here and there while she expressed herself. It was quite a protracted, venting session during which the young lady tossed blame in all directions. I sat there—speechless. She even perceived favoritism—to her detriment, of course. Nothing was in Jaydweh's favor. It took our big brother, Darty, along with Hilary and other family members, to calm her down.

Then, after she left the floor, Hilary got up and raised the lodging fallout. So, for nearly half an hour, if not more, we saw barely any smiling faces in the room.

Hence, when Johnson stood up and introduced his topic, the mood of the audience changed.

150

"When I was in school," Johnson said, "anytime I said I was hungry, the man could send me food money. He paid my rent. He paid all my school fees. And I got out of the university...exact[ly] eight semesters—that's four years. So, I want to take this time to gown my sponsor." The crowd

applauded as Johnson opened a black plastic bag and revealed an African shirt and a matching cap. Big Brother Darty walked over to Johnson, and both men put the "gown" on me.

"When I graduated," Johnson continued, "I did this same thing to Roland," he told the folks at the meeting place. Then he emphasized the significant role Roland, whom he called "The Mastermind," had played during the educational endeavors of KBE (Konnenee "Butyes" Emmanuel), Josiah Saylee Winn, Jr, and himself (Johnson). It was a timely intervention that helped the family members to restore their lost smiles.

After November 13, 2018, which was the day I reentered Monrovia from River Gee, I visited just about every family member in the greater Monrovia area. I visited both immediate and external family members. The family members I visited are too many to count; I'd rather not start. But I will name the places I did not just visit but spent a night or two.

Five days before my departure date of November 28, 2018, I left Bornyonnoh's home and went to Hilary Winn's place the early morning of November 23, 2018. I spent the night there after a well-attended family meeting (during which the family confronted me over the now-infamous lodging debacle, or fallout). The family prepared a goat and rice meal, and we ate together. We brought the goat from the interior (Jarkaken), along with a few chickens. We ate the chickens en route to Monrovia. The chickens did not make it out of Fish Town, but the goat—which we tied up and fed on the roof of our sports utility vehicle (SUV)—made it to Monrovia for the big occasion.

A feast after a powerful family meeting; many "feathers were ruffled" before this moment

I went home to Bornyonnoh on the 24th of the month, only to turn around the next day, the 25th, for the Big House, where I spent that night with big brother Doezs and his wife, To-do Winn. In the afternoon of the 26th, I went back to the meeting place, at Brother Hillary Winn's place, and spent the night there. Then the early morning of the 27th, I went to the home of my younger sister, Mrs. Lucia Nowen Winn-Davis. I spent the entire day and night there. From her place, Bornyonnoh, Tinpan, and others took me to Robert's International Airport, a familiar site; I spent six months at the Robert's International Airport during the Ebola pandemic.

From the passages below, you will realize that I did, on average, spend close to the same number of days with the immediate family as I did with external family members.

153

My brief visit to River Gee County, Liberia

Note: I left the United States on October 28, 2018, but I did not make it to Liberia until November 1, 2018. I stayed an entire month in Liberia.

Just four days in Monrovia, I left the city for the interior. I traveled to Jarkaken, River Gee, with Johnson Sayjela Winn and Roland Tinpan Winn. Admittedly, Roland helped me the most during this trip; I am very grateful for his assistance. My cousin, Johnson, too, left his work—something I did not quite relish—just to get me home to Jarkaken. I really appreciated him for his assistance, too.

By the way, the trip from Monrovia to the interior of the country will forever be memorable. We left Monrovia in a chartered SUV, a four-wheel vehicle, on November 5, 2018, and arrived in Jarkaken Town on November 7, 2018.

The two men joined me on the dangerous road trip, and I am glad they did. We got stuck a few times along the way. But the two men kept us going. They dug us out of the mud. In places where we could not help ourselves, they walked miles to nearby towns and sought help. That was the case when we were approaching Zwedru, from Sinoe (We had to use the coastal road). We had some energetic Liberian youths come over and get us out of a deep, muddy spot—so deep, three of the four tires were submerged. We survived the muddy road network in Liberia.

These young men, from the Krahn tribe, helped to dig us out of the mud as we approached Zwedru, on the Grand Gedeh side of the Sinoe-Grand Gedeh thoroughfare.

While in Jarkaken, I joined several men—Jahwaleh, S. Kpadeh Winn, Toe Juty, Gbogbeh Toe, Johnson Winn, Roland Winn, Woday Winn—and visited Puwaiken village in the early morning of November 8, 2018. I went to the village to assess the field, a swamp rice field, which I was helping the family to cultivate. Some work was required to get water to some sections of the farm. We also had to do something about the route to the village of Wodaiken, which was cut off from Puwaiken and the rest of the world, basically in any direction, by muddy waters. We had to dress down—way down—before crossing the 400-meter muddy sludge between Puwaiken proper and Wodaiken village.

(A hardened corridor now connects Puwaiken to Wodaiken, thanks to Komoh and Suhsuh.) I also asked my family, Bocuwao, to conduct a traditional marriage for me—to present a bride price (dowry) to the family of Bowionpo, whose

155

daughter I had at home back in the States. Annie and I had done the contemporary version several years earlier at a courthouse in Newport News, Virginia. We agreed to seal the deal using the traditional system. So, the two families—Bowionpo and Bocuwao—met at the home of Mr. Fulton Sayon Pah, the uncle of Annie. It was at her uncle's place where the families conducted the ceremony on November 9, 2018.

The night following the dowry payment ceremony to the family of Bowionpo, I went to the home of my younger sister, Benda Kaylor Winn, in Karweadolo, a borough in Jarkaken. But I did not stay the entire night at her place. My brothers came and got me just a few minutes before 2:00 a.m.; country devil had popped up in front of Kpadeh's house. Thus, I spent the rest of the morning of November 10, 2018, in Kpadeh's house.

That was all the time I had in the town of Jarkaken. Because of the bad roads, I had to start the journey back to Monrovia the next day, November 10, 2018. By 11:00 a.m., we left the town of Jarkaken and drove a short distance—about a forty-minute drive—to Fish Town, River Gee. Other family members were eagerly waiting to see us in the city.

We visited the village of Puwaiken early morning of November 8, 2018. We went there to see the family's farm—a swamp rice field. We—all eight of us: Jahwaleh, Kpadeh, Toe Juty, Gbogbeh Toe, Sayjela, Tinpan, Woday, and I [Komoh]— walked the two-hour-long route to the village.

Getting to Wodaiken was a challenge; swampland basically cut the hamlet of Wodaiken off from its neighboring villages, particularly Puwaiken. In fact, we had to dress down before crossing the 400-meter-long muddy sludge between the villages.

156

[Today, however, a hardened corridor connects Puwaiken to Wodaiken, thanks to Komoh and Choloplay Suhsuh.]

The next day, I asked my family—the Bocuwao Family in Chedepo Jarkaken—to conduct a traditional marriage for me by presenting a bride price or dowry to the family of Bowionpo, whose daughter I had at home back in the United States of America (USA).

Paytee, daughter of Paytee Jarbo, and I had done the contemporary version several years earlier at a courthouse in the city of Newport News, Virginia, USA. But we decided to seal the deal using the traditional arrangement. So, both our families—Bowionpo and Bocuwao—met at the home of Sayon Pah, the uncle of Annie. It was at her uncle's place where the families conducted the ceremony on November 9, 2018.

The night following the dowry payment to the family of Bowionpo, I went to the home of my younger sister, Nyangbe Kaylor, in Karweadolo, a borough of Chedepo Jarkaken. But I did not stay the entire night. Folks came and got me in the middle of the night; the townspeople had gathered at Kpadeh's house, and they wanted to meet me.

Thus, I spent the rest of the morning of November 10, 2018, at Kpadeh's house.

157

That was all the time I had in the town of Chedepo Jarkaken. Because of the bad roads in Liberia, my entourage and I had to start the journey back to Monrovia on November 10, 2018. We left the town by 11:00 in the morning; our destination was Fish Town, a forty-minute drive from Jarkaken. We had other family members there, eagerly waiting to see us in the city.

But, just a few minutes outside Chedepo Jarkaken, we met several elders walking from the towns of Jarkaken and Geeken. They were going to the nearby town of Putuken, a main road community, to attend a court hearing over a land dispute, which, they said, was between the people of Chedepo (Putuken in particular) and Killepo (Kanweaken, specifically). We made a quick decision to get out of our truck and instructed our driver to take the men to Putuken while we walked leisurely along the Jarkaken- Putuken road. It was a gesture the men appreciated. Mr. Charles Worjolo, a native of Geeken, and other elders couldn't believe that I, a man from the USA, had no second thought about getting out of my car in order to allow the locals to get to court on time. "It is no problem, old man. He [the driver] will come back for us," I told him. Indeed, it was

our pleasure to do such a favor for the men.

The truck returned shortly for us, and the driver took us straight to Fish Town City, the provincial capital of River Gee County. We went to Woday's house upon arrival. The family members we met there were exceedingly happy; they turned the place inside out, like the experiences we had in Jarkaken, River Gee.

"It is our custom," a young man stood up and said while we sat on long benches in Woday's living room. "This is something we do whenever we have visiting guests. We give them kola nuts. To our strangers who walked through the

158

elements—including landscapes infested with snakes and wild cats—just to get to us, we offer this kola nut."

"We accept it," I said.

"As you can see, we present it whole. That symbolizes unity. Let us be one." "Bless the kola so we clan split it," a voice said.

"No, pray first, then split it," another said.

"We do the prayer before splitting the kola nut. Let's pray. Our God, we thank you

for getting us to this time of our lives. We thank you for the safe arrivals of our stingers. We thank you for the joy among us. You made this kola possible. Bless it, so it can be a remedy for any ills in our bodies. Amen."

"This is Choloplay," a man behind the camera introduced the presenter of the kola nut. Then he said, "This is Nelson," pointing to the man who prayed. "This is Kofa. This is Rose, the wife of Woday, and this is Nelson's wife, Mercy. We are inside the Fish Town house."

"We use kola nut to get the reason behind a stranger's travel. As you can see, we have finished the kola, so we are curious," Choloplay said.

"We are here to visit. This is our destination. We are not passing through today," I

said.

"Welcome. You are free to move about. Go anywhere you please, but please stay

out of the chief priest's compound."

The crowd burst into laughter.

"My Full of Fan!" Rose appeared in a clown-like outfit, a black male blazer over her traditional lapa wraparound. We burst out laughing at the sight of the ridiculous outfit. Then she revealed her character: Darty, her brother-in-law, who traveled to the rural countryside three years earlier to attend the funeral of his father, Josiah S. Winn, aka Full of Fan.

"I love my father the best," she said in fancy Liberian English. "And my father loved me, I love him, too. Our best warrior. Today you leave us. My mother...my mother died [too]. And my father!"

She paused and asked her audience to introduce the voice of another character, Chebo Wayee, a peer member of Darty.

"And Chebo Wayee said, 'My friend, have my sympathy.'"

"Chebo Wayee, my friend, this is what happened to me," the crowd intensified its

laughter as Rose does some manly moves in her funny suit.

"Have my sympathy," a make-believe Chebo Wayee said in the crowd.

"I am done. My life is over. E say naakon; e say gbeiyekon. I have no mother; I have no father. Only Elizabeth Winn is left. My father! Josiah Winn, I love you. Aye, my love and my lord. My creator is Josiah Winn."

"Please be comforted, Doesz."

"Chebo Wayee, my friend, you see what happened to me? Of all my father's children, I am his favorite. Because I am poor, he never ate anything from me," she said and ran off with laughter.

We rested a little at Eric's place, an acre of land on which he built two small houses. I noticed the lawn was cut and neatly maintained, a testament to hard work. I saw a great deal of vegetation several meters beyond the well-maintained lawn. I saw tangerine and mango trees in the yard. I saw several pineapple plants in the yard, too. The family had a few chairs under the trees. Thus, we retreated there and took a cool, shaded break. We spent an hour or so there and watched as folks—from their daily errands—filed into the two small homes. We saw the kids as they returned home from school. Pictures aside, I had never physically seen all the Fish Town children until that day, November 10, 2018.

We rested a little at Eric's place, an acre of land on which he built two small houses.

Their stories had to be the same about me, too. They had never seen me in person, either, until that day. They were all born in my absence. Hence, it was no surprise when one of the children (perhaps around the age of ten) failed what we naively thought would have been an easy test. Asked who was the "American man" among his visiting uncles (I was there with Roland and Johnson), without any hesitation, the little boy pointed straight to the smartly dressed Uncle Roland. "Him!" he said with conviction. Like me, Roland was not an everyday uncle for the children. He was an outsider, a Monrovian.

It was a typical Liberian yard. However, Eric's area, to me, appeared isolated.

Soon, however, I realized that that was deceptive because the sprawling city of Fish Town lay just behind the thin layer of vegetation.

We rested a little at Eric's place, an acre of land on which he built two small houses.

Upon arrival in Fish Town, we told the families our plan was to leave the city in the early hours of the next day, November 11, 2018. And so, I wanted to see as many family members in the provincial town as I possibly could.

We visited Cousin C. Farley Sayee. I wanted to see Oldman Joe T. Sayee, but Farley told us the old man was, in fact, in Jarkaken. I was disappointed because I learned in Monrovia

162

that the old man was in Fish Town, so I did not bother to look for him in Jarkaken. We saw Cousin Paytee Sayee. We saw Cousin Napoleon Decontee Beweh, son of Aunty Lucy Jowa Winn. We also saw Aunty Elizabeth Wedlyn Winn, the younger sister of Aunty Lucy.

We went to Uncle Newton's house. It was not far from Woday's compound. It was just down the main road, a cross-town road along which many residents lined their houses and businesses. After a few minutes' walk, we were there. Known for putting huge emphasis on words of appreciation, such as "Tato!" in Chedepo, the uncle received us with passion. It is something I relish about him. It is his natural way to greet or express gratitude. On this November day, he was no different: "Tato! Tato! Tato!" he went down the line and greeted us.

He had great things to say about Eric. "Woday is not a lazy person," he told us.

That was one of several commendations he highlighted to me and members of my entourage. Uncle Newton validated what I knew already about the hard worker.

But, of all the experiences I observed or the events in which I participated while I was in the city of Fish Town, none came close to the historical conversation we had with our uncle, Newton Nyanley Winn. He gets the privilege of being called Winn, thanks to his decades of teaching at Kaytoken Junior High School, where the students (and, therefore, the entire youth population in and around Jarkaken) simply called him Winn. And so, even in our family, we call him Winn, and that does not create any ambiguities. "I am going to Winn's place" is as clear to us as day is to night. The person is going to Uncle Newton's place.

Anyway, what I like best about Uncle as a narrator is that he is very good at remembering the names of historical people.

163

He is good at connecting people, as in how people are related to one another. He injected satire in his narratives with relative frequency, so we did not realize how fast an hour and a half had elapsed. Moreover, he kept us totally involved during the conversation, mainly as active listeners.

Truly, we got oral history lessons from one of the best. Uncle Newton is an excellent narrator. We got the best of him even though the deliberations occurred in an impromptu fashion. He presented the discussions to us in such an impressive manner.

I walked away from that November 10, 2018, briefing with this declaration: "Uncle Newton N. Winn is in a category of his own when it comes to narrating oral history." He did not just tell the story in such an eloquent fashion; he did so without any embellishment. There were a few exceptions, though; there were moments during which he purposely explained certain narratives in humorous fashion. We knew he was joking in each of those moments. We had to know because his jokes had punchlines, which induced, as my Pastor, Sony Quaye, would say, our "crackling laughter." But he was authentic throughout the deliberations.

The proof, as you continue through this document, is self-evident. His narratives contain specificities: names of people; the parents of the people he talked about; places they had lived; the husbands or wives they married while they were there, and the children who had ensued from such relationships; he talked about dates; granted, they were mostly the years during which the events he narrated had transpired. He named the peer groups of many of the personnel in his stories, which is particularly helpful because that allows members of his audience to relate in real time. For example, "Khordi Sayee and David Chulu are the same generation," he said. And that gives us a real-time clue

164

on how old our long-lost uncle, Edward Khordi Sayee Chea, would have been today.

Uncle sat under a tiny palm tree in his yard; we all gathered around him. The sky was darkening, thanks to a patch of soon-to-fall rain, which stubbornly hung over us; a few intermittent rain droplets landed on us and on the giant house in which he lived with his young wife, Mrs. Esther Slohblee Swen-Winn, the daughter of Swen Tuwaju. It was not too dark; we could clearly make out things, even in the distance. Their house was painted in a teal color. It was incredibly close to the edge of the cross-town road. The city's road project, which was in full swing when I visited, was eating away at his yard. The more the engineers leveled the surface below, the deeper the drop when seen from Uncle's yard.

We were many the day we visited Uncle Newton N. Winn. My nephew, Kofa Toe Tweh Weah, the son of Agatha (Saylee Gbasay) and Toe Tweh, was there; Johnson Sayjela Winn, son

165

of Uncle Newton and Rachael Girl, was there; Roland Tinpan Winn, who is the immediate junior to me, was there; Woday (Eric) and Nelson Targiour Winn, my brothers, were there. Lastly, a small child—no more than five years old—was there as well. I did not ask, but I figured he had to be the son of Uncle and his young wife, Esther.

"We accept the kola; thank you for it," Roland said.

"A stranger brings blessing; that is what we say in the land of Chedepo," the wife said as she gestured for prayer before the consumption of the kola and rice with palm butter soup, which was surprisingly enough to feed all of us. "Surprisingly," because we did not forecast our trip, at least I did not tell her or her husband that I was going to pass through the city of Fish Town to see them before going back to Monrovia. Most importantly, going through Fish Town was not in our initial plan, the plan we had when we left Monrovia for River Gee. That was the reason for the surprise—that such a feast was waiting when we arrived at Uncle's house.

For some reason, the other members of my entourage looked to Johnson to conduct the prayer, and I could tell that he, Johnson, did not relish the task. "But I am a stranger," he protested as he gazed in the direction of the veteran Fish Town folks: Eric, Kofa, and Nelson. "It doesn't matter, man," Nelson fired a firmed and forceful rebuttal. "Pray for the kola." And that was the end of the tussle over a prayer. Reluctantly, Johnson gave in and conducted the prayer. We ate the kola first, then we jumped to the rice and ate it, too.

Then we took some time to greet each other again.

166

Moments after I entered Chedepo Jarkaken

Chapter XIII:
The Gazebo Narratives

Even though I did not expect the old man, Gbeh Chea Nyanley, to narrate our family's past, I was, nevertheless, delighted by his decision to discuss the history of our greater Bocuwao family. So, I gave Johnson a signal to begin recording him.

"Saylee's mother was Swen Chie." The old man jumped straight to our family's past. "And she, Swen Chie, also had another son; his name was Sloboh. It was this second son, Sloboh, whose wife—Wedlyn—I am about to discuss. Wedlyn and Sloboh had three children. They had Wedlyn Chea, Wedlyn Wleh, and their sister, Saytowon. As for Wedlyn Wleh, he grew up with my father, Saylee Winn. It was my father who found him a wife, but that is beside the point," he said.

The family of Bocuwao was prone to tragedies; we learned. And uncle was telling us about some of the tough times our forefathers had endured. He used the illness and subsequent death of Wedlyn to highlight these aspects of the family's past. Wedlyn's death, he said, was the first he had observed as a small child.

"They went for her," he said. "She was beyond sick. She was almost dead when Sagiah Kayjeley, Gbalee Duhl, and Khordi Sayee brought her to town. I think it may have been in the year 1955. And I was only six years old. I was born in the year 1949, September 1949. So, if you do the math, I was six years old. To put that in perspective, this child right here," he pointed to a small child, "is not quite six years old yet, but he is observing us now; he is seeing what we are doing here. So, as I was saying, they went for her and brought her to town."

They had to take her to Winn's place. Winn was the son of Saylee, the older brother of Sloboh. So, it was at Winn's home in the big town where they took the sick woman. Sloboh had no home in the town proper. So, he took his sick wife to his nephew's house. And Winn, Sloboh's nephew, was an important person in the town [Jarkaken]. He was a title holder. He lived a lifestyle that was very restrictive because of his title. Here is uncle:

"She couldn't go into my mother's hut," Uncle continued. "It was a taboo to take a corpse to her house because she was the senior of Winn's two wives [Teaty and Kaygba]. Winn was a Jakwi," a title he had for the town of Chutuken and later for Jarkaken. "Moreover, the country devil and a corpse cannot be inside the same hut. There are two title holders who must lead polygamy relationships because of the nature of their job descriptions: Jakwi and Bodieor, the chief priest. Each of the wives must have a hut. The high priest cannot see a corpse. If someone close to him dies, they will take the corpse to his second wife's place. And that was the case for Sloboh's wife, Wedlyn. They took her to Kaygba's hut as opposed to Teaty's hut."

He took a break from Wedlyn's story and went to another tragedy, the death of a

much younger victim—Khordi Sayee.

"Khordi Sayee was Wedlyn Chea's son [Sloboh's grandson]. He was born in the year 1942, and he died in the year 1967."

He was 25 years old when he died. Based on his age, he had barely made it to the seniors of Kofa (Kofajesinyo). The young man's death occurred probably in the final days of February or later in March. Uncle remembered some details.

"[The news got to us in the evening.] It was just after we had burned our farms in that year (1967). The farms burned to such an extent that we had no work left to do. It was quite rare. There was barely anything left to clean up before planting. The fire cleared everything. For forest farms, that was extraordinarily uncommon. The fire simply consumed everything in its path. It even went on to the adjacent wooded area—well beyond the limits of the farms—and burned huge sections of the forest undergrowth.

Maybe that was a telltale sign for a looming trouble, which came in the form of his death. And so, we got a terrible message, saying, 'Your son who just graduated [from high school] has died.' It was a shocking story. People were crying in Puwaiken. Some people left the village for the main town the same day. They went at night because the news got to us late in the evening. He was the first high school graduate in our greater Bocuwao family."

Then he remembered another painful death.

"The death of Sophia Tiawolo Quelley—the daughter of Chea Quelley—was in the same manner as Khordi Sayee's. By the way, her namesake is the small Tiawoloh we have with us now. But the original Tiawolo was the daughter of old man Gbeh Chea Nyanley. So, Quelley Tiawolo was the namesake of Nyanley Tiawolo. Sophia Tiawolo Quelley graduated in Pleebo, Maryland. She was in a polygamy relationship; reportedly, Sophia's mate was responsible for her death. I will table that there, but that is another calamity out of the slew of calamities we suffered, historically."

Uncle moved on to another episode of that turbulent era. He discussed some early challenges of some family members, mainly the unpleasant life experiences his older siblings—

Winn Saylee (Josiah) and Sagiah Kayjeley (Paul)—had endured.

"Kantogbe, the foothill where the village is today," he said, "was the location of our farm the year Khordi Sayee died. Many of the farms in that year were in a general area. The families were together, so it was a massive field. And just a few days after Josiah, my brother, started his farm, he decided to halt the work on his farm. At that time, he had no hut in Puwaiken. So, he tabled the farming work and began to build a village hut. And, by the time he finished the hut, it was too late to continue the farm—a forest farm. Thus, he needed a location with younger bushes [as opposed to a forest farm] to make a farm for that year. He went to Wedlyn Chea, the son of Sloboh, who was the founder of the village of Puwaiken. He had lived there the longest and had cultivated a wider area around the hamlet. 'Please give me a location with young bushes, so I can make a farm,' he asked. 'Chie Gbeye,' Wedlyn Chea called my brother [by a nickname] and said, 'Come here.' Then he pointed to a forest in the distance and said, 'Do you see that? That is a forest. We cut that down first before young bushes can grow in its place.'"

"Who-wa," I said, Chedepo's equivalent of "wow," and moved closer to the narrator. Literally, I picked up my chair and moved much closer to him. I was surprised to hear that my father was refused a farming spot in Puwaiken. "He was not running from cultivating a forest; the timing was not conducive because he had lost a great deal of time building a house. He wanted to put a roof over the heads of his family members first before farming," a thought formed in my mind.

"For that reason," he picked up where he had left off. "He ['Chie Gbeye'] had to leave the village and the hut he had just completed. He went to the town proper to stay. For that year's

171

farming, however, he farmed near Saylo. Where is Saylo? You guys travel on that road all the time," he said.

No one among us knew about Saylo, especially as a location. Prior to the conversation, I had not an inkling that a foothill existed in our region by that name. In fact, when my uncle said Saylo, my thoughts ran to our uncle by the same name: Kwiyeyee Saylo (Elijah S. Jowah). I was under the impression that Father had gone to his cousin (and fellow Sorpotonmo member) to look for young bushes.

He described the location of Saylo.

"When you leave Jarkaken, the first hill you will go around is Koso (Kloso), and, by the time you complete that go-around, you will get to the foothill of Chutu. You will have the option of either trekking over or going around the foothill of Chutu. Adjacent to Chutu is a tiny foothill—it is between Chutu and Kloso—we call it Tarwulu. Tarwulu is connected to the foothill of Chutu. The point at which you clear or pass Chutu lies at Wlenorgbae, a creek. From this creek, you will get to Deorblemgehn, where the people in the Dilamo reservation conduct their ritual (petitioning of their gods). To the left of this site, while facing Chichi Creek, is the reservation's resting site; it is our burial ground. Our father, Kargee Choloplay Saylee, is buried there. Our important people—heroes, great hunters, and the family's oldest members—are buried there, not in the cemetery near the town. From this location, you will get to Seorwle, another foothill. From Seorwle, it is just a short walk to Chichi, the northern Gee River. Just beyond Chichi is Perlo (Joyl), the long foothill we walk over foothill.

There is another hill to the right of Chichi. This foothill is located downstream. We call it Kantogbe. Once you pass between Perlo and Kantogbe and hop into Gbaenorgbae (a creek), there is the tiny bump we call Saylo. It is not quite a hill.

172

Saylo is to the right while the traveler approaches Wolorplu." He continued.

"In other words, Saylo and Wolorplu are in the same vicinity. When you pass Chichi Creek, you will climb Joyl, a foothill. Go down Joyl, and that will take you across Gbaenorgbae, a tiny creek. The tiny foothill of Saylo is to the right. That was the farm we had that year in 1962, the year Susannah was born. Because he was refused a location with young brushes, he had to go that far back to find a farming location that year. Wedlyn Chea showed him a forest," uncle continued, with emphasis on the event that had transpired, which led to his brother leaving Puwaiken to seek a farming location several miles away. "He said, 'Young bushes just do not pop up in the middle of the forest. You must cut the forest down, clear it, make the farm, and then wait for subsequent years before you can see young forest springing up on that spot. It just does not appear. I know we are laughing about this," he said, "but Chea's point was this: if he had given him a place with young bushes, perhaps he would have requested another place the following year, and the year after that one, too. 'You have to try and cut down your own forest; you are still young,'" uncle said with an obvious satirical angle on what had seriously inconvenienced his older brother at the beginning of his life. "But it was a mockery," he added.

It was a good thing that Father completed it. The year he spent farming near Saylo

foothill, "Wedlyn Wleh, the younger brother of Wedlyn Chea, entered the new house. Wleh and his wife, Pinnyonoh, spent the entire year in the hut."

"On Wedlyn, the wife of Sloboh," he went back to the sick woman, who was hurriedly taken to the town to prevent her from dying in the village. He also explained what would have

173

been levied as a fine had she been dead prior to transferring her to the town. Fines were levied for passing dead people over the village perimeter lines. He also explained how the animals they collected as fines were sacrificed, killed, and eaten. He talked about the peer groups on the elder's council that ate the fines.

"They brought her to town in a blanket, suspended from a stick. If they had allowed her to die before bringing her to the town, it would have been a serious problem for the family of Bocuwao. The town would have levied a fine—such as a goat—from the family of Bocuwao for passing over perimeter lines, which community elders refer to as korgbaeken. They were emplaced herbal protections—the town's watchdogs—that guarded the town and its people against all forms of evil, especially witchery."

He continued, "Whenever a very sick person was brought to the town (i.e., passed over korgbaeken) and the person died later, no fines were levied or charged. However, whenever a dead person was transferred to the town over the perimeter lines, the family was fined a goat. This was usually after the family had buried their loved one. The goat was taken to the town center. The elders prepared and ate it at the center of the town, while seated in a section of the town center that was aptly named (korgbaeken). If the person had died a normal death (sick or natural), the goat was slaughtered. However, if the person had died of trauma (shot, or killed by a fallen tree, for example), the goat was not killed in a normal fashion. Instead, it was killed in a painful, seemingly heartless fashion.

The head of the goat was violently smacked on the ground until the animal was dead." He went over the categories within Chedepo's Gbor, the elders' council.

"The first four peer groups on the elders' council (Gbor) from the youngest peer group on the council up to the fourth

174

peer group—are the ones who eat the goat whenever perimeter lines are violated in the village. Collectively, these four groups of elders are called **dinyomopo** ["blood eaters"]. The peer groups above them—from peer group five through peer group fifteen—are tested, seasoned, and experienced leaders. Those ten peer groups are known collectively as Bolibo. Being a member of this category ('the experienced elders') truly makes you an elder in the community. Yet, even in this group are subdivisions: two: "u teba chimae bo" and "upa bablo bo." From the tenth peer group to the most senior peer group is the board of elders, if you like. If you make it to this level, you are believed to have entered the hall of fame—u pa bablo bo—for the town's elders.

Decisions of extreme importance to the town or even the region are made in the presence of these peer groups. The ninth peer group, whose members are knocking on the door of the hall of fame, marks yet another prestigious stage in the world of Chedepo elders.

They are identified with a phrase: u teba chimae bo, which loosely means "they are next in line to become hall of famers." There is still another category of elders. Elders within peer groups sixteen and up are called "dle korti blo." They are said to be draggers of walking sticks; in fact, the phrase loosely means "cane draggers." When a town crier wants to assemble all the elders at the town centers, he says, 'Everyone is summoned to the town center, even the cane draggers are not exempted."

Then he went back to the dying woman.

"Anyway, that was my first time hearing that someone had died. That someone was Chea and Wleh's mother, Wedlyn. When they brought the lady home in some old-looking bag, Teahswen [Peter Winn, his half-brother] and I couldn't make sense of what was going on. They used the bag to transport a corpse or a very sick person. In fact, the locals called the bag 'Sakublomon,' [this translates into "corpse picker-upper"]. It had its origin in the Firestone area, where it was used by rubber tappers. They laid her down and placed the Sakublomon over her. She was under it—fighting [She had not died yet.]."

We laughed

"Teahswen and I said, 'O, there is a monster creeping under that thing.' Of course, they were not happy because we called their mother a creeping monster. So, they beat us. And they threatened to put chunks of pepper in our rear ends. We ran off. If we had stayed, we would have risked the pepper chunks in our rear ends."

We laughed.

"That was their way to control us. We were kids who were quite chatty. The pepper in the rear would have been the quick fix. They were incredibly saddened, but we belittled the situation. Anyway, from that time in my life to now, we have been losing family members to death. And that is the reason I went that far back."

He went back to Khordi Sayee.

"Before his death, he graduated from school and came home. He did not want to go to school, at least initially. He was a mama's boy; he enjoyed childhood. Every time his father, Wedlyn Chea, tried to send him to school, he used to run to Jahgeleimo, Kaity Chulu's village, to his grandmother. Khordi Sayee and David Chulu are the same generation. Gbornyonoh, the mother of Khordi Sayee, was David Chulu's oldest sister.

She came to the Bocuwao family to marry her first husband, Gbalee Duhl, who was Winn's brother. Gbayee Duhl and Saylee Winn's mothers were different. They shared a father, Kargee Choloplay Saylee. Winn's mother was Nagbe Jowa. Her father was Tuwolo Nagbe. The most recent Tuwolo Nagbe, who was a member of the Sorpotonmo peer group—which was the same peer group as our father, Winn Saylee—was the namesake of Saylee Winn's maternal grandfather. The first Tuwolo Nagbe was Jowa's father. Jowa was a Wion Nyenpanpo girl. For Duhl, his mother was Tuwobo Gbalee. She was a Gbeapo girl from the town of Flewloken. Gbornyonoh and Duhl had Jowa Doe, who is the father of Sayee, the one who is in the United States. After the death of Duhl, they took his widow, Gbornyonoh (the daughter of Kaity Chulu), and gave her to Wedlyn Chea to marry. Chea and Gbornyonoh had Khordi Sayee (Edward) and Mongee.

Duhl, the son of Saylee, paid the dowry for Gbornyonoh," he continued with what I considered to be a disclaimer. He told us about the reluctance of some oral historians— himself clearly included—to explain certain historical events to an audience of young people because of the fear that some may be reckless with such information.

"But the truth is," he said, "we are the same people regardless of what I told you about the house that was moved into, or the farming spot that was denied. When Sagiah Kayjeley [Uncle Paul K. Winn] wanted to marry Sayleebi Worjolo's daughter, Nyenneh, who is with Konboel in the town of Killepo Kanweaken, he went to Gbayi Wliya. He needed financial assistance from the Bocuwao family to pay a dowry to the family of Nyenneh. However, Gbayi Wliya, the leader of the family at the time, told Sagiah Kayjeley, 'I would have given you the money for dowry, but your parents—Teaty and Winn—do not have female children. Whose female children's money are you going to use to pay your dowry?"

He continued.

177

"So, in 1961, Kayjeley left from here [Jarkaken] and went to Nimba [Yekepa, Nimba County, Liberia]. He left school and went there. Luckily, upon arrival, he got decent employment. This is a true story; I put the kola nut and rice we've just eaten in this story. Wedlyn Wleh went to him and asked him to complete his money. Wleh told Kayjeley that he only had US$12, which he had made from the sale of a baby chimpanzee. He killed a mother chimpanzee, and when he got to its carcass, the baby was sitting next to its mother. It was that baby chimpanzee he sold to some Mandingo people for US$12.

He wanted to pay dowry to the family of Magwulu—to Gblana and Charlie Wah [Wleh's fathers-in-law]—for his wife, Pinnyonoh." In short, it was Kayjeley who completed the money that Wedlyn Wleh used to pay the dowry for his wife, Pinnyonoh. He gave him US$28, and that completed US$40 for the dowry money. Then he added US$7 to pay his way from Yekepa to Chedepo."

Targiour was baffled. It was quite ironic, so he wondered aloud, "Kayjeley, whose brother was denied a farming spot [and who did not marry a local woman because Gbayi Wliya denied him money for dowry payment], was the one Wedlyn Wleh went to for

money to pay dowry for his wife?"

"Yes, and it was your father, Josiah, who took Khordi Sayee to Firestone. He even took him to the city of Harper to meet Hon. Hilary Brewer, the superintendent of Maryland County at that time. He told the superintendent that Khordi Sayee was his own son. The people knew my brother. When Josiah got his first tapping job, he was a fifth grader. They took a test, and he scored the highest in his group. By the way, I did not start from the beginning. Our father did not want him to go to school because of his status as the first son. Back then, the locals frowned upon first sons entering schools. Obviously, there was an inherent disadvantage to that decision. Moreover, there was an additional downside. Youth members who were not in school were forced to carry loads for visiting government officials. Every time an official of the government entered the town, they compelled them to carry the official's loads from their town to the next town. The parents could not do anything to get their children out of carrying government loads. My brother carried loads to Chedepo Putuken. After that trip, they told him to take another set of loads to Chedepo Geeken. He managed to escape. If you know where we are in Jarkaken, the road along which I have my house (along with Dowolo's), that was the main road that went to Putuken. He went to the mission town and registered for school that year. School was a church project. He was an astute student when he entered. He outperformed all the other students he met in the school—Jasper Chea and others. He was always the first in the class."

But the threat of a father who did not want to break a ridiculous norm still hung over his son, Josiah S. Winn, Sr, according to Uncle Newton. Hence, like the load-carrying incidence, which sent him to a mission town for school, the continuous threat to get him out of school prompted yet another decision to seek a faraway mission community for enrollment.

"But our father was still not happy about my brother entering school. He wanted him to leave school. So, my brother did not tell anyone about his next plan, not even Mr. Sampson Chea, who was his teacher. In other words, even his school did not know. At the end of the school year, with no formal transfer, he left the school and went to Potupo Japroken and registered at the mission school there. Mr. Landerus was there. Mr. James Hinneh was the Principal in Japroken. My brother was in Japroken when I was born (1949)."

179

He lightened the moment with a joke. Well, we thought it was just a joke until he told us that it did happen—for real.

"One time, he asked me to fetch water for him. I refused, but he made me go. Then later, he told me to go all the way to Cheanorgbae Creek and fetch cold water for him to drink. I asked what my pay was going to be my pay. He told me, 'When your mother had you, the palm nuts I brought to town—which our mother used to prepare the palm butter that you ate—if you pay me for the palm butter, then I will pay you for the water.'"

We laughed.

"Because you will drink it, too," Nelson added. "I am not lying," Uncle said.

"And so, he went to Japroken," he returned to the runaway student. "Like I said, he did not tell his teacher, and the teacher was asking about his whereabouts, especially at the beginning of the new school year. 'Where is the smart student, Josiah, whose performance during a school program made our school look really good? He gave our school a good name. Where is he?' He started to ask around. They told him, 'He went to Potupo Japroken.' So, he wrote a letter to Principal James Hinneh, saying, 'Josiah Winn, a student in your school, has stolen some books from my school.' The principal in Potupo sent him back to the Chedepo mission school. Upon seeing him, Sampson started laughing at him. He told him, 'I thought you were the man.' The next day, he drafted a formal transfer for my brother and allowed him to return to Potupo, though not until he gave him this powerful life's lesson: 'You must learn to respect others, no matter how smart you are. Why didn't you tell me you wanted to leave? I would have sent you away with a transfer."

Nelson, arguably the most involved member in the audience, added, "And you left without telling me."

180

"From Potupo Japroken," he continued the story, "he went to Firestone. He lived with Brown Nyenaon Sayee. He went to school in Firestone, and he went up to the 5th grade before something happened."

My curiosity level went up. Our father told us this repeatedly while he was alive. And every time he told us the story behind his leaving school in the 5th grade (and the reason he never returned) seemed ambiguous, in my opinion. In one recorded explanation, which he did in Wodaiken Village on January 19, 2004, father told our older brother, Mantee (Saylee Sayjolo), that "he left school [in 1955] because of school," a phrase he later explained in the same recording to mean that he left school to make farms, sell his yields, and pay the school fees for his siblings and his own children, later. It sounded plausible, but I received such an explanation with some level of reservation. So, on November 10, 2018, when Uncle Newton told us in Fish Town that "he [Josiah] went up to the 5th grade before something happened," I was ready for some breaking historical news, and I am glad my cousin, Sayjela, was rolling the video.

"One day," he continued, "during the recess period, he went outside and left his book in the classroom. It was not uncommon back then to be bewitched over school, because of one's smartness. While he was outside, someone put green leaves inside his book. And when he returned and opened the book, almost instantaneously, a powerful glare—a shine with dazzling light—overwhelmed him. He almost lost his sight. That was how he ended school. Our father sent for him, and when he came home, our mother, Nyangbe Teaty, took him to Gbeapo Podloken, where he was treated by a man named Saylee Masan. He was our maternal uncle. After he worked on his eyes, he told him to abandon school; if he went back to school, the issues with his eyes would resume.

And that was the reason he never returned to school. So, he stopped in the 5th grade, but he wrote until his death. Today, it is hard to see a 5th grader who can write a letter.

Anyway, that was the ending for him.

But the luck was still there," he continued the story. "When he started tapping for rubber, he met a man named Charles Ford. Originally, he came from the Toe's Town area—from Gbazon. He was the overseer. It was this man he worked for in Firestone. The man was barely audible whenever he talked. He talked the same way our son, Domini Toe, used to talk. One day, he called my brother, 'I don't want you to tap for rubber anymore. I don't know how to read and write.' Every overseer had four 'Jam men.' He wanted my brother to be his timekeeper. His job was to keep a record of the rubber as they weighed it. And that was what he did; no hard labor. He just recorded the figures from the scales. That was what he did for Charles Ford."

Uncle said our father almost traveled abroad, but "the specter of a father who did not want to break a preposterous norm still hung over" our father. He wanted his first son home, as usual.

"While he was working for Mr. Charles Ford, an American man came to the area.

He was the superintendent (or 'Ma-seh'). He controlled a division, which had three overseers. One overseer had four headmen. The division he controlled was Camp No. 6. The man was James West, from Missouri, USA. He took my brother to his place and gave him a job there. He did lawn work and washed clothes. James West wanted to take him to the United States, but, somehow, that news got home to our father. When he got the news, he said, 'Toe Duwelee! What America! My first son? I will not let that happen.'"

182

Then quickly, he explained something only a few of us knew—that our father was not the first son for his parents. There were other children before him. As usual, Uncle Newton was armed with the details.

"Saylee was not Winn's first son. Winn had two children before he had your father. So, he was not the first son. He was the first because someone had to be the first. We could not continue to count the dead family member as the first. So, that was the reason he assumed the role of the firstborn. But Saylee Winn's first child was Gbasay. She would have been the same age as Wiah Toe [Joe Weah, 1922]. She would have been a member of the Flepotonmo peer group. She was old enough to get married when she died. Then our father had a male child. His name was Sagiah Kayjeley. He would have been the same age as Sayee Teahfore (Joe Sayee, 1929). He would have been a member of the Petonmo peer group. He died, too.

The death of the two children led Saylee Winn to Chedepo Geeken. Winn wanted to secure protection for the lives of his future children. So, he went to Joe Pah's grandfather. His name was Bayor Pah (aka Tajigba Pah; Gbeyee Pah), a warrior. He was a veteran of the Killepo war. He fought in that war. And this warrior was one of the best hunters in Chedepo. He was a great hunter, too. Whenever Bayor Pah went hunting, all he needed to see were prints of animal hooves. He used to put his powerful juju in the prints, then he sat and waited for the animal(s) that left the prints to return to where they had left the prints. The power of the voodoo compelled the animals to come back to the spot where the hunter had applied his juju. He always had a kill or two.

But he had no children. One day, the elders of Chedepo went to the town of Chedepo Putuken, a main road community, to attend a popular carnival, a festival the locals called 'Kla Nyonohmo Saaju' [for Cesarean section, C-section,

183

or surgical birth]. While in Putuken, Bayor Pah began to boast about his hunting skills among his peers.

Oldman Khorwea was a native of Chedepo Putuken. His daughter, Khorwea Teh Mganyen, married one of our forefathers, Knoh Toe, whose name Daisey Gbeh gave to one of his sons, Knoh Toe, the father of Wenny Toe and others. The first Knoh Toe left his wife, Khorwea Teh Mganyen, behind in Chedepo and traveled to a faraway country. He went to Ghana, and he died there. After our father Knoh Toe's death, the family of Bocuwao said, 'Gbeh Chea Nyanley, as the surviving brother of Knoh Toe, it falls on you— according to our family's customs—to go for Knoh Toe's widow and marry her.' She was in the town of Putuken. 'We, the family of Bocuwao, have paid a bride price to Khorwea, so get your brother's widow and take her as your wife.' And that was how Khorwea Teh Mganyen and Gbeh Chea Nyanley became a couple. Together, the couple had two children. They had Nyanley Chea, and they had Warlen.

So, it was this Khorwea, the maternal grandfather of Nyanley Chea, who was a member of Gbeyee Pah's peer group. And the two men—Pah and Khorwea—met in Putuken, where many elders across the land of Chedepo had gathered for the popular Kla Nyonohmo Saaju carnival. While they were in Putuken, Pah stood up among members of his peer group and began to boast as a skilled hunter, a celebrated marksman. At the time, Gbeyee Pah had no children, and, indeed, he was a great hunter, as I explained earlier. He was telling his friends in Putuken, 'Pick any animal in this area; I have killed it. I have done this; I have done that...' And that prompted his friend, Khorwea, to stand up. He said, 'Pah, my friend, find a seat and sit down. Spare us all those hunting stories. Let us have our peace. Why is it that every time we gather, all you want to talk about is your hunting skills? When you kill your animals, while entering the town with your kill, are there any sounds of children rejoicing? Are there any hee-yoo, hee-yoo sounds welcoming you home? Whenever you are bringing home a kill, who runs to you? And when you are butchering the meat, who sits around you? You kill it, bring it home, and you and your wife eat it. That is all, isn't it?' Of course, children are the ones who do all the things Khorwea was talking about. So, he damned his friend; he damaged his soul. He was shamed in the gathering of his peers. Pah was quiet; he was embarrassed. Khorwea was blunt; he told him he had no children."

"Who eats the intestines and the heart?" I asked as a joke because children typically eat the guts of a hunter's kill.

"He was embarrassed by his peers in Putuken. So, after the event in Putuken, he returned home to his native Geeken. But the event in Putuken was weighing on him heavily, so in a few weeks' time, he traveled to the land of his mother's people— Blorpo (Kru people). He went for reproductive treatment. And his mother's people helped him. He wanted children, and they gave him children. They told him he was going to have many children if he had a female as the first child. If he had been a male, then he would have remained his only child. He was lucky, even though he was old before he had his children. And God blessed him with a first child, who was a female. Her name was Pah Wlayee. She got married in Klosoken to a Dowao man; his name was Nyuan. Pah Wlayee and Nyuan had Geesay Doe [James Doe Young]; they had Pah Chie; and they had Keh Tiah, who was the father of Esther Mgheln Tiah, the one-time girlfriend of Winn Saylee. She and I had our houses together in Jarkaken. Keh Tiah also had Geeyea. Behind Pah Wlayee, Gbeyee Pah had a son, whom he named Teahwea. He was a member of the Gbetekleotonmo peer group. He was the same peer as our father, Duku Gbeh (Rev. Luke Cojolo). Boyah, the man who is with you in the United States, his father, Kosolo Nyenkan, was Gbeyee Pah Teahwea's peer group member. He was the father of Seeo, who is the actor in

Geeken. Teahwea's namesake is Joe Pah, who is married to my daughter, Sonny Ma."

Nelson knew Seeo, "He insults all the time."

"He also had Wardel, who is the father of many children. He has children in Ghana.

Then he had Komoh, the father of Joe Teahwea Pah. He stopped there."

"Anyway," he continued, "it was this man whom Winn went to. He did not take the money for himself. He cooked for him. He told his wife, Teaty, 'Prepare a special meal—felteah—so we can go to Bayor Pah.' They went to him early in the morning. He told Pah they were fertile, but they were losing their children. 'My children are dying.' He told him your next child will not die. The next child was your father (Josiah, 1931). Our father said, 'The one whom I have saved? He wants to go to America? It will not happen, unless he doesn't see my face.' He was followed by Kayjeley again.

Bayor Pah requested a BB cartridge, along with a shotgun. Then he asked if Winn knew how to fire a rifle. That, if he didn't, he (Pah) would have either shown him how to fire it or had someone else fire it for Winn. Our father said he knew how to fire the rifle; he just didn't hunt with it. He gave Winn the following instructions: 'Go to the road that leads to Firestone. Start heading out to the road at the sound of the first cock that crows.

Walk that Firestone-bound Road. Call his name four times, then fire the rifle. And within

In a few days, your son will return.'

"And that was what he did. He told him that after my brother had returned, he was not going to return to any distant land, certainly not to stay. And that was the case for the rest of his life. He did travel, but never with the intention of making any distant land his home. And that is how my father, Winn, through his friend, Bayor Pah, brought your father home from the Firestone area in the 1950s. So, we all know the story now—how it ended. The white man, James West, the Missouri man, did not take him to the United States."

As if to test Bayor Pah's work, Uncle said our father went back to Firestone in the 1960s. "While he was there, he took a test in order to work at the Firestone Hospital. He went with Teaswen [Peter Winn, another uncle of ours], who did not want to go to Firestone anyway. So, it was Teaswen who told on our brother, 'He said he is going to get a job here; he came to look for money for taxes, but it looks like he wants to find a permanent employment and stay.' The specter of a dad who wanted his first son home persisted, "O," the old man said, "Saylee is at it again?"

"Does he want me to fire another BB cartridge?" I said as a joke, basically putting words in our grandfather's mouth.

"He came back, and he was here until his death. He did not go back to Firestone— certainly not to stay. Just to make it clear, he did travel after he came back. He just never went to any faraway area with the intention of staying there. But the point I want to make is this: the America he wanted to travel to, you have been there. In a way, he did go there; he did travel to the United States through you. And that has been the basis or premise for the James West angle of this story. 'This person talks too much,' we often hear that. If you can connect the dots, if you can give the reasons behind the talking, it is easy to understand the whole conversation. If a storyteller cannot do this, the story will have no head, no tail.

The story will lack genuine meaning."

"Such a conversation will be confusing," Nelson said.

"But I am telling you these things to highlight this point: most of the time, it is tough to start life. The events that transpire at the beginning of one's life are often tough. My brother left seventeen male children alive the day he died. He also left four female children alive. Therefore, he left a total of twenty-one children alive when he died."

He talked about Saylee Gbasay—again.

"As I said, Gbeyee Pah helped Winn and Teaty for Winn Saylee to live. He went to Killepo and got his first wife, Bolju (your mother). And their first daughter was Gbasay, who was the wife of Toe Tweh. She was the namesake of Winn and Teaty's firstborn.

They did not enjoy her, and she died, so when Agatha was born, it was her grandparents who named her. When your mother, Bolju, was in labor for Saylee Gbasay, my mother, Teaty, who was a nervous wreck, was worrying to such an appalling level. She was nervous about any normal situation, which posed the slightest challenge. Such was the case when Ethel was in labor."

He continued, "My mother called me one early morning in 1957; I was only eight (8) years old. She told me, 'Saylee's wife is in labor. Nyanley, take me to the waterside—at Portornorgbae creek. When I took her to the creek, she told me we were not actually going for water. She wanted us to go to the village of Nimeneh Sneh, the father of the country doctor known as Kaykay. 'I want to ask him how grave a situation my daughter-in-law is in. Is she going to deliver in peace without any incident? So, let us go to Nimeneh Sneh's hamlet. Where Sneh Wiah was, that was his father's hamlet. He was a

188

powerful country doctor (deajeor suwa). Anyway, we went to his village, which was known as Dakadolo. We went to Sneh early in the morning.

Gbasay was born in the month of September; her birthday was September 19th. It coincided with the date on which her parents were married, according to Winn [Saylee—January 19, 2004]. While entering Sneh's hamlet, the road was a straightaway. He sat outside in the morning, chewing kola. When he looked up, he saw my mother walking up and he said, 'Here comes the nervous rack woman; Teaty, you are coming to inquire about your son's wife.' Back then, the country doctors told you why you were there, not relying on clients' explanations, which is what we have today. 'Let's eat this kola so you can go back. You didn't get to Portornorgbae Creek when your daughter-in-law gave birth. She has a girl child. When you get back, and what I am telling you is not so, come back and reclaim what you have given me. And that was what Nimeneh Sneh did that I saw as a small child."

He switched to old man Saylee, our great-grandfather.

"Saylee and Sloboh's maternal grandfather was Swen. He was a Killepo man. His hometown was Killepo Kanweaken. Swen was a member of the Wiondwehpo family, which they also refer to as Dewlepo. Swen had three daughters. His first female was Swen Chie. She was the wife of our great father, Kargee Choloplay. Swen Chie and Kargee Choloplay had two children. They had Saylee, the father of Winn; and they had Sloboh, the father of Chea and Wleh. Swen's second daughter was Swen Sai. She was married in Klosoken, too. Her husband was Tela Gbegbe. Swen Sai and Tela Gbegbe had Worjolo.

Then Worjolo had his father's namesake, Tela Gbegbe (again). It was the second Tela Gbegbe who had Karplo. He also had Choloplay, who used to live in the Chenwniken area.

189

Swen's third daughter was also married in the town of Klosoken. Her name was Swen Gbasay. Her husband was Gbasay Klay, a Bowionpo man. Gbasay Klay and Gbasay had Klay Doe, the father of Gbasay Klay, who we knew as Isaac K. Doe. So, the three sisters were married in Klosoken."

The above evoked what my senior brother, Wleh Snoteh, told me just a few days after I had returned to Monrovia, from Fish Town, River Gee. He talked about the Killepo Swen, who was the father-in-law of Kargee Choloplay, Tela Gbegbe, and Gbasay Klay.

He provided a few synopses on Swen's daughters, mainly on Swen Chie. The subject was relations, particularly, our family's long relationship with the clan of Killepo, fueled by intermarriages.

"We are related to the Tela Gbegbe family," he said. "We are related to the Gbasay Klay [Isaac Doe] family, too. In fact, Wleh and Saylee used to trek Jarwalo, a foothill, to get to Klay in the Chenwniken reservation. They used to visit Klay, and he used to return with them to our Dilamo reservation. Your mother, Bolju," he continued, "her namesake—the first Bolju—was married in the town of Klosoken. She had Bolju Chefane, who was the father of Keh Tubo. Bolju Chefane also had my mother, Danyonoh. Bolju was a Killepo girl who came to Klosoken. Your mother—who had the first Bolju's name—was a Killepo girl, and she came to Klosoken [Jarkaken] and married here. Our greater family, as I said earlier, has a strong relationship with the people of Killepo. But that is our link on the Killepo side," he said specifically of me and him. Our mothers used to be closed among the Puwaiken women. They used to care about one another. Today, they are gone. Only God knows why."

The scene quickly became somber. As was often the case, their stories tended to end with regrets. I noticed every time the family talked about their fore relatives, their connection or attachment to them was still strong, regardless of how much time had elapsed since their deaths. That was apparent at Snoteh's place. He and his wife, Rachael, had summoned me to their expansive compound in Monrovia, a very beautiful compound with several homes. Its vegetation reminded me of Chianyenken, Wedlyn Wleh's Dilamo hamlet. The family was readying a traditional blessing ceremony for me. At least that was how they presented it initially, but it morphed quickly to being for all the orphans in the compound that day. All the folks in the family (and passing visitors) who had lost both parents were automatically qualified—and, therefore, allowed — to eat the sumptuous meal Rachael had prepared. The families had not seen me since the death of my parents until this 2018 trip. That was the reason, Cousin Snoteh, himself a traditionalist, told me not to depart for the United States without first observing the tradition.

"This role should have been played by either Bokuwo or Nyanley," he said. "Since neither is here, the responsibility falls on me," he said with a grin. Then he talked briefly about the women of Puwaiken.

"All the women you left in Puwaiken are gone," he said. "Only Nowinnie Warlen—she is very old now. I do not relish that type of longevity; she looks like a chimpanzee now." We laughed.

"Only a few of the Puwaiken women are here now. Betty Swen, the wife of Togbe Bafeh (George Bafeh's mother), is here. She is a member of Debepotonmo peer group. She is older than Elizabeth Snoh Winn. Only those three are here."

191

Then he began to conduct the blessing, which is referred to as Bulayjebebea. He wished us long lives. "You will not die a premature death. Your children's children will be tired of you before you will leave this world. Your hair will be as white as this Bulaye [a form of mushroom used to symbolize purity] before you leave this world, with as many years as the grains of rice in this bowl..."

"Well," I interrupted, "I suppose I will be as old, if not older, than Nowinnie Warlen," the crowd laughed.

According to Saylee Sayjolo, Nowinnie Warlen traveled to Klosoken in 1931. She went there to help her sister, Nyankpe Teaty, wife of Saylee Winn. Her reason for traveling to Chedepo was to babysit Winn Saylee, who was born in 1931. Warlen was a Koloe family girl. Warlen was a member of Gbeapotonmo. Her peer group members included Toe Wiah (Borbor Toe), Teaty Pley (Wayee Pley). She was born on March 15, 1919. She was 12 years old when she came to Klosoken to babysit. Soon, she became the wife of a Weltehken dweller, named Nagbe Jayee Sloboh, the brother of Knoh Toe, Tarwiah, Gbeh and other siblings. Their father was Darseh Gbeh. Nowinnie Warlen died on November 30, 2020 in Jarkaken, River Gee. She was buried on December 2, 2020 next to Winn Saylee, the child she left Gbeapo as a young child to babysit.

Anyway, it was a familiar ceremony. But the last time I saw this version of the blessing was several years earlier. Hence, he guided us through the process. We took turns and chewed tiny chunks off the mushroom-like substance. We poured out the saliva- soaked stuff on the backs of our clinched fits. Then we back-handed the stuff to our faces. And for the rest of the afternoon, we walked around with bulay residues on our faces.

Truly, we have a long history with Killepo, and Snoteh's narratives connected some dots.

Now, let us go back to the narratives of Uncle Newton. Prior to diving into the melancholies of his paternal grandfather (Saylee, and his own father, Winn, too), the uncle took time to explain to me that the name Chie was given to two persons in our family history. He realized that in my initial drafts, I wrote, "Saylee and Sloboh's mother was Toe Chie." And he said that was not correct. He said I was not the only family member who got that wrong. Many people in our family seem to be obsessed with the name "Toe Chie," one of the two historical people with the name Chie. So fixated, uncle said some family

193

members (myself included) tend to assign the "Toe" identifier to either Chie. So, he sent me the correction below.

"Saylee, the father of Winn, had two wives," Uncle Newton said. Then, inadvertently, he jumped to the second wife, Tuwobo Gbalee, in order to explain the ambiguity around the now infamous Toe Chie. He did not talk about his grandmother, Winn's mother. Therefore, to understand who Saylee's first wife was, I conveniently turned to my older brother, Mantee (Saylee Sayjolo), my usual lifeline.

"Saylee's first wife was Nagbe Jowa, the namesake of Aunty Lucy Jowa Winn," Sayjolo told me. "The original Nagbe Jowa was our grandfather's mother. She was a hometown woman. Nagbe Jowa's father was Tuwolo Nagbe, a Bowionpo family man. Tuwolo Nagbe also had a son named Nagbe; he was Nagbe Jowa's brother. Nagbe Jowa's brother, Tuwolo Nagbe, was the father of Worjolo, whose wife was Tela. Nagbe Worjolo and his wife, Tela, had Tela Gbegbe. Tela Gbegbe had Gbegbe Karplo and Gbegbe Cholopley," Sayjolo explained.

In other words, the grandfather of Tela Gbegbe was Tuwolo Nagbe, whose sister was Nagbe Jowa, the mother of Saylee Winn. Grandpa Winn's mother was Tela Gbegbe's Grandaunt.

Then there was Tuwobo Gbalee, his second and younger wife. She was a Gbeapo girl, from the town of Flewloken. She was the mother of Gbalee Duhl. Tuwobo Gbalee also had a daughter named Toe Chie. So, historically, there are two people with the name Chie in our family — Kargee Choloplay Saylee's mother was Chie. However, her full name was Swen Chie, and she was a Killepo girl from the town of Killepo Kanweaken.

Then Saylee and his second wife, Tuwobo Gbalee, had a daughter they named Chie. She is the Toe Chie."

He dived deeper into the family tree.

"But Saylee, the father of Winn, had four female children. The first of the females was **Saylee Welayor**. She got married in Potupo Juwelpo. She had Young, the father of Theodore Young.

Then he had **Saylee Teaty**. She got married in the town of Chedepo Klaboken. Her husband was Waytoh. Teaty and Waytoh had Waytoh Snoh. Jalawle, the father of Tarsleh, engaged Teaty's daughter, Snoh, for his son, Tarsleh, to marry. Snoh and Tarsleh had Tarsleh Qwenne. It was this Qwenne who married to Bayor Pah's son, Teahwea, the father of Seeo Jah and all those people...."

"Soklo Seeo Jah and others," Nelson said. He demonstrated his knowledge of the

families Uncle Newton was talking about.

"Yes," uncle agreed. "They are children of Winn's sister, from one mother and one

father. Teaty had Bornyonnoh, who was married in Kanweaken.

"Next to Saylee Teaty was **Saylee Wedlyn**. She got married in Gbeapo, in the town of Dweaken. Her daughter, Jlalene, used to come to Jarkaken with cooked food. She used to bring meals from Gbeapo Dweaken. She went fishing in her town, cooked her catch and then brought us very sumptuous fish and rice meals. Then Saylee had **Saylee Kaylor**. She got married in Tienpo. Kaylor's children's children are in the persons of people like Sneh Wiah. Saylee had two wives. His head wife was Jowa. She was the mother of my father, Saylee Winn. She was the mother of **Jowa Doe**; he was a member of the Sapannetonmo peer group. She had **Jowa Choloplay**; he was a member of the Jelepotonmo peer group.

195

Of course, she was my grandmother. My father, **Saylee Winn**, was a member of

Saypaytonmo."

He continued the story.

"Then, Jowa Doe was bewitched; they said it was Karplo who bewitched him. The sickness was so serious, even the country devil came to town. But it was too late for Jowa Doe. He died. So, the townspeople decided to go to the outskirt of the town to figure out what or who killed Jowa Doe. While they were heading to the meeting place, then Jowa Choloplay [Jowa Doe's brother], was bitten by a snake. He died, too. The two brothers were buried on the same day. So, Saylee Winn was the only child left in his mother's hut. His other siblings were all females; they had all gone to marry their husbands in other communities."

So, in a nutshell, these were Jowa's children: Saylee Welayor, Saylee Teaty, Saylee Wedlyn, Saylee Kaylor, Jowa Doe, Jowa Choloplay, and Saylee Winn.

"Later," Uncle Newton continued, "Saylee went to Gbeapo Flewloken, and engaged a second wife. Her name was Tuwobo Gbalee. Saylee and Gbalee had **Gbalee Duhl**. He was a member of Wamegntonmo peer group. He was the same generation member as Tenblo Chea, Teah.

Wlehley, and Chenekan, the father of George Kwi Karmon. When Gbalee Duhl was a Kofaju [15-Year-Old], his brother, Saylee Winn, was a kofajesinyor [26-Year-Old]. Gbalee Duhl was a traveler. He hardly sat still. Also, Tuwobo Gbalee had **Sagiah Kayjeley**. Then she had **Sagiah Wiah**. So, in all, Tuwobo Gbalee had three male children."

Then he jumped to another gloomy chapter in the lives of Saylee Winn and the second wife.

"Then Saylee's son, Kayjeley, died," Uncle Newton continued. "And Winn was devastated. In fact, he said, 'I am leaving this village [Klosoken]. I am going to my friend, Snoh Young, in the village of Wlewlohken.' Snoh Young was a powerful herbalist. He used to thwart the effects of people's voodoos. He used to unplug witches ["Sawolo"].

Whenever he was in his form and a young child saw him, that child was overwhelmed by his powers and died. Sawolo kills. You, the English speakers, call Sawolo 'juju.' When Saylee ran from Klosoken and arrived in Snoh Young's Wlewlohken village (because of the death of his children), he met death there, too. It did not take a very long time for the next tragedy to hit Saylee's family. His son, Sagiah Wiah, died there—in Wlewlohken.

One sunny afternoon, Sagiah Wiah saw a creeping monster in a spirit form and died. It was Snoh Young's sawolo that killed Sagiah Wiah. After that tragedy, Saylee said, 'Death is everywhere. I cannot run away from it.' So, he returned to the town of Klosoken."

He continued, "Thus, it was in the town of Klosoken where Saylee and Tuwobo Gbalee had **Toe Chie**, their first daughter. She was a powerful woman. She got married in the town of Chedepo Geeken. Her husband was Tarwloh. Toe Chie and Tarwloh had Sloboh, the father of Geeken's singer. Toe Chie also had Quennyonoh, Yonwan and Wesseh. Toe Chie's daughter, Quennyonoh, was the namesake of Winn's sister.

Quennyonoh (Toe Chie's daughter) got married in B.F. Goodrich, on a rubber plantation in Bomi County, Liberia. She later died there. For Toe Chie, she was a powerful woman. She knew the issues, both current and historical issues. She died in

197

B.F. Goodrich as well. Moreover, Tuwobo Gbalee also had **Saylee Sinamen**; she was with us for a long time."

"Menmen," Nelson said. "She was married in Killepo Kanweaken."

"Tuwobo Gbalee had **Saylee Quennyonoh**; it was this person whose name Toe Chie gave her daughter, the one who was in Goodrich (discussed above). The original Quennyonoh got married in the town of Chedepo Geeken to Jarwindai. While Jarwindai was away, Sloboh Nowinnie took Quennyonoh from Jarwindai and took her away. (Sloboh Nowinnie's father was Kaygba Nowinnie; he went everywhere with a kola). Joe Wesseh Chea's daughter, Quennyonoh — that is the namesake of Winn's sister. And those were the children of Saylee.

So, in a nutshell, these were Tuwobo Gbalee's children: Gbalee Duhl, Sagiah Kayjeley, Sagiah Wiah, Toe Chie, Saylee Sinamen, Saylee Quennyonoh.

Again, Saylee had two wives: Nagbe Jowa was his first wife, and Tuwobo Gbalee was his second wife. As I said earlier, Winn was the only child left in his mother's house when his sisters were married off to other communities. If Winn had died, like the rest of his male siblings, we would not have been here."

He went back to Gbalee Duhl, Winn's half-brother, who was a traveler.

"Anyway, Winn was by himself until Duhl came back from traveling. He used to live in Klepo Karlorken. He lived there for so many years, cutting the undergrowth of their cocoa. Occasionally, Winn used to get him. But, every time Winn succeeded and brought him to Chedepo, Gbalee Duhl used to go back to Klepo Karlorken. It took Winn asking people about how to really bring him home for a permanent stay. And that effort, which involved a bit of voodoo intervention, if you like, paid off; Gbalee Duhl eventually came home. Upon arrival, the two brothers (Winn and Duhl) looked for money and paid dowry for Bornyonnoh, the daughter of Kaity Chulu. She was David Chulu's oldest sister. Gbalee Duhl and Bornyonnoh had one child, a male named Jowa Doe, the namesake of Winn's older brother," he said.

The brothers lived together in Wotuken, where they made up for lost time; but, soon, the elder brother had to relocate to another community, a decision that permanently parted the two brothers.

"Winn and his brother, Gbalee Duhl, lived in Wotuken, which was Wiah Nyonoh Nowinnie's village. Then Winn moved to Chutuken. He wanted his younger brother to move to Chutuken also, to be with him; however, Gbalee Duhl was reluctant to move. In fact, he refused to move there. Duhl had his eyes on the younger widow of Wiah Nyonoh Nowinnie. Her name was Welyee Jowa, the mother of Jenkins 'Adjaphie' Weateah Norianton who used to live in Tabou, Cote d'Ivoire. She was a family woman. There was a family dowry on her head, so the assumption was that other men were interesting in this relatively young woman. Hence, Winn wanted his brother to leave Wotuken, to avoid the perceived tussle over the young widow. But Gbalee Duhl was determined; he wanted her.

Anyway, he succeeded. However, their relationship was short-lived. He caught a mysterious illness—a cough—and died in Wotuken. Doe was his only son. When Gbalee Duhl died, Saylee Winn gave his widow, Bornyonnoh—the mother of Jowa Doe—to Wedlyn Chea. And Bornyonnoh took her son, Jowa Doe, with her to the home of Wedlyn Chea. And that is why Doe's son, Sayee, who is in the USA, has Chea as his last name.

His father, Jowa Doe—a member of the Sorpotonmo peer group—grew up in Wedlyn Chea's house. Sayee is the grandson of Winn's brother, Gbalee Duhl. The dowery that was on Bornyonnoh was paid for by Gbalee Duhl."

In the original drafts that Johnson printed in Sinoe and delivered to Uncle Newton in River Gee on November 10, 2020 (a date that coincidentally marked the two-year anniversary of the gazebo narratives), I inserted, "He went there to be a title holder, a Jakwi." In other words, I told my readers that when our grandfather left Wotuken for Chutuken, he was in fact going there to be a title holder. My comment was based on an audio recording I have of my own father. On the cassette, my father said the old man, Saylee Winn, "served as a Jakwi in the towns of Chutuken and Jarkaken." After the death of Jakwi Teba Teh, who was the father of old man Neneh (Oldman Gray), Saylee Winn became Chutuken's Jakwi. He did the job until the town of Chutu fell, and the people moved to Jarkaken, where Saylee Winn served as a Jakwi again. Uncle Newton pointed out that, while the above is generally true, his father did not exclusively go to Chutuken to be a title holder there. In fact, he said it was not the reason he was there. Here is Uncle Newton:

"Winn did not go to Chutuken to get a job. He did not go there in search of any position. He went there because he liked the community of Chutuken. One of the key reasons Winn chose the town was the town's proximity to the farming areas within the Dilamo reservation. He ran to the town after they lost the hilltop community of Klosoken. While some Bocuwao family members were going to Jarkaken, he chose Chutuken. The family of Bocuwao has two subfamily groups—Wiahchie and Nyansunupo. The subgroup of Wiahchie, which is Winn's subfamily group, is traditionally assigned the Jakwi job. The job does not belong to Nyansunupo, the other branch of Bocuwao. But after Kloso fell, the family members from the Wiahchie side of Bocuwao went in droves to the villages of Wotuken and Chutuken, which were built by Bocuwao men. Our father Wiah Nyonoh Nowinnie was the owner of Wotuken, and our father Teh was the owner of Chutuken.

Nyansunupo members, however, went in droves to Jarkaken. Anyway, the people of Jarkaken wanted Winn to be a Jakwi in their village, but he refused to go to Jarkaken. He said, 'I will never leave Chutuken. In fact, I do not want that job.' At the time, no Wiah Chie person had a hut in Jarkaken. They were in Chutuken and in the Dilamo reservation. 'No one from my subfamily group has a hut in Jarkaken; all of us are either in Wotuken or Chutuken,' he told the people of Jarkaken.

'Who will protect me when I go to Jarkaken? If I get in trouble, if I am fined and if I need moral and immediate family support, who will be there for me? Who will defend me? Who will have my back?' Those were his concerns, and these were the basis for his refusal to go to Jarkaken.

In 1942, the elders in Jarkaken increased their pressure or appeal for Winn to come to their town," he said. "Quayee Swen, the father of Karwolo, was the Jakwi in Jarkaken. But the elders in Jarkaken were complaining that they were experiencing accidents on the farm every time they were helping Quayee Swen. Sometimes, they told Winn, that there were conflicts and seemingly endless fist fights on the farm, too. They suspected that they were going through those things because the job was held by a Nyansunupo man (Quayee Swen). 'We went to a country doctor,' they confided in Winn, 'and you are the one we see there as the perfect person for the job. You are our favorite of the people we have considered.' They told Winn."

For this reason," he continued, "Winn's mother, Jowa—you know, it is good to have a mother who has a loving people behind her. If you have people behind you, you are rich in a sense. His mother had powerful men in Jarkaken. Moreover, many of Winn's peer group members were in Jarkaken. Just a few of them were in Chutuken. A majority of Saypaytonmo [Winn's peer group] members were in Jarkaken. His peers told him that since he was concerned about moral security, personal security, and family support in Jarkaken, they were eager to fill any roles for which Winn had concerns. 'We are your family; we are members of the same generation. We care about one another. We will go to battle for one another. It is our responsibility, and we owe you that when you come to Jarkaken,' they assured him. 'We are inviting you to come to Jarkaken. Jakwi job benefits the entire community.' They told

202

him that they were concerned about his personnel security as well."

He discussed the involvement of Winn's maternal uncles.

"His mother's brothers played crucial roles in the effort to get Winn to Chedepo Jarkaken. Winn had many maternal uncles. One of them was Nyaandior Tubo, and another uncle was Partoloh Nyensowa. They told him to go to Jarkaken. They reassured him that he and his family would be vigorously protected. That nothing will happen to him, which was Winn's primary concern. His safety. Family safety. The involvement of Jowa's brothers, coupled with the guarantees from his peers, gave enough security assurance to Winn. He agreed to relocate to Jarkaken. That was in 1942, eleven years after fire destroyed the town of Klosoken. Winn's refusal, which was an outright stubbornness for others, lasted over an extended period. It was during Winn's rebellious period that his wife, Nyankpe Teaty, suffered back-to-back health abnormalities. She suffered. She even had a miscarriage. She was reportedly bewitched due to Winn's prolonged refusal or stubbornness to go to Jarkaken for a permanent stay."

He returned to how Winn's peer group, maternal relatives and the entire Jarkaken community supported his relocation; they also supported him as a Jakwi, and that made him a successful title holder.

"It took his peer group's motivation to come to Jarkaken. That was his main push. They were extremely happy when he agreed to go to Jarkaken. Jubilantly, they carried him from Chutuken to Jarkaken [roughly over a mile and half, or two]. When Winn entered Jarkaken, all the conveniently-located town lots were occupied or claimed. But one of his maternal uncles, Tuweli Swen, gave Winn a centrally-located town lot. He told him, 'Since you have agreed to come to Jarkaken, I am giving you a town lot. I have two. So, you can have one. And it is for you for as long as you will live, it is for you.' His peer group members pledged to build his hut in two days, which they did." The town said, 'Nothing will happen to you!' A thunderous 'Bati!' enchantment came after their collective declaration. 'We dare anyone to do anything to you,' his peer group emphasized the town's commitment. And that was how our father entered Jarkaken from Chutuken in 1942.

He took the job of Jakwi from 1942 to 1974," Uncle Newton continued. "In fact, his death occurred on August 8, 1974, which ended his long career as Jarkaken's Jakwi. So, if you do the math, you will know how long my father lived in Jarkaken and how long he served the people of Chedepo Jarkaken as a Jakwi. Each of the many years he served in that post, he cooked sumptuous meals for the town of Jarkaken. And from the period he took the job, Winn did not experience any major illness. Definitely, no one bewitched him. He lived a very long life. His peer group members loved him, and he loved them back, too. The house (his) was always filled with his friends. They were very many. He loved the job; no one troubled him while he was doing it. There is no Jakwi compares to his reign. He was a member of Saypaytonmo, and that group really cared about one another. My friend Alexander Boyah—who is with you in the United States—his grandfather, Nimeneh, was Winn's friend. Wolo Nyenpan was Winn's friend. William Choloplay's father, Tylor Choloplay, was Winn's friend. The man we call Nyusoon was Winn's friend. As I said, they were many—Sayee Bafeh was another. Mgatoh was Winn's friend. Also, Kpawle Sloboh was one of my father's many friends. These were the people who influenced Winn's decision to leave Chutuken for Jarkaken. They were kind to him. They gave him gifts, such as pieces of meat when they came home from hunting. He was never in any conflict with anyone."

The point is," he continued the story, "he went to Chutuken after Klosoken was destroyed. Unlike Jarkaken, he did not go to Chutuken to serve as a Jakwi there. For the record, the town of Chutuken was abandoned in the year 1942. All the residents went to nearby Jarkaken. They had agreed to a consensus to live together again. They were members of a single community (Klosoken), but after that community was ruined, they went mainly to two communities: Jarkaken and Chutuken. It was in 1942 that they agreed to move to a single community, again. And they agreed that that community should be Jarkaken. Families used to go to Chutuken to help haul people's properties to Jarkaken.

They made the moving family responsibilities. As the new family members entered Jarkaken, the families used collective efforts and teamwork to build their huts in the new town. It was a thrilling reunification period."

We returned to Winn as a loner. How he battled tragedies after tragedies, and how incredibly close such tragedies were to him. But, somehow, Winn lived until he was in his mid-80s.

"For Winn, being alone was a way of life. He was used to it. He lived until he had outranked fifteen generations of elders [Gbor, the community's council of elders].

Bocuwao have been dealing with death for centuries, but their fatalities increased exponentially after they [Bocuwao] set the town of Klosoken on fire."

I was shocked, not that I did not know about the town being at blaze but that my family was responsible for the burning of the town of Klosoken.

"So, without any doubt, was it the family of Bocuwao that set the town of Klosoken on fire?" I asked

"Yes," he said. "It has always been a small family," he said of Bocuwao. "However, burning Kloso made it worse. A great many of our people died after the incident. The people said, 'Okay, you people want to burn our town to the ground? You will smell yourselves.' For a long time, it was hard to have a Bocuwao person in every peer group. Bocuwao is a small family, and, in Chedepo, the family exists only in one town—Jarkaken, (or Klosoken before it). Even in Tienpo, where the family is called Bilaye, they are in a single village, too. Winn and Quayee Swen's brother, Tuwleh, were the only members of Saypaytonmo. [Tuwleh and Quayee Swen were one mother's children.] But the year in which the two—Winn and Tley Tuwleh—were the senior of Kofa, Tley Tuwleh died. And Winn was the only Saypaytonmo member in Bocuwao for the rest of his life. This is the reason why Winn's peer group members—I saw many of them, like Wolo Nyenpan and others—referred to him as 'Ju Dole,' ["Only Child"]."

"Wow, he was lonely," Nelson reflected on the life of his grandfather.

"At the traditional town center, whenever members of a peer group eat, they have to ensure all the families that make up the town's population are present before eating. If a peer group eats without full representation, its members will be fined. They will pay for the food. Because Winn was the only Bocuwao family member in his peer group, his peers used to look for him during events like eating at the town center. Because if they ate without Winn, they knew they would have paid for the food. They used to say, 'Only Child, let's go.' Whenever they were helping a title holder on their farm, for example, and the women brought food for them, Winn was usually the last to join the rest. He would say something like, 'I am coming; let me cut down this tiny tree.' They would yell, 'No, no, come here, Ju Dole!'"

"I guess he took full advantage of the situation or condition. He probably did that to get on their nerves," Woday said.

"So, being alone was a norm for my father; it was not something he relished but he

learned to live with it.

He stayed on the issue (his father's loneliness) for a few more minutes.

"Of Jowa's children, Saylee Winn was the last. My father was his mother's last born, and the same is true for me. We both watched our older siblings died. Only God alone knows why. But Winn's situation was a lot worse. His situation was filled with incredible sadness. Every time they gathered during his time in this life, he hardly had anyone on his side. Why? Because the family of Bocuwao killed the rest of his brothers. So, he was the only one from his immediate family in our greater Bocuwao family. As you may have heard already—and it is worth repeating—had Winn been childless, there would have been no 'Winn' in this life."

Uncle said Grandpa Winn's solitude was incredibly painful and emotional; that his Father lived a very distressed life.

"During the days of Winn, the families of Bocuwao, Dowao and Kaytiao hardly had members in new peer groups. That's how small they were back then. As I said earlier, when the peer group of Saypaytonmo enlisted, the family of Bocuwao had just two members in that peer group. Saylee Winn was one, and Tley Tuwleh was the other. The two were peers until they were seniors of the Kofa section [around 25 years old]. Then Tley Tuwleh died. His namesake is Tuwleh, the one we call 'Biju-biju' in our family. Tley Tuwleh and Quayee Swen, the father of David Karwolo Swen, were one mother's children.

Their father was Jah. Tley's namesake was Jah's daughter (Biju's sister), Tley.

Her husband was Kpatoh Sloboh, who was living in the village of Blalorken [Magwulu's village on the Dilamo reservation]. Quayee Swen and Tley Tuwleh had a half-brother. His name was Wailabo Serkpeh whose daughter was Welleh's wife; they had Nyonohtae. But I will leave that there."

He went back to the loner, Saylee Winn.

"Winn was the only Bocuwao member in his peer group until 1974, the year he died. He outranked fifteen peer groups on the elders' council before his death.

Coincidentally, Nyankpe Teaty (a member of Wamegntonmo peer group) died at that same stage in life as her husband, Saylee Winn. Their son, Saylee (Josiah), however, outranked them when he died. For me," Uncle Newton continued, "I have outranked fourteen. If I am not dead by the time the next peer group gets a promotion to the elder's council, I will have made it to my father's final stage in life. I was born on September 29, 1949. And, on the day I was born, there were three births in the town of Jarkaken, according to family members. The country devil was in the town, and the townspeople were helping the late Luke Gbeh on his farm. It was a harvest season. This is the man we knew as Rev. Luke Cojolo. On the day I was born, Nyenpan Snoh, who was married to Teaty Paley, was born in the morning. Then Rev. Luke Cojolo's daughter, Wolo, was born in the afternoon. My birth, however, was in the evening. The devil was in front of my father's house, as is often the case whenever the devil enters the town. That was the case when the townspeople came from Rev. Luke Gbeh's farm. So, the devil was in front of my father's hut when I was born."

208

The town proposed a name for him, which would have saved him some early childhood scuffles; he did not have such security in Nyanley.

"So, the people wanted my father to name me 'Kwi,' the name of the country devil. My father said the town's proposal was an honor; however, 'One of my fathers, Nyanley, the son of Choloplay, had a dying wish for me. He wanted his namesake to come out of my house. So, I will name my son as Nyanley. Please do not consider this a disrespect.' He told the townsmen. So, I would have been Kwi, if my father had not stood his ground. The name, Nyanley, is a homonym. It has dual meaning—really, it could have as many meanings as one would like. In Chedepo, 'nyan' means 'to defecate,' but that is not what I am. Also, 'ley' loosely means 'everywhere.' But I want you to know that I am not defecating everywhere," he joked. "The name refers to someone who is ahead of his peers; someone who is ahead of his time—as in a farsighted person, a forward thinker, a leader, and a pioneer. The key word in the meaning of Nyanley is 'ahead.' The name is actually pronounced as 'Nya-neon' ["the one at the front"]. Over time, however, it took on its current 'Nyan-ley' pronunciation. But as a child, I used to fight all the time because my friends were calling me the version that suggested I was 'defecating everywhere.'"

He moved on to more relations.

"Winn's father was Saylee. Saylee's father was Choloplay's. Choloplay's father was Kargee. And I can go up to ten but we can save that for another time," Uncle Newton said. Then he named Saylee's wives and their children, who are recorded elsewhere in this document. He also talked about Winn and Teaty's struggle with keeping their own children alive.

"Teaty was a Gbeapo woman. She came from Podloken. Teaty's father was Nyankpe. Teaty's mother was Tarwin Wlayee. She was a Potupo woman, from Gbakebeya. Nyankpe and Chea were brother. Chea had Waselyee. Chea also had Kehyee, who was married in Klaboken. Kehyee had Wlenyonoh, the mother of Cecelia Quayee.

Teaty's first child was Gbasay. She was born in 1924. Then she had Kayjeley. He was born in 1928. When these two children died, Winn and Teaty went to Bayor Pah, who was Winn's Gbormagniaye [Winn's comrade on the elder's council]. With the help of Pah, our father, Saylee (Josiah), was born and, as I said earlier, outlived his parents. Bayor Pah told Saylee Winn and Nyankpe Teaty that their next child, a man, will be prone to anger, petite, and after his birth, he told the parents to bring him back to him (Gbeyee Pah) so he could fortify his life. That was what they did. They had another child. Saylee Winn said, 'This is my son, Kayjeley; he wants to live.' The parents named him Kayjeley."

Soon, their winning streak was seemingly over.

"The couple had two children after Kayjeley. They had Teaty Kpadeh; he died. Then they had Teaty Jolopoh, and he died, too. So, Winn and Teaty went to Tienpo to one woman. She was a singer. Her name was Bello. Bello was getting ready to go to the farm. But soon after she took a pinch of powdered tobacco (snuff) and sneezed, she told her husband, 'We are not going to the farm.' Her husband wanted to know why. 'We have strangers in route to us. I am looking at them — a man and his wife.' The man asked if the strangers were close to the village, and the wife responded that they were not. 'They will arrive in the afternoon. So, I must get things ready. Their situation was unlike what we have today. Nowadays, when you go to a country doctor, they ask you to explain."

210

I concurred, and added that "explanation is the basis for treatment now."

"They used to see," he continued the conversation. "By the time my parents got to Bello and her husband, the folks were hauling evening water [around 5pm]. And Winn and Teaty entered the house. The couples had never met before; surprisingly, however, Bello called them by their names before they could introduce themselves. She told them that she saw them long before they got to the village. And that they were there for children. 'Aren't you from Klosoken? Don't you have country doctors in Klosoken? Sleep tonight and you will go back tomorrow.' As they were getting ready to leave the few huts settlement, my father asked, 'Are we getting any herbal package? Any tangible thing to take back with us?' Bello told them to go straight back. She told them not to make any significant deviation from the main route. 'You will have a child; I will give you a child. But the child you are getting is quite reserved; he will keep to himself. It will not matter how much commotion is around him, he will not budge. No, he is not stupid or crazy; he is meek. You have a choice of hardheaded ones, too. But the one I am looking at is cool, calmed and collective.' And Winn told Bello, 'A child is a child.' So, Bello gave them final instructions. 'As you enter the community, you will see an animal—a creeper. Whatever it might be, take it home and prepare a soup with it, with small rice **(boka).** Only the two of you must eat it. And when you do that, your wife will conceive.' Then the couple left Tienpo."

Bello's prediction was spot on.

"By the time they got to the perimeter fence (a fence used to surround the village in the past), they saw a snail on a hot summer day, creeping towards them. And it was the animal the couple cooked and ate. The result was Bocuwao Welley, who is with you over there [USA]. Behind Welley was a

211

miscarriage. Your grandfather was not too enthusiastic about the Jakwi job in Jarkaken, where they wanted him. And he hesitated. We learned the miscarriage had something to do with Winn's refusal early on to leave Chutu in order to be a title holder in Jarkaken. [Of course, he did go to Jarkaken later. Quayee Swen, a Nyansunupo man, was the Jakwi in Jarkaken when Saylee Winn came to town. Quayee Swen turned the job over to Saylee Winn, a Wiah Chie arm of the Bocuwao family.] After that miscarriage, my mother had another pregnancy. And that was me. So, like my father, who had shut his mother Jowa's proverbial delivery door, I, too, was the one who shut my mother Teaty's proverbial delivery door."

He moved on from how well his father, Saylee Winn, had adapted to life in solitude to other subjects of interest.

By this time, the rain had forced us into a nearby gazebo. By my recollection, he talked about the gazebo at the beginning of the conversation. He told us that the gazebo belonged to Eric Woday Winn, or that it was Eric who built it on the family's seemingly elevated roadside land. It was the makeshift shop Eric used to sell cell phone units (or minutes) to customers in Fish Town, River Gee. The little shack came up in the conversation because Uncle Newton used it as a supporting piece of evidence to validate his earlier claims about Eric, the hard worker. Woday "is a smart and determined person. He is not a lazy person," he said of my brother.

At first, Uncle exhibited a reluctance to retreat to the tiny cabin because it had what he described as "a dusty floor." However, as soon we had begun receiving Fish Town's powerful—and I mean marble-sized—rain droplets, the verdict to use the gazebo as a refuge was unanimous and swift.

Chapter XI:
Fire in Klosoken, a once Thriving Chedepo Town

One of the old man's [Uncle Gbeh Chea Nyanley's] topics of interest was the question of who set Kloso on fire. I, Saylee Komoh, asked the question because I wanted to confirm what I thought I had heard earlier from him during the November 10, 2018 discourse, a series of anecdotes and labelled as "Gazebo Narratives." Of particular interest to me was the issue of alleged culpability (guilt or fault) of the Bocuwao family, which is my family group in Chedepo.

In truth, I thought he had answered my question on whether the family of Bocuwao was responsible for the burning of the town of Klosoken. In fact, I was pleased with the answer he gave me immediately after I had asked my question: "Did you say the family of Bocuwao, our family, was responsible for the burning of the famed Chedepo town?" He heard the inquiry clearly, and his response was swift. It was an unambiguous "Yes!"

The old man, after all, was narrating the oral accounts of our people, so I knew better not to press him too much for specificities or minute details, such as asking for the dates on which the events he narrated had happened, the exact times the events took place, or even the years during which the events he narrated transpired. I knew better not to do this, and I did not expect such information. In fact, I was fine with generalization or basic explanation, provided or as long as there were correlations or connections, which enhanced the understanding of his stories. But little did I know that the old man had such a detailed explanation on the tragedy that befell the people of Chedepo. He even named the year— "the year

213

was1931," he said with conviction. His recounting of the events was so meticulous—and convincingly indisputable—I walked away accepting as a fact that, indeed, the family of Bocuwao—mine—was guilty as charged.

From his narratives, I was—we were, I should say, because we were many under Eric's Gazebo—informed on the reasons we, the members of the Bocuwao family, paid so dearly for our crime at the famed town: Klosoken. This was not an endorsement for what happened to our family after the catastrophe; no rational person can be satisfied about the post-fire ills that members of the family of Bocuwao had endured. But the old man's accounts provided the clarity and basis that any reasonable person requires to reach an educated decision. The term "crime," which I used above, may be a misplaced term because, as you will see later, the incident bore the resemblance of an accident as opposed to a planned, deliberate, or calculated effort to set the town ablaze (on fire.)

How exactly did we pay "dearly" for our sin at Klosoken? We paid with our lives.

Many lives were disrupted when the town was burned, and many people—particularly those who were witched—were extremely angry. As a retribution or revenge, some ill- minded people—some of the witches from the charred village—began to bewitch some members of the Bocuwao family. Events that contributed to the fatalities within the family of Bocuwao were more pronounced immediately after the now infamous Klosoken fire.

Such subsequent tragedies were painful for our people; they took a severe toll on the population of the entire family. Note that the family of Bocuwao is inherently small—it has always been a small family (in terms of headcounts). But it got even smaller when rampant retaliatory killings befell its members

214

after the occurrence that obliterated the community of Klosoken. "For a long time," the old man said, "it was hard to have a Bocuwao person in some of the peer groups around that time."

On Bocuwao's Stereotype: While the old man was explaining our family's culpability in the events that had befallen the hilltop community of Klosoken, he also provided the premise or basis for what had been a nagging stereotype for the family of Bocuwao. The people of Chedepo Jarkaken—the only town on the entire Chedepo landscape where the family of Bocuwao is—have labeled the family as stingy or mean. This generalized label— that Bocuwao is a mean or stingy family—is clearly a falsehood, which has been around for many, many generations. Thanks to the old man, we know now, as a matter of fact, that the occurrence that gave rise to this lingering stereotype happened in the town of Klosoken, the previous home for the families who dwell in today's Chedepo Jarkaken. So, this label has been around for a myriad of generations.

The falsehood does not go away even with the apparent generosity of the family. The stigma continues. And Bocuwao's elders, like our old man—Gbeh Chea Nyanley—make it their duty to explain the stigma away, using available or known facts. I cannot say, with absolute certainty, that they have succeeded.

My own father, old man Winn Saylee, the older brother of old man Gbeh Chea Nyanley, had tried to set the record straight—that the family of Bocuwao is not stingy. He told us—his children, and any group of people who cared to listen—that we, the members of the family of Bocuwao, are not a mean people; that it was a stereotype, which had developed from an actual historical occurrence in Klosoken. It was a simple

215

corrective or punitive action, not an act of being stingy or mean.

The correlation is evident in the brothers' accounts. On December 5, 2005, for

example, my father told a gathering of the people of Klosoken (Jarkaken) in Saylee Kpadeh's (his son's) living room, where they had come in their numbers to welcome me (from the United States) to the town.

"There's something I want say quickly before I take my seat," my father said as he neared the end of his remarks. The members within the mostly-male audience were surprisingly well-behaved. They stood up, one after the other, as if rehearsed, and offered their remarks. The men were pleased that my father did not conceal the presence of me and my siblings who were members of my entourage to the town. They had many examples of people who did the opposite; they concealed their family members who came from far-away places from the townspeople. So, the general sentiments were centered around the fact that our father was always opening his doors to the townspeople. "Even when your brother, Bocuwao Welley, came, it was the same as it is today—everyone was free to meet him," one elder said.

I had preceded my father on the floor. In my message, I told the townspeople that, before I left the United States, I realized that I did not "have enough money to bring a gift for everyone" in the community; that, if I had tried to do such a thing, I would be stuck in River Gee County, Liberia. "I will not be able to return to the United States," I told them. They got a good laugh over the statement. "For this reason, I brought with me gifts for the towns youth: two soccer balls, a set of soccer jersey and air pumps for the town's young people." I also added that I wanted to see "the elders in the town," primarily to read to

216

them a letter I had brought from Mr. David K. Chulu, then the Chairman of the Jarkaken Self-Help Development Association in the Americas, for which I was a general secretary. Then I added, "I have a gift for you, too; I am not just meeting you to read a letter." It was this ending statement that had prompted my father to get up and take the floor.

"You, the people of Klosoken, he said with a wide smile, say that we, the family of Bocuwao, are stingy," the crowd laughed. My father said this while looking at Wiah Toe (Mr. Joe Weah), then the oldest man in the village in 2005.

"You will continue your remarks," Wiah Toe politely interjected. "All of you in this room can attest that I am a truth teller. I am not a liar, but the people in this community say that we, the family of Magwulu, are a bunch of liars."

The crowd roared in a thunderous laughter. Old man Wiah Toe had a point. Like the family members of Bocuwao, the members in his Magwulu family—located in Chedepo Jarkaken and Chedepo Geeken, respectively—are stereotyped as chronic liars.

"You say that we are a mean people," my father picked up from where he had left off. "That we do not even give people common water to drink. And that, if we must give our drinking cup to someone whom we had refused a drink to fetch their own water, we go to the extent of drying out that cup, just to ensure a droplet of our water is not left in the cup," the audience roared in a thunderous laughter.

Mr. Alfred Deateah Kenta, a member of the Kaytiao family, got up and interrupted my father, "In our church [the Liberian Assemblies of God], every time we were, say boarding a plane, Kofa [Isaac K. Noring, a Bocuwao man] would generously fill it up with whatever we needed. Go ahead with your remarks!"

217

"In our tradition, we, the **Kofa** [13-26-year-olds], are in the bushes," my father continued. "We are chased out of town and sent into the bushes by switch-wielding Gborjlu [24-26-year-olds; the youngest peer group on the town's elder council]. Kofajlu

[13-15-year-olds] are the ones we traditionally send to fetch things for us. And then you tell one of them, 'Go fetch water for us to drink' but you get 'no' as a response. And this does not happen just once; it happened repeatedly. That was what happened, and that was the basis for a fitting corrective action: 'The water we have brought, you will not drink it. In fact, if you want to use this cup, we will have to dry it out, so you cannot get a droplet of the water we brought.'

"So, that is the meaning." Shedrick Choo Wesseh, a member of the Dowao family

and son of old man Duwa Wesseh, remarked.

"Yes, that is the meaning," my father continued. "'Bocuwao people are mean; Bocuwao people are stingy.' Pick any Bocuwao's hamlet. No traveler leaves our hamlets without eating; you have to eat before you leave," he said. "We, the family of Bocuwao, are not a mean people; we are a generous family." He sat down as the town rendered an applause.

"Wiah Toe, did you hear that?" Joe Wesseh Chea, a Bocuwao man, called the town's oldest man. He exhibited clear satisfaction for how well his cousin and peer group member had set the family's record straight.

Now, a few years later, the old man's baby brother, old man Nyanley, also tried his best to set Bocuwao's record straight. Unlike his elder brother, whose audience encompassed the entire makeup of the town's population, uncle's audience was quite small. In fact, we were no more than seven persons,

218

forced under a tiny gazebo by a torrential Fishtown rain. Uncle's version was a comprehensive one though. Unlike his elder brother, who—though repeatedly interrupted by members of his audience—provided mere synopses to the townspeople, his uncle's version of the same story contained specific details. Who did what? Why did they do it? Where did it transpire? When did it happen? Even though it all goes down. All these elements complete a story, and all these elements were apparent in uncle's story. Moreover, he kept his voice raised the entire time we spent under Eric's gazebo, a calculated effort to win over the sustained noise from the Fish Town rain, which was pounding the corrugated sheet metal roof of the tiny shack, where we were seeking a refuge. Again, Uncle cared very little, if any, about summaries; he went all in.

"Our people [young people, 13-26-year-olds] used to go into the bushes to conduct a variety of training activities; that was their equivalent of going to school," he said. For example, "They went there to learn how to tap palm wine, which they presented to the peer groups within the **Gbor** [elder] section. Now, in today's peer groups, it is different.

Young people are going from one house to the other, looking for palm wine or cane juice to purchase. Back then, that was not the case. It was all palm wine—no cane juice. It was straight palm wine. So, the peer groups within Kofa had no choice but to learn how to tap palm wine. The collection itself was call '**Gbornormo**,' for elder's wine, loosely. And, every time the peer groups were chased into the bushes during Kofa's traditional farming season, they had to spend the entire day there—into those bushes. In fact, they referred to that training activity as 'Wailay Chonu,' [loosely translates into "staying in the bushes"].

Kofa's season was around the Christmas season; this meant that the townspeople's harvest

219

was over, and it was still early to begin the following year's farms."

He went on to describe the palm wine collection process.

"Every farming reservation [**Sonjigba**] had a designated collection point. They built tents at those regional points. In our region, for example, the collection point was located at **Deorblemgehn** ['under Dior's tent']. The location was not in name only. Our people built an actual tent at the location. I saw it with my own two eyes. I went in it. It was to the right of the reefs (bamboo plants). It [the tent] is not there today because the storms blew all that stuff away. The location of Deorblemgehn [at least, where it used to be] is not far from Chichi creek [norther Gee River is so small here; it looks like a small creek]. It was a two-story tent. There was a first step, and there was a second step. It had a giant clay pot under it," uncle said.

From his hand gestures, I made an educated assumption that the collection pot could have held 15 to 20 gallons of palm wine.

"The pot sat on a small platform, which was built specifically for it," he continued. "We used to see it on a regular basis until the stuff was removed from that location. Our people planted a cola tree there; it is still there. So, for Gbornormo [the elders' palm wine], they used to send Kofa to the bushes. By the time the sun set over the horizon, it was time for the young men in the Kofa section to proceed to their palm wine trees and collect the palm wine. They took the palm wine to the location of the giant clay pot and consolidated it there.

In our region, there are two famlies that own that faming region—Bocuwao and Dowao. The family of Bocuwao petitions the wishes of the people in our region [including the wishes of the people who live in the entire Kaytoken area, i.e., Chedepo

Jarkaken and Chedepo Geeken, according to Winn Saylee—January 19, 2004]."

He briefly talked about the family of Magwulu, the latest to join Bocuwao and Dowao in the Dilamo region.

"Putting something where it does not belong—the family of Magwulu went over there in 1931," the same year Klosoken was set ablaze. "And they have been there [with us] since that year. Even Killepo Torwloken was not over there," he added.

"Anyway, that is how Gbornormo was collected. The mothers of Kofa's peer groups used to farm in a general area. Then later, they picked one woman's farm and apportioned it among themselves. The women planted cassava on the consolidated farm. Every time Kofa went into the bushes, they used to go to their mothers' cassava patches to collect cassava, which they cooked and ate while they stayed out there, waiting for the sun to set over the horizon. They were not stealing the cassava. The women knew their children needed cassava from their patches. In fact, the women did not go to herb or country doctors—as some people used to do—to protect their cassava patches from thieves. 'Bocuwao are mean.' This is how the stereotype started in Klosoken," he said.

Then, without expanding on the stereotype, as I would have liked, the old man briefly tabled the subject. He switched to the tragedy that destroyed the ancient town of Chedepo Klosoken.

Fire in Chedepo Klosoken: "The man we call Wayee was a prominent Bocuwao family member. He was a father of many children. One of his children was had Jayee Teh, the man who had his village over the foothill known as Joyl. Old man Wayee also had Wiah Teatay [who, according to Wleh Snoteh, had Young]. Moreover, old man Wayee also had Wayee Dweh; he had Sarlee Young, and, finally, he had Gbayee Wiah. Sarlee Young was older than Jayee Teh; Sarlee Young

221

was Jayee Teh's immediate senior. By the way, Jayee Teh was the Jakwi who died in the town of Chutuken before Saylee Winn became a Jakwi in that town—Chutuken; Winn later moved to Jarkaken and became Jakwi there; he did not seek out the post in Jarkaken, instead, Quayee Swen, a member of the Nyansunupo branch of Bocuwao, had it prior, he ceremoniously turned the job over to Saylee Winn—Winn Saylee, January 19, 2004].

Sarlee Young," he continued, "like his peers, stayed an entire day in the wild. By sun down, he collected his palm wine and poured it in the giant clay pot. Then they brought the palm wine to town. Of course, it was dark when he got home. After they turned in their palm wine to the elders, Sarlee Young went to his father's hut in Klosoken. He was tired and hungry. Again, it was very dark, and the people in Klosoken had no flashlights back then. They were using torches to see in the dark. Young's mother, Sarlee, told him, 'Young, your food is sitting on the hut ceiling [*wulo*], near the entrance [*mormonbo*] to the ceiling.'"

He set the scene. We glued to him—attentively. His voice was piercing through what (by this time of the narratives) had been the sustained noise from the Fish Town rain, which was pouring the metal roof of the shack that was shielding us from the elements.

"Our people used to put things near this entry and exit opening to the ceiling because it was easy to find things there. Often, there was no need to get on the storage ceiling to retrieve items from this common storage area, which was known as mormonbo. As soon you climb up the ladder, it is that immediate area. His mother, Sarlee, told him to 'feel for it; do not take a torch up there.' Sarlee Young did not listen. He wanted to find his food fast, so he lit a torch and climbed to the hut ceiling, where his food was, indeed.

222

In Klosoken, all their dwellings were rounded huts, and because of the shape of their rooftops, the people used a different form of thatches for roofing. Unlike '***Matin,***' which are palm leaves fashioned like large, square-shaped sheets, the huts in Klosoken used the version called '***Bubu.***' This type of roofing was more flammable [than Matin] because they were bundles of dried palm leaves. They tied up the bundles of leaves in such a creative way that the roofing was waterproof. And that was how they built their huts."

Uncle moved on to talking about one popular commodity in the town of Klosoken—palm oil. I was thinking in the back of my head, "How does that relate to the subject under discussion?" In fact, I fleetingly considered asking the question out loud. But I changed my mind because I did not want to throw him off topic. He was clearly "in the zone," as we say in the writing community. So, I continued to listen to him, along with the other members of my entourage.

"They used to make and sell palm oil," he said. "They used to sell the oil to the Krahn tribal people. The town of Killepo Torwloken [now in River Gee] was not over there—from Chedepo, it was straight into the Krahn tribal areas. Our people used to take their commodities to Gborlu, a location near the Krahns; the people of Killepo were on the other side, and Germans were the key business people. The Germans had oil tins or containers, which looked compressed or flattened. The people in Klosoken called them '***Chansene Pafurlo,***' ["flat kerosene"]. It was in those same Bocuwao quarters where Sayee Gbey Parteh lived. By the way, Sayee Gbey Parteh was the one whose penis was hailed as the biggest in Klosoken and its environs."

We laughed.

223

"Sayee Gbey Parteh," he said, "was the one who gave us, the Bocuwao family, the record in that area. He inherited it from birth. It was God Himself Who gave it to Parteh."

We laughed—and I mean with "crackling laughter."

Every time the old man tried to move on, Targiour and Tinpan, my younger siblings, were seemingly urging or egging him on, "Sayee Gbey Parteh!" And so, we stayed a few more minutes on the funny, manhood story, perhaps more than was necessary. Targiour and Tinpan were on the loose. When we learned about Sayee Gbey Parteh's bizarre record, there was no dried eye left under the tiny gazebo, where we had sought refuge from the rain.

"Any way," he managed to move on.

"Sinneh, the son of Sayee Gbey Parteh, and Wayee's huts shared the same courtyard. Sinneh had a Chansene Pafurlo in his overhead storage; it had oil in it. Sarlee Young took the torch to the hut ceiling to retrieve his food, and what his mother dreaded happened. Inadvertently, he dropped a flame on the ceiling (storage) floor. Of course, the ceiling was extremely flammable; the bamboo materials were dried up, so they were extremely combustible."

He talked about the calm before the chaos.

"Sarlee Young came down with his food, sat down and he began to eat. Two men (Teh and his friend) from the Wulopotonmo peer group were sitting by the main entrance— the male entrance—drinking palm wine and sharing jokes. Sinneh and Wayee sat in their courtyard and chatted, too. The people who were in the Ponwaon family quarter were the first to see the fire. They started to yell, 'There is a blaze over old man Wayee's hut! 'There is fire over old man Wayee's hut!' The father of Sarlee Young was Wayee. It was his [Wayee's]

224

hut that was on fire. Wayee also had a son, as I mentioned earlier, named Wayee Dweh, the father of my friend Wilmot K. Dweh (in Australia).

The town of Klosoken was upside down. Their homes were extremely close to one another. Coupled with the flammable nature of their choice of roofing, it was a challenge to contain the fire. People were saying 'put water over it!' Instead of dust, which puts fire out quicker, they were saying 'get water!'

The people in Klosoken used to drink from a tiny, hilltop fountain. It was called 'Portorwan,' and I know you have not seen it. It is a tiny spring. It does not dry. Back then, people used small clay pots to collect and store water. But, really, how much water could they hold? Not much.

When the fire was getting serious, people were throwing things in it in their efforts to contain it. Sinneh, the father of Chelateah Sloboh, whose children include Paul Sinneh and others, grabbed a Chansenc Pafurlo—a metal tin—and tossed it into the fire. The tins were very popular in Klosoken in the 1930s because they were used to store liquids, mainly oil, which they transported to the Krahn tribal people and also to the Germans for sale. (The Krahn tribal people, by the way, have been digging gold for many, many years.) Sinneh's Chansene Pafurlo contained a lot of palm oil, which he mistook for water. It made the fire even worse. And that was how Klosoken was set ablaze. That was in 1931."

He talked about a dugout drum, which he said one man used mysterious powers and save from the inferno.

"We heard that one old man in Klosoken saved the **Kofa Toku** [a giant talking drum for the young peer groups] during the fire. I cannot remember his name," he said. "But I can tell you this much: My grandfather, Saylee, the father of Polee Winn, curved that drum. He curved it by himself. The tree he

225

used to carve the drum came from *Tokuken*, [that's how it is called now because the toku came the top of that foothill; its actual name is *Jelatoh*]. When you are going to the village of Puwaiken, just a quarter of a mile after the ruins of historic Weltehken village, the foothill is in that general vicinity. It is glaring; it is very tall, not a bump. The powerful man reportedly used his juju and told the drum, which was firmly anchored to 'Get up! Fire is coming!' The drum, as I said, had been tied up in the home of the *Chikpaamo*, a traditional title holder who acts as a host for Kofa's activities. Basically, we are told that the drum untied itself and flew downhill to safety. The powerful old man said, 'We are going to build another drum; there's nothing wrong with that drum.'"

Then, finally, the old man faced me directly and said to me, "And that is why I said we, the family of Bocuwao, burned the town of Klosoken, and, as I said earlier, we paid for this incidence with our lives. Saylee Winn, my father named one of his sons '*Bocuwao Welley*' ["Bocuwao families have died out; we are finished"]. When the people asked him for the meaning of such a unique name for my older brother, he basically told them to let it sink in. 'An orphan does not explain parables,' routinely, my dad [Polee Winn] used to tell this to members of the townspeople. Our people died because of many unruly elements took revenge against us when a member of our Bocuwao family caused their beloved Klosoken, a once thriving Chedepo community, to burn. At one point, death and illnesses were overwhelming. If two people died on a given day, that was nothing. Indeed, the family of Bocuwao lost so many people after the Klosoken incident. And you wanted to know," he continued while we—he and I—stared directly at each other. "It was our family member, Sarlee Young, the son Wayee and his wife, Sarlee, who set the town of Klosoken on fire. He was old man Wayee's oldest son. He was Jayec Teh's big brother. Jayee Teh, the man whose village was called Joyl, was Wayee's son. Jayee Teh was a member of the

Wulopotonmo peer group. His brother, Sarlee Young, was a member of the Jelapotonmo peer group.

Because of the tragedy at Klosoken, our family suffered. We died; they killed us. It was for this reason that Saylee Winn, my father, went to a country doctor. Her name was Bello, and she was well-known for her excellence in fertility of reproductive treatments. Ballo was a native of the land of Tienpo. Anyway, my father got a child from her. And he said, 'My son's name is Bocuwao Welley,' and the people were asking him to explain the name. The people of Jarkaken [who are the former dwellers or residents of Klosoken] were very curious about the name. 'What does it mean?' They used to ask my father. He rarely provided genuine responses to them because he did not want to tell people what he felt they already knew. He would say, 'My people, I am an orphan. I have no mother; I have no father. We have a saying in this land that 'An orphan does not explain parables.' So, the name is just that—a name; it is just an innocent name. It means what it says—no underlying meaning there is to it.' They kept asking; they kept pressing him to tell the meaning of the unique name: 'Is it a namesake for a long-ago forefather within the family of Bocuwao?' they wound say, an attempt to get Winn to open up. But Saylee Winn stood his ground. He said the name was coined; that he, Polee Winn, he made it up, which is the true. His son was the first to have that name in the family of Bocuwao, and it meant nothing more than what it said—that the family of Bocuwao is killed off, crushed, and annihilated from the Chedepo landscape [Bocuwao, unlike the other families in Chedepo, is in just one community—Chedepo Jarkaken]. But whenever Saylee Winn was with his peer group members and other confidants, he told them his genuine mind. He told them what they knew and suspected to be the name's underlying meaning. 'Don't you, the people of Klosoken, know what you have done to my family, the family of Bocuwao?

227

Don't you know how you killed us because of our sin at Klosoken? That's the meaning of

Bocuwao Welley. You killed us. You even killed off our properties, i.e., our cattle and other domestic animals.' That is the meaning of that name because we suffered calamities after calamities because our son, Sarlee Young, unintentionally set your town, Klosoken, on fire."

By this point, we were consumed by the fiery incidence. But this excellent storyteller was not done yet. And so, the old man went back to the young men and their palm wine.

"Whenever the members of Kofa went to the wild, as I explained earlier, they cooked and ate cassava from the cassava patches (farms) of their parents. Boiled cassava has the propensity or tendency to stick to the throats of people. Every time they were in those bushes, the family of Dowao would be over there, and the family of Bocuwao would be here [he made hand gestures, and illustrated how the two were apart or separated]. Do you know who the seniors of Kofa send to fetch things for them?" he asked a rhetorical question, not expecting an immediate response from his audience. "It is the members within the Kofajlu peer group, the13-15-year-olds who are the youngest of the youth members within the entire Kofa section [13-26-year-olds]. One day, as they were getting ready to cook cassava after palm wine tapping work, the oldest of the Bocuwao's Kofa sent a young man. 'Go and fetch water, so we can cook this cassava.' He refused. 'No, I will not do that,' he said. 'I am not getting that water.' So, a senior member of Kofa [a 26-year- old] went and fetched the water himself. They used the water to cook the cassava. They had small containers, so they asked the same young man who refused to get the water earlier to go for water for drinking. Without any hesitation, the young man refused to go and fetch water again."

228

He set the scene further.

"During this time, they were using snail shells as cups. So, they sent someone else for the water. And then they sat down to eat. As I said earlier, boiled cassava is quick to attach itself to the throat. When they started to eat, the one who refused to get water—not once, but twice—was the first cassava victim. He began to struggle because the food had lodged at his throat. He needed water to get the cassava down his throat. The senior of Kofa who fetched the water said, 'You will not drink the water I brought. If you want to drink, I will gladly give you the snail shell so you can fetch your own water. But I will first ensure that a single water droplet from this water will not be in the snail shell I will give you. I will dry it out.' And that is the basis or source of the stereotype in Jarkaken [and Klosoken before it]. Whether naively or intentionally, they glossed over the facts gave rise to this punitive action. All you hear is that we, the family of Bocuwao are a mean family. We do not give people things; that we are not charitable at all. These are falsehoods. That we go to the extent of drying out our cups before we let others—who we had refused water—use our dried cups to get or fetch their own water. It was a punishment, and it happened a long time ago—in the days of Klosoken."

Satire: Laugh it up: "Sayee Gbey Parteh!" The name of the historic Bocuwao figure with an apparent killer penis, surfaced—again. And, with the name came another episode of crackling laughter.

"It was a long one," he said. "It was about an arm's length. It had its own rope, which he used to put it away. And every time he wanted to use it," he said while we were laughing painfully and tearing up, "he would undo the rope and reveal exactly the segment of the manhood he wanted to use. Truly, it was a big one. Sayee Gbey Parteh did not like it either. Because

229

of his personal luck, we, the family of Bocuwao, are credited today for having huge penises.

So, every time you hear anyone says that about us, blame Sayee Gbey Parteh. He did not go to any herbalist to request it. He did not go to any country doctor in search of a big manhood. It was pure natural," he said. "The Almighty God Himself made that mistake. The thing is, Sayee Gbey Parteh has been dead more than a few centuries ago now. Why can't they [the people of River Gee] leave us alone, already?"

Even though Sayee Gbey Parteh's story is authentic, the old man was saying some of the above things to get us laughing. And he laughed at his own jokes, too. Unlike the previous Sayee Gbey Parteh episode—when Targiour and Tinpan were egging him on— this latest version was completely unprovoked. He managed to gain control of the conversation, which had clearly gone off course. But the end would not come sooner; and there was not a single dry eye left under the darkening gazebo.

"Our people are not good," he said with obvious sarcasm. "The next story [about Sayee Gbey Parteh] is either true or fiction. They said a popular and attractive Potupo woman heard about him and came to Klosoken to befriend him; it was more like a challenge. 'What can this one guy do? Who is this guy?'"

"Alright," Roland joined in. "If anything happens, you have no one to blame but

yourself, lady. You are looking for trouble."

"Parteh who has no march in this area," the old man picked up with more jokes. "Potupo people have some crazy people," he said, mockingly. "But that is pure human nature on display right there. Every time people are told not to do something—

230

something that they know about to be forbidden, and perhaps evidently or historically known to be unsafe—there are those with the inclination to do just that."

"My son, there's a snake! There's a snake! But you still want the pointing finger to

land on the snake before you will stop proceeding in its location," Roland said.

"Well, she came to Chedepo," the old man said with relative composure or self- control. "The lady reportedly prepared a sumptuous meal. Then she dressed up in the finest Potupo attire and brought the food to Sayee Gbey Parteh in Klosoken. Upon arrival in the land of Klosoken, the lady went to the Bocuwao family quarter, where Parteh was living. 'You are my **signi** [Chedepo for a date, which is a form of wooing of courtship],' she allegedly told the lucky man when she arrived in the town of Klosoken. The local people who knew all about Sayee Gbey Parteh enormous natural gift were baffled by the woman's risky behavior. They were saying, 'Look at the trouble the woman is bringing to herself; she is walking into a waiting danger.'

And so, the couple ate and then went to sleep. He just loosened up a tiny, frontal segment. And the Potupo woman said, 'Really, this is it? Is this all you have? I walked the long road for this? So, he said, 'Well, let me loosen up the next segment then; in fact, I am releasing the entire cobra.'"

"Come out of the hole," Targiour said, and we laughed.

The segment came to an end, leaving us with teary eyes and, for some—myself included—minor headaches and pains because of the crackling laughter.

Chapter X:
War in Chedepo Jarkaken

The National Patriotic Front of Liberia (NPFL) war started on December 24, 1989, in Nimba County, northeastern Liberia. It started near the town of Butuo, which lies along the Liberian-Ivorian border. For several months, the war was just news to many Liberians because the impact was not as immediate as it had been for those in Nimba and the western Grand Gedeh County areas. But that calm was short-lived in many parts of the country. By the middle of that year, in fact, the war was not just news anymore. It was a full-scale war between the government of President Samuel Kanyan Doe and the NPFL rebels, led by Mr. Charles Ghankay Taylor.

By this time of my life, I was far removed from Chedepo Jarkaken, my hometown. It was almost a ritual or rite of passage within the Winn family—though not limited to the Winns alone—to leave the town in the mid to late teens, especially for those who were going to school. In fact, by this time, many of my older, school-aged siblings were away from home. S. Kpadeh Winn ("S.K.") was at the Assemblies of God (A. G.) High School in Zwedru. Mantee Sayjolo Winn ("Brother Man") was at Tubman Wilson Institute (TWI), Zwedru. Later, both S.K. and Brother Man attended AG, where they obtained their high school graduation certificates. Susannah S. Winn ("Ma Sue"), my oldest sister, was at the prestigious Zwedru Multilateral High School (ZMHS). Moreover, a few years earlier than Ma Sue's exit from our village, Brother Sandy Darty Winn, the immediate senior of Ma Sue, also left the village. He was a student at Bishop Juwlie High, a Catholic school also in Zwedru (Tchien). Then Chester Taynue Winn and Lucia Nowen Winn (Lucia is not my senior.) left a lot earlier than me—around 1985.

So, I followed the tradition in the area and left the town as a teenager to pursue higher education elsewhere. In fact, I went to Tchien (Zwedru), which is the provincial capital of Grand Gedeh County, Liberia in the year 1988, a year before the start of the NPFL war. I traveled after I completed 6th grade in my village. My mother, Mrs. Ethel Bolju Winn, sent me to stay with her niece, Ms. Saratha Chie Toe.

Kaytoken Junior High School, which is the main school in Jarkaken, ended at the 9th grade level. So, it was not uncommon for junior high students to move out of the town and enroll at communities with high schools. And the only high school near Jarkaken at the time was Gbeapo Central High in the city of Kanweaken, Gbeapo District. For some reasons, many junior high school migrants from Chedepo District, where Jarkaken is, hardly went that route; instead, they went to much larger cities—Pleebo, Harper, Zwedru—with many school options. I am not sure whether my parents' decisions to send me to Zwedru was mainly to give me the options to pick a school from Zwedru's many high schools. I do not think that was the case; in fact, I am leaning toward the likelihood that my auntie, whom we called "Sister," her own children included, wanted a child from the interior (the country side) to help around the house.

Sister wanted the best for students. She was an employee at the Southeastern Regional Education Office in Zwedru. In fact, she sent her kids to schools with both academic and name recognitions. In our house, which was in the borough of Kudah Bye Pass, we had students at the prestigious ZMHS, where my oldest sister also attended. This school was—technically—a high school, but, practically, it was sandwiched between a high school and a community college. The younger ones in our house, however, went to Saint Philomena Elementary School, a Catholic institution.

Like the other students in our jam-packed house, Sister gave me the opportunity to choose any high school I wanted to attend. But I could not gain access to my preferred schools in my first year in Tchien because of the time of entry in that year. I got to Zwedru late in February 1988. By that time, new student's enrollment windows in many of the schools in the city were closed, especially at the ones I was eyeing in 1988. I wanted to enroll at Gbagba Elementary and Junior High School, not because it had "both academic and name recognitions,"—maybe it did—but I knew about it long before I left my rural village. S. Kpadeh Winn, my older brother, was a student there when his time came to leave Jarkaken, so it automatically became an option: apparently, it was the first option I had on my mind when I arrived it the city. But, like many Zwedru schools in late February, the window for new students to enroll at Gbagba was shut; there was no room for me or anyone who wanted to enroll that time.

That was the reason she enrolled me at Antoinette Tubman Day, a combined elementary and junior high school. It was known popularly as "A.T. Day" and it was "a day [afternoon] school" as opposed to "a morning school." Even though I loved every movement of my year at this school—met B. Swen Parteah, a friend of mine to this date, there—I could not wait to leave the afternoon school at the end of year, 1988.

We, the students at A. T. Day, were called "giants;" the term was used in a disparaging manner. Note that we wore black pants and pink shirts, so we couldn't hide, if we wanted to do so. Why hide? Well, we were routinely picked on; we were bullied by some (maybe most) of the morning school students.

Whenever we came in contact with the morning school students, they raised what was then a provocative or confrontational chant. It was a one liner, with the propensity to morph or transform into more disparaging lines. One morning

234

school student—a provocateur—would say in a loud and thunderous voice, "A.T. Day!" His audience will respond, "We are the giants!" Then the initiator or provoking agent would follow up, "What kind of giants?" This is where the lines [responses] morphed or took varied. Some said, "Kala eaters!" Some said, "Donut eaters!" Pick your food. It went on until you (the A. T. Day student) were out of sight from them. This was a daily occurrence because our school started after their school ended. In fact, A.

T. Day used the campus of Gbagba, so I was not at attending at Gbagba Elementary and Junior High School in 1988, but I used Gbagba's campus that same year. Anyway, we were the "giants" who, they claimed, ate or finished their left overs. There were fights on or off campus, between departing Gbagba students and reporting A.T. day students.

I was a young boy. I was not comfortable with what was going on. We were a laughing stalk. This, to be honest, was one of the reasons I moved to Robert Baker Richardson Baptist High School (RBRS). The Rev. Shelton Seidi, from Chedepo Putuken, Lower Grand Gedeh (now River Gee), was the principal of RBRS when I reported there.

Anyway, when the war started, I was a ninth-grade student at RBRS; that was in the year 1990. By June of that year, we started to hear more pronounced sounds of ambulances as they returned Soldiers and other casualties of war from the western parts of the county to hospitals around the city. So, my guardians rightly decided that our safety was more important than the pursuit of education. So, in June 1990, we packed up and left our Kudah Bye Pass neighborhood for "Lower Grand Gedeh," which later gained regional autonomy as River Gee County in the year 2000 under President Charles G. Taylor. We assumed safety was waiting for us in our eastern hometowns. So, we left the city of Zwedru. Within a few hours

235

of turbulent ride, we arrived in the fundamentally Grebo region of what was then a Krahn county. My guardians dutifully dropped me off at my parents' house in the town of Chedepo Jarkaken. Then they continued on to theirs: Killepo Torwloken, which lies just a stone throw away by way of the now infamous Dilamo road.

But relocation to the River Gee region didn't provide the kind of safety we had hoped to secure when we left Tchien (Zwedru). In fact, barely eight months after entering the country, the rebels—seemingly with no one standing in their way—reached the little- known town of Chedepo Jarkaken on August 24, 1990. Like the rest of the country, the town lay vulnerable. The rebels entered the town from all directions. And in just a few hours, the rebels had the town of five thousand people on a complete lockdown. But remarkably, however, some of the people who the rebels targeted, like the Krahn and Mandingo tribal people, government officials and other people of interest, managed somehow to leave the town before the rebels achieved a total lockdown.

There was a family of Krahns in our **David Dia** *[David's town]* neighborhood, informally named for the late Kolobah (Chief) David Toe, who was one of a few people from our Bocuwao family to serve as a paramount chief in the area. They (the family of Krahns) rented Uncle David Karwolo Swen's tiny shop. On the day the rebels entered the town, they were among the lucky rebel targets to get out of harm's way. As they headed out of the town, they met my family by the Geeken Road Cemetery. The graveyard, where many members of the family are resting—to include Grandma Nyangbe Teaty (Sunset 1982) and my brother James Jowa Doe Winn (1979-1989)—is sandwiched between Jarkaken proper and the ruins of the historic community of Klosoken, which was destroyed by fire in 1931, long before the town of Jarkaken gained prominence. We were on our way to the town after several

236

hours of work along the Dilamo Road, which connects the town proper to our Dilamo (Deormo, Deorken) farming reservation.

We learned about the activities in the town from the runaway family members. "The rebels just captured the town!" They told us. Immediately, safety became a concern for us, especially for me—again. We stood there and watched as the family ran away with only the clothes on their backs. We stood there, literally a few meters from our paternal grandmother's resting place, and pondered whether to enter the town or to turn around and go back to Wodaiken, the few-hut farming outpost our father established in 1975. We agreed to enter the town.

As we were entering the town, we heard the loud voices of town criers, dispatched to inform all residents in the community at the time of the rebels' entry to report to the town center. So, we went straight to the town center. It was late afternoon when we gathered at the center of the town. Many residents were still on their farms. But to their credit, the announcers had managed to assemble a large crowd. It was very quiet at the town center while the people awaited the rebels' briefing.

Suddenly, a few horrible-looking men, the so-called "patriots," gallantly marched to the town center from the vicinity of Teaty Nyenkeyla's house, which was just a few yards from the *Tugbakou'u*, or the People's Hut. They were no more than ten in all, by my recollection. And they were not uniformed at all. Many of them were partially dressed in the traditional military battle dress uniforms (BDUs). Some men had on BDU trousers, but there were no matching or corresponding tops; others had on BDU tops, but no matching bottoms. Elaborately, they had different shades of red on their clothes. Also, affixed to their headbands were varied shades of

237

red strings. A few men held their weapons at the ready—as if they were about to shoot them; but a great many of them simply slung theirs behind them (across their bodies). They were mostly tribal peoples (Mano, Gio) from Nimba County, but we also knew a couple of local NPFL converts in their ranks. Using the locals who joined them as interpreters, the rebels briefed the town and laid down these seemingly impromptu ground rules:

1. They demanded that all former and current government officials come out of hiding; they compelled the ex-officials to renounce President Doe and his government. Lastly, the rebels demanded former officials to embrace the NPFL rebels.

2. They made it clear that the local Grebo tribal people were not their targets, even those who were in the government at the time, provided they adhered to their rules: they had to renounce President Doe and embrace the NPFL.

3. The rebels were explicit: Krahn and Mandingo tribal peoples were their targets.

4. Those who knew the whereabouts of any Krahn or Mandingo tribal peoples were ordered to turn them in to the NPFL. And anyone who failed to adhere to this and all other NPFL rules, they said, would face death as their punishable.

5. The rebels' color was red. They asked every house in Jarkaken to display a red piece of cloth as a sign of support and solidarity for the NPFL.

6. The fighters repudiated the term "rebels," as the government called them. Instead, they demanded to be called "Freedom Fighters."

238

7. Adultery—basically any form of infidelity—was a cause for summary execution. "If you follow somebody's woman, you will die," the rebels said.

8. The NPFL declared all crimes, including murder, theft and rape, punishable by death.

9. There was a new order; they said. The Doe government was a thing of the past. The NPFL was the new order in town.

10. Depending on the number of boys in a given home, the rebels said a certain unspecified number would be slated to fight for Charles Taylor's NPFL. The rebels did not enforce this—at least not in Jarkaken.

11. "No one in the town owned any domestic animals," they declared. All the animals the rebels met in the town were for the "Papay," as they called their rebel leader. They told the locals that anyone seen tampering with the animals liable to be put to death.

One unmistakable message stood out: a state of lawlessness had just taken over the town. The presence of guns, coupled with several threats from the rebels to carry out summary killings over minor crimes, made the rebel briefing very gloomy and quite bizarre.

Despite all the NPFL's talks about death, dying and killing, somehow one resident at the town center gathered enough courage and raised his hand for a permission to express his thoughts on one of the rebels' impromptu rules. When granted the floor to speak, the courageous citizen told the rebels, "Many people in this town do not speak English. They will not be able to call you [Freedom Fighters] in English." So, he wanted to know if the rebels—I meant "freedom fighters"—could settle for "Wowanyo," which is the Grebo's equivalence

239

of freedom fighters. Thankfully, the NPFL acknowledged the resident's concern. In addition to (or instead of) freedom fighters, the rebels agreed to be called Wowanyo, for "saviors" in Chedepo, the variety of the Grebo language spoken in and around Chedepo Jarkaken. Gradually, the Chedepo equivalence evolved, particularly among the elderly, into "Wunwonyo", another Chedepo word for "Fighters." But the predominately Nimba fighters couldn't figure out any distinction.

The get-together at the town center lasted a little over an hour. The rebels did not shoot their weapons a lot on the first day, something that was uncharacteristic for the NPFL. In fact, I did not hear a single shot that day. The only shots heard by other residents were those informing the locals that the rebels were in the area. Thankfully, I missed those initial midair shooting aspects of the rebel entry because I was still busy with other family members trimming the edges of the footpath that led to Puwaiken, our village.

In the following days, the local government officials in and around the town started to come out of hiding little by little. They renounced President Doe and his government and embraced the NPFL.

Our father, Hon. Josiah S. Winn, Sr., was the Township Commissioner of Kaytoken Township at the time. After attending the briefing, we told him to do the right thing. He was among the first to show up and "embrace" the rebels. He and all the Township's Nine Council Men, headed by Hon. Fulton Sayon Pah (now the current Township Commissioner of Kaytoken Township), kept their jobs. Moreover, a great many of the local officials retained their jobs as well. They included, but not limited to, Hon.

George Wesseh—a member of the Kaytiao family—retained his post as the Quarter Chief. (Hon George Wesseh was a humble individual; he was one of the town criers the day the rebels entered; the other town criers were Mr. Teaty Playe and Mr. John Chea (Tinkpe/Worwlee Duwah). Hon. Henry Nyemah Jah was the Paramount Chief at the time; he retained his post. Hon. Kaynyonoh Wiah, a native of Chedepo Geeken, was the Justice of the Peace. His office was in the living room of Mr. Wiah Toe (Borbor Toe). He retained his post, too.

All of these officials, who had occasionally received wages under the ex- government prior to the arrival of the rebels, were now rehired as unpaid civil servants under the Charles Taylar rebels. No pay would come their way "until the Papay sets up his government," the rebels said. In any case, many of the government officials, particularly the remnants of the Doe administration, were nothing more than rubber stamps for the NPFL. They did not have any significant influences at all; people hardly took them seriously, except during moments when they were the backing of the rebels.

In just a few days after the town had fallen into rebel hands, the town was completely jam-packed with NPFL rebels. Chedepo Jarkaken was a magnet for NPFL soldiers because it was one of few places that still retained some semblance of civilization. Prime Timber Products (PTP), a thriving timber company, was still operating in the town. In fact, while much of Liberia was in the dark by this time of the Charles Taylor war, the timber yard and Karweadolo, the borough of Chedepo Jarkaken adjacent to the company's sawmill facility, had electricity around the clock. The latest waves of rebels who descended on the town were among those who had convoyed with self-proclaimed "General Noriega," a Taylor deputy who came to Chedepo Jarkaken to join the rest of the rebels who were looting PTP, the timber company.

On the day the general arrived, the rebels killed three cows and maybe one on each day that followed. In fact, domesticated animals were systematically fired upon. The rebels were shooting at cows, goats, sheep and any animals they had craving for on a given day. It became so normal that some community residents ran to the sounds of gunshots in the hopes of getting a piece of cow meat from the rebels. Sometimes they got the rejected parts of their kill: the ears, the head, the guts and so on. Other times, the rebels threw their kill in the back of a cattle truck and drove away. No one had the courage to question the rebels as they were slaughtering the town's animals. Mostly uncommitted local women and girls, who were lured to the rebels by fear, were seen cooking for the NPFL bandits.

Mr. Friday Doe was the acting manager of PTP. Instead of living in a company- provided bungalow on the grounds of the company, Mr. Doe elected to rent a giant concrete building right in the middle of the local population. He chose to live in the borough of Karweadolo, which was not too far from his office at the PTP yard. Mr. Doe's compound had electricity around the clock, and the lights from his massive compound practically lit up Karweadolo.

Routinely, the Taylor rebels demanded and subsequently obtained their fuel, food, cars and even their housing units from the timber company. And any sign of rejection of their never-ending demands by Mr. Friday Doe, himself a stubborn Kru tribesman from Sinoe County, usually triggered dangerous rebel reactions, which sent the rest of us running for protection or cover.

The rebels used to unleash intimidating onslaught of gunfire in and around Mr.

242

Doe's home. Mr. Isaac K. Doe—not related to the company manager—rented his compound to the timber company. Hence, we saw or heard many of these awful rebel activities firsthand. It was unpleasant, especially at night, because we saw tracer ammunitions, or simply tracers, which are "bullets or cannon-caliber projectiles that contain small pyrotechnic charge in their base. We frequently saw these rounds—red, hot bullets—flying over our homes. They were using AK-47s [Russian made rifles] and their relished "Sister Berettas" to fire these dangerous bullets over our homes, which were mostly traditional thatch huts.

Whenever Mr. Friday Doe was not around—whenever he was not in the company area—the rebels had market women and other ordinary people to harass, intimidate, or even torture. Mind you, as the rebels and the folks coexisted for some time, some people mustered enough courage and guts to repudiate some of their unwanted behaviors, such as looting and bullying.

In other words, the rebels did not always get what they wanted from the people. To increase their chances to loot the local population, they instituted several dangerous behaviors. One of the dangerous behaviors the rebels were engaging in included what they coined as the "digging" of their victims' "potatoes" Whenever they were challenged or feared of being challenged by their looting victims, the rebels demanded the victims to spread their feet apart—as much as a shoulder width apart. Then they pointed their rifles a few inches from the victims' feet and began to fire off multiple bullets around the victims' feet. This was enough to have even the toughest or rebellious victims turn over whatever the rebels wanted from them. At other times, the rebels resulted to another form of torture, which they also coined as "duck fat tabay." It was a tie-down method that was so cruel it destroyed their victims' chest. Some victims had their chest cavity punctured; others had broken ribs. As dangerous as these were, the rebels used these methods regularly on their victims.

Mr. Kennedy Kehgbeh Jah was one of the first victims the NPFL war claimed in the town of Jarkaken. He was a native of Chedepo Geeken, a town that is just a stone throw from Chedepo Jarkaken. Mr. Jah was a career soldier in the Armed Forces of Liberia (AFL). He spent a better part of the warring period in the interior (the country side). That was possible because he had been absent without leave (AWOL) at the onset of the Taylor war.

The old soldier was fondly known as "Kill the Bitch," a would-be fatal nickname he unpredictably acquired in the Liberian army long before the Charles Taylor's National Patriotic Front of Liberia even thought about launching its campaign. Like many previous government employees, the old soldier had come out of hiding, as the NPFL had demanded, so he could denounce his former Commander-in-Chief, President Samuel K. Doe, and embrace the rebels. Well, that turned out to be a wrong decision.

As a former AFL fighter with an obviously demeaning epithet, the so-called 'freedom fighters' quickly analyzed the epithet and concluded it was directed at the NPFL rebels. Therefore, for several days, the freedom fighters tortured the old soldier. The rebels tightly handcuffed him, dragged him in the streets and flogged him at will while his folks watched painfully and helplessly, too. The freedom fighters upgraded their improvised cuffs to "duck-fat tabay," their signature hands-behind-the-back tie down method, which, as described above, was very effective at tearing the ribcages of their victims.

For the record, his torturers were exclusively members of the rebels who came from Nimba. These were people who mainly originated from the Gio and Mano tribes. They had seniority

244

over the local NPFL converts. With little influence, the local "Wowanyo" reluctantly looked on as their superiors from Nimba County smacked Mr. Jah around. He must have been in his early to mid-fifties. He was a Ponwaon family member.

Relatives of the ex-soldier in both Jarkaken and Geeken vigorously sought his release. They managed and came up with huge cash amounts, which the rebels had demanded but without any success. The rebels appeared to be drugged all the time; they didn't really care about life. They took the money and the proclaimed guilty soldier. He was duck-fat tabayed and tossed in the back of a previously-owned PTP truck. His graphic body was later found in the town—between Karweadolo and the PTP Camp ("Campoken"), the sawmill yard. He was reportedly tossed out of the moving cattle truck and sprayed with Sister Beretta and AK-47 bullets.

Now that the families in Chedepo Jarkaken and Chedepo Geeken had failed to save his life, they embarked on yet another battle: the quest to bury his remains. This was not an easy task either. The NPFL's firmed grip on its live victims was just as strong as it was on its dead victims. In fact, for folks to touch or remove anyone the rebels had shot or killed—in the early days of the rebels' activities—the folks had to obtain what the rebels called "burial permits." The so-called permits were never written; they were not tangible permits you can display for others to see, or show other NPFL soldiers as proof. The permits were verbal removal permits; and they were not readily available.

The process to obtaining a permit was exhausting and frustrating for the petitioners, who were usually the relatives of the victims. First, the victim's relatives had to find permit fee. The fee was not set at a particular figure. It varied on a case-by-case basis. Next, they had to find an approving authority—an NPFL soldier who was more influential within their ranks and

245

who could give orders that other soldiers were required to obey—to grant the permit. That was the problem. Finding the right freedom fighter was the challenging part because there was no specified permit authority. The person granting the permit today might be the wrong person tomorrow. It was not uncommon at all for victims' relatives to get numerous run-arounds during the process, occasionally losing their hard-found fee to the "wrong" freedom fighters.

Laying to rest "Kill the Bitch" took a few days. These were days of negotiations— the families begging the rebels to bury the many they had shot dead along a major road (the Jarkaken-Putuken road). Within those daunting days, while his lifeless body stayed by the side of the road, relatives and other concerned Jarkaken citizens frantically negotiated with the rebels for a permit to bury his decomposing corpse. It was obviously not easy to obtain a permit for the old soldier. At the end, the folks' efforts paid off. The soldier's family members from both Jarkaken and Geeken finally secured a burial permit to remove and bury his remains. He was, I believe, buried in the vicinity where the rebels carried out the execution. Mr. Jah must have been the lucky one because he was buried. Other NPFL victims did not get that respect.

The next war victim in Chedepo Jarkaken, Mr. James Quiah, was never buried— thanks, but no, thanks, to the so-called freedom fighters. Originally a Krahn native, Mr. Quiah was practically a Jarkaken citizen. He came to Jarkaken while in his mid-teens to work for Bell Timber Company (BTC), which preceded PTP. When BTC left, Mr. Quiah stayed back in Jarkaken. He even married to a local Bowionpo woman, with whom he had a family. He was so assimilated that many people in and around Jarkaken did not know that he was a Krahn. He spoke fluent Chedepo, perhaps better than Krahn, if he spoke it at all.

In truth, the few who knew about his Krahn root had to be the older people because they knew how he came to the area; they knew his history. Others could tell by his somewhat unique Krahn name – Quiah.

Prime Timber Products, the new company that replaced BTC, employed Mr.

Quiah as a security guard. Mr. Quiah manned a tiny gateway shack, tasked to regulate motor and human traffic at the main entrance to the sawmill compound at the camp (or "Campoken"). He was quite a popular gentleman. Many children knew him; they had to know him because, in order to collect "payday" on Saturdays, the children needed to gain access to the gated compound where workers received their wages. It is fair to assume that James' friends probably didn't like to be bothered by nagging kids, but that didn't deter him. He let them in anyway. At other times, the kids pleaded for nighttime entrance to Campoken so they could collect giant seasonal beetles, local delicacies that briefly flew around lampposts before helplessly collapsing below. At night, there were fewer activities, so the kids usually got their wish. They gained access, thanks to James, and posted themselves by the lampposts.

Mr. Quiah had to leave the town when the rebels entered. He faced almost instant death when sighted by the rebels because he was born a Krahn, a tribe he neither knew well nor interacted with. Mr. Wlehlay Young, a compassionate and courageous local, a member of the Bowionpo family, the adopted family of Mr. Quiah, took the Krahn native to his farmland. It was an outpost on the Tartymo farming reservation. It was a few miles outside the town, and the Krahn native found safety there – well, for about a month before something tragic happened.

The rebels had promised not to target the truly local residents when they captured Jarkaken, except those who broke their laws. The courageous Young had broken their law by providing sanctuary for a man whose only crime was being born into the Krahn tribe. And living in a town where death was the ultimate penalty for crimes, however petty these were, the refuge provider—Mr. Wlehlay Young—had legitimate concern for the safety of himself and his own family, especially after someone in the town had maliciously leaked into rebel ranks that a Krahn man named James Quiah was hiding somewhere in the town.

Angry for being duped, the rebels put out a timeline demand for Mr. Quiah. By late afternoon, Mr. Wlehlay Young reluctantly turned himself over to the rebels; he became their instant prey. He was duck-fat tabayed and unabatedly tortured by the rebels. Like the first victim, the rebels tossed the Krahn native in the back of a cattle truck and drove away. His lifeless body was found just two hundred meters from the town—between Hon. Joe Teahfore Sayee's house and the cemetery along Geeken Road. He was reportedly thrown out of a moving vehicle and riddled with AK-47 and "Sister Beretta" bullets.

"What a shock [his death was]!" Winslow David, son of Mr. David K. Swen, interjected. "What a day that was! He was shot dead by few of the rebels on their return from Torwloken when the Krahns launched their first retaliatory attack."

The town begged the rebels to bury their honorary citizen, whom had kids with a local woman, but to no avail. Mr. Quiah was never buried; thanks to the "freedom fighters."

For some time, the town was largely peaceful, if you excluded the routine firing of rebel weapons into midair and also their periodic looting of market women. The community was concerned about its residents' safety, so the mostly women

248

merchants who had previously been trekking to the main road community of Putuken, were advised to avoid walking the approximately hour-long distance every Saturday to the region's main marketplace.

The township commissioner, the equivalent of a city mayor for the town, Hon.

Josiah Saylee Winn, Sr, offered his front yard on Saturdays for the people of Jarkaken to trade local products. The township charged each merchant who set up table ten cents selling fees. Old man Pupuo Dweh, the father of Joseph T. Weah/ "Bob Blue," collector the fees for the township. The Jarkaken market didn't get a great deal of support from the locals. Many of the sellers had the same products, and there were hardly any buyers. Their usual buyers were outsiders, including transient Liberians who parked and rested while heading to and from the east. The buyers hardly, if ever, went to Jarkaken. Instead, they stopped at the main market in Putuken.

While Jarkaken and its surrounding villages were relatively peaceful, other places that were not so far away could not claim the same level of safety. The timber companies named above, for several years, had an improvised "airfield" between Putuken and Jarkaken. During "normal time," as Liberians often refer to the calm before the Taylor era, only single-engine planes with fixed wings landed on it. This so-called airfield was nothing more than a roadside stretch of land, essentially a leveled dirt strip. When the rebels arrived, they dug huge holes on it and laid logs there to prevent other factions from landing on it. They also turned it into a killing field, literally. The NPFL rebels who primarily lived in Jarkaken patrolled other places, too. Every night, as they returned home, they dumped their captured, tortured and subsequently murdered victims on the area's airfield, leaving horrible scent in adjacent areas. While

249

heading to the commercial town of Putuken, we had to hold on to our noses, an attempt to avoid the fouled odor. We also tried to run the entire course of the airfield, which was well over two miles long. Sometimes we saw lifeless bodies on the dirt strip; other times, it was just their horrible odor. The bodies dumped on the field from the far-away communities were considered buried by the rebels. No one dared to ask the rebels any questions.

The break in Jarkaken's relative calm came when the rebels intensified the killing of domestic animals. A local rebel, Boelfueh (Big Boy), went on a shooting rampage. As a local rebel, he was not an influential soldier. In fact, he would not have been ab approving authority for giving a permit to anyone. He had to answer to those that came from Nimba—the mano and Gio NPFL soldiers. They ran the sure, and for a cow to be shot, the pronouncement had to come from an influential NPFL. Hence, I can say with certainty that Boelfueh did not wake on that day and thought, "I want to eat a cow, let me go and shoot on."

His seniors sent him to kill a cow. Like many of the rebels, especially the locals they picked up along the way to the east did not get a former gun training. Hence, with no formal gun training, the local rebel removed his weapon's selector level from "Safe" to "Automatic." He sent a barrage of rounds through a cow at knee high. The cow died on the spot; in other words, he dutifully accomplished his mission.

But, in addition to the cow he killed, the local soldier also— and it's fair to say unintentionally—killed Gbala Worjolo. He was a middle-aged man who had been recovering at home after a long day of farming work. The fellow died on the spot. Still, some of Boelfueh's bullets ended up into the body of Gbegeah Saylee, another middle- aged man. Gbcgcah Saylcc

250

was the lucky one. They rushed him to a hospital in Maryland County, Liberia, and surgery saved his life.

By this time, the rebels in the southeast, with all their cruelties, did not discriminate when it came to punishing its own members. For the fear of being punished by his fellow rebels, including the likelihood of a swift justice—or imminent death—the cattle warrior (Boelfueh) managed to flee across the Cavalla River, and into the Ivory Coast.

The rebels really didn't provide any security for the people. All they cared about was personal comfort; therefore, they left the people of Jarkaken and other Grebo towns extremely vulnerable. After PTP was long gone, the rebels stayed around just enough to deplete the company's resources and the cattle in the area. Then the NPFL left a skeleton team — containing mostly local rebels – and went to larger towns like River Gbeh, Pleebo or Harper to increase their chances to loot well-to-do people.

Most Liberians and the world over know that, indeed, the Krahn tribe people were the real NPFL war victims. Other tribes suffered, too—namely, the Mandingo tribal people. But the Krahns were the main or core victims. The narrative of the NPFL rebels, who were mostly people from Nimba county, was that they were the first victims.

President Doe, a Krahn native, had allegedly killed thousands of tribal people in Nimba when General Thomas G. Quiwonkpa, a son of Nimb, launched a failed coup d'état (1985). This infuriated President Doe, and he reportedly directed his revenge to the Nimba people. And so, Taylor, with a maternal Nimba connection, launched his rebel group to revenge for his people. Hence, the Krahn were their primary targets. And they suffered brutally at the hands of the NPFL. The Krahn people lost so many lives and properties.

Some Krahn towns were wiped off the map entirely.

But the Krahn people wrongly took on the Grebo tribal people for their [Krahn's] losses. Instead of heading west toward Nimba County, where the NPFL came from, Krahn militia men headed east toward the Grebo people. The remnants of Krahns near River Gee took advantage of the vulnerability created by the absence of the core rebel fighters. They were infuriated with Grebos for "hosting the rebels," as if Grebos had any choice in the rebels' unilateral decision to capture their territory on gunpoint and stay.

Well, the absence of the core rebel fighters in the Grebo areas paved the way for members of the Krahn militia to leave their hideouts and attack Grebo areas, mainly at night. In Jarkaken, the Krahns killed several residents who they encountered on the way to the town. Some names that come to mind are: Teacher Chea, Jaja Chea, W. Kpakehn Gbegeah, Evon Gbeh, Peter Dough Gbeh, Kayee Taynue, and so on. They also burned homes containing some elderly, including Finanyonoh Jarbo and Wayee Dweh, before hurrying back into their safety zones. In some Grebo regions, entire towns were set ablaze.

To counter the Krahn militia, the authorities in and around Chedepo Jarkaken ordered it residents on farmlands and other remote areas to come to town. And a twenty- four-hour local defense force—comprising aptly of local militia and rebels—was initiated in the town.

During the Krahn violence in and around Jarkaken, one could have easily counted the entire local rebel forces. They were many in the beginning of the war. But, by the time of the Krahn retaliatory attacks, the local rebels—those who were still active—were so few, they could not have been more than ten. Because of their small number, the people did not get a

252

worthwhile support from the local rebels. They play a bare minimum role.

But to be fair to the local rebels, however, they were too weak a force by this time of the war, and we can blame them, too, for the situation they had found themselves in. True, they were not receiving any supplies; however, many of them had recklessly depleted their bullets long before the Krahn retaliatory attacks. The rebels were notorious for firing on the town's cattle. They could have caught any cow they wanted without firing a shot; instead, they wasted tons of munitions on domestic animals.

They also spent lots of their ammunitions "digging" their looting victims' "potatoes," the bizarre and dangerous rebel behavior during which the rebels fired bullets between the feet of potential looting victims, mainly the folks who resisted them. In fact, only a handful of the local rebels had automatic rifles, so their defense against the town militia—the defense they provided—was not any better (if not worse) than what the ordinary citizens of the combined force offered. I suppose the rebels' weapons were for mere intimidation because, by the time the hit-and- run Krahn militia men exploited the period of reduced security, the local rebels had long seized or discontinued firing off rounds into midair. Either they, suddenly, became gun disciplined, or they no longer had any bullets left to shoot off. The latter was certainly true. How else could anyone logically explain the reasons for their lack of midair gunfire? It was a dangerous act—the firing of bullets above flammable homes and defenseless people for little or no apparent reasons. Ironically, however, the act became the norm over time.

Therefore, the sudden lack of this "show of force" raised doubts about the rebels' overall strength.

Karpeh Toe, one of the first to join the NPFL rebels, left the town to fight in other parts of the country. We heard early on that he had gone to Tulubor-Fartu (Monrovia- Firestone), as our people call the rubber plantation area near the city of Harbel, in lower Margibi County. He died during the war, but he was not a direct victim of the war. "Karpeh Toe returned to Jarkaken via the Ivory Coast about five years after he [had] left [the Jarkaken area]," Winslow Saybeh David added. However, "[Karpeh] fell from a palm tree and died on the 30th day of his return." His cousin, Komohbutu Quayee, a member of the Sapannetonmo peer group and son of old man Welmo Quayee was an early enlistee.

He left Jarkaken early in the war. He was among the local freedom fighters who traveled but never made it back home. "Komohbutu died of his wound [sustained on the battlefield] at Phebe Hospital [in Suakoko, Bong County, Liberia] after his leg was amputated there," according to Alex Dweh (Bay), the son of Mr. Isaac Dweh and cousin of Komohbutu. Details on these two cousins, especially their whereabouts during the early days of the war, were not always forthcoming. We heard things about them in bits and pieces. Komohbutu's death was confirmed by his elder brother, Sam Quayee; the town openly mourned his loss.

Also, according to Mantee Sayjolo Winn, the family of Bocuwao lost two young men in Pleebo, Maryland County, due to the war. Abell Toe (Nyemah), son of Temblo Chaylen, and his cousin, Sorpo Jowah, son of Elijah Kwiyeyee Saylo Jowah, lost their lives in the Pleebo area.

And while many of the local rebels were out of the fight, dead, missing, or in faraway places, Tarnu Williams assumed the charge of the few who were still active in Jarkaken. Tarnu (or Smallboel, not related to Boelfoel, the cattle warrior mentioned above who killed Mr. Gbala Worjolo) was a stubborn, no-nonsense rebel leader. He was a tough and inflexible figure.

Truth be told, the rebel needed someone his caliber to lead them because they were constantly arguing and flexing their muscles (fighting or threatening to fight others). Tarnu was hardly stationary though; he appeared to be on the move all the time. He shared his time between Jarkaken (River Gee area) and Maryland County. Rebel Junior (or RPG Junior) was extremely influential, too. His parents' home was across from the John Cholopray United Methodist Church, near old man Welmo Quayee's place. In Tarnu's absence, it was the slenderer, equally no-nonsense teen who took charge of the local rebels. He was instrumental, along with Tarnu, in bringing much-needed order to the conflict-prone rebels.

JDF fortified the town to the best of its ability. All the main roads entering the town were gated and manned around the clock. The Jarkaken militia was comprised mainly of volunteers, but other services (such as providing food and drinks for the gate guards) came

by way of levying collections from members within the community's peer group system. The town's women also played an essential role in defending the town; they cooked for the checkpoint guards.

JDF conducted day-to-day duties with improvised weapons. The traditional hunting rifles that lock and load only BB cartridges—one cartridge at a time—were the militia's primary weapon system. (Of course, there were local rebels with machine guns, but we know by now that they had no munitions by this time of the war.) Some men sat by their assigned entry- and exit-controlled points with machetes or

255

"cutlasses" while others simply carried strange, but harmful, homemade weapons.

Many of the militiamen were confident that mere gunshots could "do nothing" to them because they had received confidence-building war protection, which the Nimba rebels called Zekay. There were many sources for Zekay, but one of the people who was known for protecting the militia (and the rebels) was old man Toe Wion, a Bonyonpo family member (either from the Wionnyenpanpo or Karpehpo section of the family). He was very popular during the war, especially during the early days of the war. Locals and non-locals alike went to him for war protections. His house used to be across from the home of Swen Martin (Wilson Swen). It was rumored that he charged outsiders fees for his work, but his protection for the local rebels and town militia cost either pennies on a dollar or completely free of charge. Whether the protections worked depended on who you questioned. They must have worked, if my opinion means anything on this subject.

Judging from the number of people who went over to his Bokutodolo home (some repeatedly), they must have realized certain benefits. In any case, the protections gave the rebel, the local defense force, and ordinary people renewed level of self-confidence. Old man Toe Wion used to tattoo his clients lightly (mainly over their shoulders or their lower backs) and inserted the war protections. When the cuts healed, they left scars (marks), which the local population referred to as jilee.

In 1994, Krahn militiamen intensified their attacks in Grebo areas. The militia overran the local defense force in Putuken, arguably a forty-minute foot distance from Jarkaken. Concerned that Jarkaken could be next, very brave young men from the Jarkaken Defense Force took up whatever they could get their hands on as weapons and set out for Putuken. They wanted to confront the militia. They wanted to stop them from entering Jarkaken. But something went terribly wrong.

The locals made numerous attempts were made by the locals to explain away what had happened, but the truth is, we may never know exactly what happened that disbanded the men from Jarkaken. They didn't function as a team when they reached Putuken. One theory that stood out among others suggested that when the defenders arrived in Putuken, there was no sign of disturbances. In fact, rumors had it that there was a traditional dance, apparently staged by the Krahns to lure residents. It was this Krahn scheme, along with the scene appearing relatively peaceful, that led to the disbanding of the forces from Jarkaken. The facts collected from the crime scenes seemed to give some merits to the claim that the Jarkaken defenders had in fact disbanded before they were killed. They didn't stay together, they didn't fight together, and they didn't die in a shootout as a team. The men appeared to have been taken away one by one into isolated parts of Putuken and killed brutally with machetes.

One of the Jarkaken defenders killed in Putuken was Shannon Toe, the son of Mr. Borbor Geegba Wiah Toe. Shannon was a virtual walking monument for the town. His name was a tribute to Shannon, the public worker who built the main Jarkaken-Putuken road in 1969, according to local historians. Shannon Toe, along with Fala Seakor Quayee, provided the leadership during the mission. Both leaders were member of the same peer group (Wulopotonmo). Fala Seakor Quayee and his younger brother, Tutu Quayee, died in Putuken. They were sons of Brown Nyemah Quayee, a combined business proprietor and philanthropist whose efforts led to the establishment of an elementary school in Jarkaken for the Liberian Assemblies of God. As a tribute, the school is named B. Nyemah Quayee Elementary. Mr. Quayee also lost a nephew in Putuken; his name was Johnson Finakan

257

Quayee. Old man Sayee Gbey Parteh, a Bocuwao man, also lost a son in Putuken. His name was Wesley Toe. Moreover, "Colored Boy," the son of Hon. George Wesseh, once a combined Quarter Chief and a town crier in Jarkaken, was also killed in Putuken. These young men—and more to name—had their bodies dismembered and tossed about in Putuken, which, according to another opinion, was deserted on that tragic day.

The town of Jarkaken had clean water system prior to the war, thanks to an experimental solar panel technology a company from Denmark brought to the community in the mid-1980s. Prior to this system, which the locals called "solar system," the people were fetching water from three main creeks. Cheanorgbae, a tiny stream at the foot of Soklotogbe, a foothill near Winnville; Portornorgbae, a tiny forest stream in the Kujaysnumo section of town; and Neplen, a large but disappearing creek near Karweadolo, were the water sources for the town. But after the European experiment, during which they used giant drilling trucks to dig incredibly deep wells (some as deep as one hundred feet), the town ditched the muddy creeks' water in exchange for clean, pristine water. The main water source was the deepest and most yielding of the wells: the one between the homes of Mr. James Poutwah Geegba Nyanfore and Mr. Henry Nyemah Jah.

The Europeans did not do the job alone. They did not bring equipment to dig holes for the emplacement of water pipes and hoses. For that, they looked to the people. In fact, for a few dollars a day, local men and women were hired to dig the holes. An average hole was three feet deep, ten meters long, and two feet wide.

Solar panels and a water pump were set up near the main well. And the water from

258

the primary well flowed to a waiting tank, near Mr. Brown Nyemah Quayee's house. From this giant tank, the water flowed to more than ten water collection points around the town, including one at faraway Kaytoken Junior High School. The tank was essentially the storage bucket from which the town collected cleaned, pristine drinking water. It was basically the only system of its kind in the whole of Liberia, West Africa.

Today, the water system is destroyed by the civil war. The water tank was deliberately fired on and punctured by several of the warring groups that frequented the town. The solar panels, the water pump, and even the wire fence around the main pump were looted and sold across the Cavalla River in the Ivory Coast. "Those solar panels were mainly looted and sold by some fellows from Jarkaken," Winslow David added. In other words, unscrupulous elements in the town—our own people—had a role to play in the destruction of the water system.

The rebels could not loot the tank, so they decided to destroy it. The tank, the pipes and concrete water collections points—to include six faucets (Sawl) stations and four or five foot-pumping (Kpachia) stations—remind the townspeople, especially the youth, of some of the destruction that went on in the town. The town needs Good Samaritans to restore its Solar System. And during this wait, the people are back to drinking from the dirty creeks of Cheanorgbae, Portornorgbae, and Neplen—again.

To say that the town of Jarkaken was truly battered by the Taylor war would be an understatement. But it is worth mentioning that while she had lost plenty of lives and few homes to mostly Krahn retaliation, the town survived the chaos.

Chapter XI:
Jumayee Dance: A Catalyst for Social Cohesion

In many parts of Chedepo District, like in most of the county, there are no bars or dance clubs; yet the people, especially the youth population, are not left idled on the entertainment front. There are traditional singing and dancing to substitute for clubs and bars.

One of such youth pastimes is the Konbo songs and dance. As it grew in popularity, so did its notoriety, thereby creating powerful enemies among the elders who ensured that it was banned and declared a taboo in some parts of the district. It was during this period of the ban that Jumayee began to gain prominence. While some youth in the district do not know why Konbo is a taboo, they nonetheless obey it. When caught in the act, they would unequivocally deny dancing Konbo, terming their strokes as those of Jumayee, the new dance form accepted to be more civil.

Even though the fine details around the emergence of Jumayee dance in Chedepo District, River Gee County, remains largely unknown, the dance has been one of the most fascinating means of entertainment and social cohesion I have ever known since the early 1980s. It is an important source of pastime for both members of the younger and older generations. It promotes peace and unity in the district and its surroundings. Ironically, this dance is viewed by some influential elements in the society as ungodly, promoting profanity, and being disrespectful to women.

"Jumayee dance began in the year 1980," Saylee Sayjolo, one of a few local historians who had knowledge on the subject told me. He was, in fact, the only person who discussed some specifics about the Jumayee dance—how it originated, and where it began. All other oral local historians spoke on subjects they were comfortable talking about; they talked about the dance when it was in its prime, and little or nothing about how it came to be, its origin.

"The name of the dance derived from *Ju Mamie*," Sayjolo continued. *Ju Mamie* originated as a cheerleading song, and it was coined by Jaye Norwan. He was a resident of Chedepo Putuken. Originally a Konbo singer, he transitioned to cheerleading songs, which they [the locals] were accustomed to singing behind the goalposts of their favorite teams.

And so, Jaye Norwan was singing *Ju Mamie* during the second half of a football [soccer] match between the towns of Chedepo Jarkaken and Chedepo Putuken. Actually, the two towns met in Putuken along with all the teams from the major Chedepo towns. They here gathered in the main road community of Putuken for a week-long soccer tournament for the Chedepo School System.

In other words, many schools across the land of Chedepo had teams in Putuken for the competition. Jaye Norwan's lyrics were in the Kru and English languages. As the game was closed to the end, he started singing the song, 'Ju Mamie, are you on the field this evening?' The term, 'Ju Mamie' is believed to be an epithet for s "lover"]. This was in the year 1980; I was 12 years old, so I was very alert even though I was still very young. For the youth members who left Jarkaken for the Putuken event, I remember some of the people who were either our seniors or who were influential people, even if they were not our seniors: Wellington Kolwleh Wesseh was one of our seniors; he was a drummer. We had Othello Wesseh; his Grebo name was Nimeneh. He was our senior. Odomeo Weah was there, too; he was our senior member. Cecelia Quayee

261

(Karpeh Welley) was there; she was a singer. We had Nancy Winkar (Sarlee); she was there, too. I also remember Jacqueline Barfeh; she was in Putuken.

The above personnel brought the song back to Jarkaken after the tournament. Other personnel for the local Chedepo towns took the son back home, and that was how the Jumayee songs and dance started. It began as a cheerleading song in Putuken and quickly spread across the whole of Chedepo.

Even though Jumayee dance did not begin in Chedepo Jarkaken, one of the most populous towns in River Gee County, but the dance developed as probably the most effective means through which the youth and adults socialize. In the early 1980s, when the son was in its prime, Wilson Swen, a renowned youth supporter in Chedepo Jarkaken, intermittently invited the youth to sing and dance Jumayee in front of his home, which he built over the foothill of Bokutoken (or Bokutodolo), a borough of Jarkaken. Because of his receptive nature, the youth became quite comfortable with him. They began to frequent his front yard, even without invitations. Increasingly, the population that camped on his premises skyrocketed. The place attracted many people, to include males and females from diverse age groups. Routinely, we saw children joined young adults, along with some tolerant middle-aged adults, and hung out at the site. And, in due course, the site goers gave the spot an interesting nickname: "Parking Station," the same terms the locals used for a bus terminal. All of this was all right with Mr. Swen. He displayed an incredible indifference, letting the noisy youth have their way in his yard.

Reportedly, disrespect toward the town women was the basis for the abolition of the Konbo songs and dance in Chedepo. Mr. Swen's initial invitations might have been his genuine acts of solidarity toward the mostly youth population.

262

Their overall level of enthusiasm had diminished significantly because of the ban on Konbo, a once relished youth dance, which they—the new generation of youth—had allegedly turned uncivil, mainly against the local females. Value-based elders and other powerful people from the district declared the dance a taint on the image of women and girls, so they outlawed it.

The morale of the local youth population went down with the ban even though it didn't last long before the birth of Jumayee, the new dance. Wilson Swen along with others, such as Sam Chebo Weah, Willington Kolwleh Wesseh and Chea Toe were among the major supporters of the new Jumayee, which replaced Konbo. Or did it? That was the main issue when the new dance came into existence. Many people, especially among the elderly, were skeptical about the new dance, fearing it was the reemergence—not a replacement—of Konbo. Supporters of the new dace, mainly the voices of the four named above, maintained that it was a unique dance; that it did not have anything in common with the banned dance. Sam Chebo Weah, a combined youth leader and chief drummer for the new Jumayee, made several attempts to prove the uniqueness and the overall significance of the new dance. He improved the image of Jumayee by demanding that singers inject more tasteful, family-friendly or sterilized songs. He made a huge—perhaps the greatest—impact on the communities within the Chedepo clan when he used the dance as a tool of diplomacy to induce peaceful relationships among the neighboring clans.

One event in 1987 that brought out the good image of Jumayee was its use to neutralize tension between two clans, Chedepo and Potupo. Mr. Sam Chebo Weah used Jumayee and football to establish peaceful relationship between the two peoples after an earlier settlement of a long-held boundary dispute turned conditions unpleasant. Prior to the settlement of

263

the boundary dispute, the Potupo children used to flock to Chedepo Jarkaken after completing elementary school and continuing their education. Depending on one's inclination, the student exodus was either blamed or praised for increased marriages between the folks from the clans. The evidence for increased marriages was overwhelming, too. The principal of Kaytoken Junior High School (KJHS), Hon. Newton N. Winn, the most senior educator during the peak of the student exodus, became one of the many beneficiaries of the student migration when he married his student, Ellen Teaty Winn, then a transferred seventh grader from Potupo Teajlayken. All this interaction was good while it lasted; soon after the government ruled on the line between the clans, however, many of the Potupo children who were attending KJHS were effectively recalled. And new elementary graduates from Potupo were redirected to junior high school communities elsewhere, avoiding Chedepo in the process, mainly the boundary town of Jarkaken.

Potupo did not like the government's decision on the matter.

And so, to end Potupo's boycott of Jarkaken, Sam Chebo Weah made a bold move.

He wrote a letter to

Japroken, a key town in the Potupo District, and challenged Potupo to a friendly soccer match. His Jarkaken Youth Association (JYA) wrote to the Japroken Youth Association (JYA). Instead of inviting Potupo to Jarkaken, Sam told the Potupo JYA that he was willing to take his Chedepo JYA to Potupo. The response was surprisingly swift. Potupo accepted the proposed friendly gesture, which prompted more than fifty Jarkaken youths—armed with nothing but Jumayee dance and a soccer ball—to descend on Potupo Japroken. My memory is slightly fuzzy on the game's outcome. I thought Jarkaken won

264

the game, but I was corrected a few years ago by Cepheus Choloply, a native of Japroken and a player at the game, that Potupo did win the match. Anyway, there's nothing ambiguous about the hearts and the minds Jumayee won in Potupo when we visited. The host community extended our stay from two to four days. All those days were used not only for dancing Jumayee and all-out feasting but also talking about how to mend the fractured peace between the neighbors.

We left Potupo with more stock of songs than we had boasted before the trip. We also swapped songs and returned to Jarkaken with great deal of chatters about Potupo's singing, particularly the talent of their lead singer, Ms. Gbeyee Jarbo. Equally, we left Potupo people admiring both the singing talent and the striking beauty of our own Cecelia Welley Quayee, the songbird from Jarkaken who ingeniously memorized every song that came off the lips of Gbeyee Jarbo. Not long after we left Potupo, they followed us to Jarkaken. We had a great time, just like we did in Potupo. There was no extended stay.

Suffice it to say that normal relationship exists today between the two Grebo districts. No one goes around anymore questioning why Bliya na (a small creek) is not the boundary, as Potupo would have preferred the government ruling. According to a longtime teacher at Kaytoken Junior High School, D. Kargbe Nyanfore, about 60 percent of the kids that attended in 2005 (more than two decades after the boundary saga) came from the greater Kaytoken area (Geeken and Jarkaken). "The rest of the children come from Killepo, Potupo and other places around here." This level of Potupo's interaction with Chedepo, particularly Jarkaken, was extremely limited or even unseen before the boundary saga. Thanks to Mr. Sam Chebo Weah and Jumayee for that progress.

Moreover, the boundary dispute was not the only crisis Sam Chebo Weah effectively used Jumayee to manage.

At my welcome ceremony in Jarkaken (December 2005), Amos T. Weah, then Jarkaken's primary nurse and sponsor of several youth activities, lauded the Jumayee diplomat for using "his Potupo experience" to nullify war-related tensions between the Krahn and Grebo tribes. Sam Chebo Weah took his likeminded youth to Pennoken, Grand Gedeh County. It was almost an exact replica of the so-called Potupo experience. This time, the Chedepo JYA won both the game and the hearts of the Krahn people, and they left their hosts craving for more interactions: "They want us to come back, but it is their turn to come to us," Amos declared.

Contrary to the good image the Jumayee dance exhibited, some opponents still campaigned vigorously against it, even after the Potupo milestone. Those in the church community considered the dance an "evil thing." Influential leaders in churches around Jarkaken said Jumayee was ungodly. They advised their membership to avoid it; going to Jumayee dance was a satanic act. It was no wonder that those who loved the new dance and comedians, such as the Timothy Tanyon children, tried to get even by mocking the people who exemplified church. They targeted Mantee Sayjolo Winn, a celebrated singer at the Assemblies of God, and his friend, Swen Doe, a youth leader at the same AG church. They called the two (Mantee and Swen) "hypocrites" because the two men sometimes used routes that passed through active Jumayee dances to get to their destinations. In other words, if a Jumayee dance was at Wilson Swen's roadside home, the two men (and all other religious gurus) had to find alternate routes instead of following a passageway that runs directly through an active Jumayee dance. "It is the same as going to the dance," they joked.

266

That was the lighter side though. The core rhetoric against the young dance, however, came from those who would rather sleep than get up at night for a dance: mostly males over age fifty who still retained ambiguity about the new dance. They said it was nothing more than a pretense, a deceptive Konbo masquerade. The so-called new dance, they claimed, "teaches indecency to our children." They blamed the dance entirely for academic failure at Jarkaken schools, including KJHS, Tom Wion Elementary (which failed a year or two after emergence), and Brown Nyemah Quayee Elementary School.

The theory that linked poor grades, rudeness, or anything impolite to Jumayee dance caught on very well at KJHS. The school had very strict position on students' attendance during such dances. In fact, the most daring of all the events that surrounded the turbulent beginning of the Jumayee dance occurred shortly after the school instituted a new set of rules. I suppose we can call them "the Jumayee policies." The school banned its student population from the dance, especially if the dance was on a school day. Violating the policies carried serious consequences, including labor-intensive (grass-cutting) punishments and an outright assault on the students. During a school-day dance, designated spies (mostly teachers or their unpaid aides) were dispatched to the dance site. The undercover team of instructors secretly took down the names of students who they spotted at the dance. They later submitted the names to Principal Newton N. Winn, and the violators were in a world of trouble.

The students at KJHS were routinely entertained during the flag raising formation and morning prayers, dubbed "devotion." It was at this formation that those who had attended Jumayee dance on school day were identified. The principal called them out of formation. Female violators were placed on one side, and their male counterparts were placed on the other side. The students knew the punishment that was coming their way because it was briefed weekly, but they had taken a change to the dance, hoping no one would care enough to wake week up at night and look for violators. How wrong! Anyway, all the female violators were given garden tools, and were assigned large rectangular grassy portions around the school building to clear. Their male counterparts got machetes and thick portions of grassy areas to cut. But some men refused to cut grass, opting instead for another bizarre alternative: to be beaten on a table or against a flagpole because it was "the quick and manly thing to do."

Well, what they asked for was exactly what the school gave them. While many of them were dramatizing the excruciating pain that came with the quick and manly thing, which included weeping, one student gained sudden fame in the town. Student Nyondo Tanyon, son of Rev. Timothy Peppeh Tanyon and the school's main goalkeeper at the time, was hailed as the ultimate man for his mind-blowing tolerance for pain. Unlike the other men who were either held down on the table or against the flagpole, Nyondo took his beating standing straight up. He was unbelievably calmed throughout the entire episode, occasionally taking a few steps here and there while the brutalities continued.

Some teachers thought the goalkeeper had cushioned his backside. They checked, but there was no padding at all. He neither resisted nor displayed any anger. He left many people stunned and baffled in town. He was the talk of the town, overshadowing the brutalities toward other students, like Saylee Seakor (a Potupo youth) and S. Kpadeh Winn among others. Ironically, some parents were pleased with the school's actions. They even submitted non-dance related wrongs to the principal.

To curb the beating of students at Kaytoken Junior High School, the youth in Jarkaken decided to restrict the dance to weekends, except when weekday dance was made imperative by event-oriented circumstances, such as death or causes that demanded abrupt celebration. It is a tradition that continues today, even long after the relaxation or nonexistence of the ridiculous school rules.

Old man Jacob C. Belleh was one of those who didn't like and could not tolerate Jumayee dance in Jarkaken. While many of the people who opposed the dance used the school or churches to push their agenda, old man Belleh was rather bold and deliberate about his intentions. He took matters into his own hands. The youth saw him more often because he and Mr. Wilson Swen were neighbors. It was common for him to get out of his house and march courageously to the dance site.

He demanded the three-drum set upon arrival. Usually, he took two first and returned for the third one. To their credit, the youth respected the old man despite his unwelcomed tendency to intrude into their affairs. They didn't wrestle the drums out of his hands; instead, they followed him home and pleaded for the set of drums. He always returned the drums, but not without conditions, including his lengthy speeches on being considerate to others. The dance kept him awake, he complained. On some nights, the old man pushed for limited dancing nights on as a condition before returning the drums. On other nights, he simply kicked the youth from the neighborhood altogether. "Go home, or find another location!"

On the nights the youth lost and subsequently regained their drums, they relocated to the giant space between the homes of Mr. Daleyee Slobert, Mr. Tuor Cholopray, Mr. Tuwle Swen Nyemah, Mr. William Nagbe, and Professor Weah. These people tolerated the youth dance, though relocation itself was not always uneventful. Sometimes, Daleyee Slobert and Tuwle Swen Nyemah balked at the youth, but the men were largely

269

moderates. I don't know of any time we were chased off that triangular area. They always let us dance there. We never permanently abandoned Mr. Swen's front yard either. We only relocated frequently due to the disturbances of old man Belleh.

Despite the forces against the dance, it was hard to avoid its enthusiasm. Many people found the dance irresistible. They were swept up by the Jumayee wave. Many kids and young adults displayed the brunt of the excitement and motivation about the dance. In fact, almost every youth member that lived in and around Jarkaken—from as far back as 1982 to the years leading up to the Charles Taylor war—attempted a Jumayee role. They were singers, dancers, and drummers. Others arrived early to set up for the dance. Many youth members exhibited remarkable talents during the dance.

There was a squad of drummers. Mr. Sam Weah and some members of his family—Mr. Odomeo Weah, Mr. Leo Weah, and Mr. Wulopoi Swen Weah—were members of the drummers. Other drummers were Mr. Willington Kolwleh Wesseh, Mr. Bonnie Walker, Mr. Albert Weah, Mr. Taynue Weah, Mr. Dekontee Tarwulu, Mr. Too Doe, and later Mr. Togba Wleh, Jr.

Ms. Cecelia Welley Quayee, or Cece, as she was fondly called in Jarkaken, was the town's celebrated singer. Many of her songs were traditional in nature, but Cece also coined or expanded others. Her lyrics contained no profanity or biases. The songbird sang other versions, such as the ones from Ms. Gbeyee Jarbo, the lead singer in Potupo Japroken. Ms. Cecelia Quayee also shared the stage—sometimes competitively—with Mr. Nyenatoh Teh and Mr. E. J. Young, both from the town of Chedepo Geeken. In my opinion, Mr. Alfred Kayee Sayee (in Chedcpo Jarkaken) would have come second only to Cece, if ranked. But that was not all the singers. There were other singers beside the heavyweights.

They included (but not limited to) Mr. Napoleon Dekontee Beweh ("Deddeh"), Mr. Matu "Reverend" Weah, Ms. Paytee Sayee, Ms. Edith Weah, Ms. Teaty Cougioer, Ms. Betty Weah, Mr. Wilfred Komoh Winn, and more. In fact, who can ever forget the contributions of Ms. Mamie Siehyewa Swen and her older sister, Ms. Edith Geesay Swen, the sisters-in-law of Mr. Wilson Swen. These young ladies hailed from the town of Chedepo Klaboken. They added a wealth of songs to the collections we had in Jarkaken?

We celebrated dancers in Jarkaken. The works of the town's graffiti artists were visible just about everywhere one went in the town. Walls with elegant clay plastering in Jarkaken were either dotted or lined with what the artists claimed were images of Mr. Sam Weah playing a drum while Ms. Payla Jarbo and Mr. Jerry Doe danced to the drum. Ms. Payla Jarbo was the younger sister of Ms. Gbeyee Jarbo, the lead singer in Potupo Japroken. Mr. Jerry Doe was a hometown kid, the son of Mr. Isaac Klay Doe. The two were probably lovebirds, but that's beside the point. It was the great appearance of their portrait that lured many homeowners in Jarkaken; the pair also deserved their moment of fame because of how well they danced off the walls. Between 1983 and 1987, only a few walls in Jarkaken escaped the Payla-Jerry painting.

Jumayee dance deviated significantly from Konbo. Its lyrics were neither sexually exploitative, nor gender based or biased, as the moral police tried to portray them. It certainly had no violent culture even though conditions were often right for triggering disturbances. For example, dimly lit nights promoted the unfortunate acts of accidentally stepping, kicking, or bumping into others. But we rarely saw any fights during the dance, which arguably averaged fifty, eighty, or sometime well

271

over one hundred fifty people. Males usually dominated the scene, but we rarely saw them fighting over dance partners. In fact, those who were not lucky to get female dance partners had a unique solution in place.

They gathered and formed an all-male dance line, which was aptly termed bachelor line. Unlike its mixed or unisex line, which was civil and disciplined, the all-male line was too noisy. It was notorious also for snaking between courtyards of neighboring homes.

Sometimes they went off the limits of the dance site.

But Jumayee in Jarkaken was not entirely free of impurities; anyone claiming otherwise would be stretching the truth. There was a popular chorus, "If you are late [to the dance], someone will take her tonight." In Chedepo: "Bo wlede, bay kpa witayorlo." But over time, the same chorus line was altered, "If you are late, you will take Sneh Wiah's monitor lizard." In Chedepo: "Bo wlede, e kpa Sneh Weah'a pen." The phrase depicted Girlju, old man Sneh Weah's daughter, a beautiful and respectable woman for whom I have the highest of regards. (She passed away a years ago. May her soul rest.) She had delayed entry into puberty while she was coming of age. At about twelve years old, she had little to no breasts. Many boys said she was too slim. They repudiated her. The young lady was reportedly kept in isolation and likened to a large (but seemingly pale) lizard. That was the closest Jumayee in Jarkaken had come to Konbo, as far as I know.

I think there was the issue of oversensitivity when Jumayee emerged in Jarkaken.

There were off-limit words and phrases that people couldn't say, for example. Girls wearing skirts above the knees were frowned upon. Equally, it was hard for anyone to have content-full conversation without being cautioned that a certain word or phrase was taboo. Some songs were frowned upon for what I will call "petty hints" on sexuality. And that was the case for a once popular Chedepo song, "Belleh tu" or "bedframe." We were told to stop singing it because it said, "Let's break the bedframe before sleeping." That was the song. "Ba chela belleh tu ple ami mon." In Jarkaken, that was one of the indecencies for which students were routinely exposed. This was one of the indecencies from which churches were trying to protect members of their congregations. It makes one wonder sometimes what were the charges leveled against Konbo that warranted its silence in the land of Chedepo.

Finally, while the new dance contained some impurities and perhaps influenced some kids in a negative way, Jumayee dance promoted and continues to promote peace and unity. It restored normal relations between the Chedepo and Potupo people during the boundary disputes. It also relaxed war-related tensions between the Grebo and Krahn people. It was and remains a major source of entertainment for the youth and young adults in Chedepo District. It was and is still being used as a pastime for those long and boring nights in rural River Gee. Jumayee dance was never half as awful as the moral pundits tried to portray it.

Chapter XII:
Jarkaken's Favorite Son

"When you said, 'We are coming,' I was under the impression you were coming with Paytee and the baby," Mr. William G. Cholopray said with apparent discontent. He and his wife, Mrs. Esther Cholopray, were excited about Wilfred Jr. He was only a few months old when I visited the Choloprays in 2011. In truth, I made a detour off the main route to the state of Maryland, where I was going to attend a funeral service for Mr. C. Harry Gbesi. He was a friend. We connected when I realized that the man we called "Doctor Gbesi" in Jarkaken in the 1980s was, in fact, his father. He also knew my uncle, Mr. Newton N. Winn; he was the principal of the ever-popular Kaytoken Junior High School when Gbesi, the son, was a student there. Hence, when I heard his death news and about a subsequent program in his honor, I did not think twice about making the journey.

I kept Mr. Cholopray posted, especially as we got closer to Trenton, New Jersey, where he was living with his family. A week before I left the city of Newport News, VA, a twenty-something-year-old family friend, Melvin, heard that my trip north was taking me to New Jersey. So, he asked if he could catch a ride. He had his folks in the Philadelphia area, the sprawling metropolis that lies immediately across the Delaware River, which separates Trenton from Philadelphia. So, Melvin and I made the north- bound trip. That was how I erroneously got Mr. Cholopray's hopes up when I told him, "We are coming." He thought I was coming with my wife and our young child; and he told his wife that we — i.e., Wilfred, Annie, and Wilfred Jr— were coming.

"I was waiting for Junior," his wife told me. She and I are related. Her maternal grandmother and my paternal

274

grandmother came from the same household in the Gbeapo town of Podloken. "I want to hold him," she said with mixed emotions. "I want to put him on my back and walk around."

"Next time I will bring them with me; I did not plan this trip."

"Anyway, we are glad you've come. We are pleased to see you," she told me.

When we arrived at Mr. Cholopray's home, he walked us to a corner store. It was no more than a city block away, and we purchased drinks and snacks there. The young man who accompanied me on the trip was of legal drinking age; however, he was a bit timid in the presence of the old man, so he opted for a few cans of soft drinks. I grabbed a six-pack of Smirnoff Ice Original, which had consistently been my go-to drink, especially at occasions where I felt peer-pressured into drinking alcoholic beverages. Ordinarily, however, I have little craving for alcoholic drinks. The host, I believe, grabbed a few bottles of Whiskey Stout, Heineken, and a mix of other refreshments from the store shelves. He paid for all the items we picked out.

Our conversation, therefore, was held over the full display of the family's generosity. It was a chance, I thought, for me to take a proverbial trip to the past and enjoy a splendid lifestyle with Mr. Choloplay, a former senior member on the National Joint Security of Liberia.

But on this day, the old man looked in my direction and suggested that the tables had turned in the United States. "You are a big man in the government of this country; I have to give you the respect," he told me. The comments were flattering, to say the least, especially coming from Mr. Cholopray, who—in the not-too-distant past—used to enter Chedepo Jarkaken and other communities across Liberia on vibrantly decorated local roads and in convoys with vehicles blazing with the sounds of

275

sirens and gun salutes. It was this caliber of person who turned to me and said that I, Saylee Komoh, was now an honorable man. By the time of my unplanned visit, I had been in the United States Army for a little over ten years. I was assigned to Fort Eustis, an army post in Virginia, where I was a Service School Instructor, with the rank of Staff Sergeant. "Thanks, but no thanks." Humbly, I returned the honor precisely where it belonged—to the rightful person: Hon. William G. Cholopray.

"You wanted to ask me something," he reminded me while we chatted over our

beverages of choice.

"Oh, okay," I remembered. During the trip to the corner store, I thought of an occurrence at my welcome ceremony in Chedepo Jarkaken, which was about him. "When we get back to the house, I will ask you something," I gave him a heads-up at the tiny roadside store. When we got back to the house, however, I was carried away with all the merrymaking, which included a sumptuous meal. I forgot to ask him. Thankfully, the old man had better recollection.

In December 2005, while I was visiting Jarkaken, I heard something about Mr. Cholopray. My father, Mr. Josiah S. Winn Sr, was speaking on the topic of a war dance in my honor. Wiah Toe (Mr. Joe Weah), the oldest town elder, declared in his earlier speech that the town was going to dance the powerful traditional dance to honor me as a warrior. After Wiah Toe took his seat, my father took the floor.

"We will sponsor the dance tomorrow; that is nothing," he said with conviction. "But what matters most is this: when the people in Chedepo Geeken hear our dugout drums tomorrow, and someone wants to know what's happening in the land of Klosoken, the answer will be, 'The man we call Winn Saylee,

276

his son, Saylee Komoh, has returned from overseas as a warrior. The people of Klosoken are happy to see him...'"

Then Mr. Alfred Deateah Kenta interrupted him with a dramatic entrance. "Pa, pa, pa; he will continue!" he told the people in a commanding voice. It was truly a warmed entrance into the living room of Saylee Kpadeh, where the predominately male audience had gathered. Mr. Kenta abbreviated the phrase "pa kwla mo," which means "get in the bush" in Chedepo, a variant of the Grebo language. The phrase is a tactful way for one speaker to ask another to yield the floor for a moment. "Then they said, 'Here comes Barleh Gbeh. He is bringing school!' Wasn't it so?" Mr. Kenta asked the crowd to validate his comments. Almost in unison, the members in the audience responded in the affirmative.

"So, did you bring school, as we know it today, to Chedepo Jarkaken? What happened that Deateah was referring to in his 2005 statement?" I asked Mr. Cholopray.

"You should have asked Deateah that question," the wife said to me.

"I did not get a chance to ask him later. I did not want to ask him in the middle of the townspeople's formal discourse."

"Thank you," Mr. Cholopray said. "I must give you a historical perspective first, then you will understand the answer, which will come later. We were many youth members who left Jarkaken and went to faraway communities in pursuit of education. We went in groups, or waves, if you like. The people in my group were, of course, myself, your uncle, the late Paul Kayjeley Winn, and Mr. Isaac Swen. We went to Wulobo Towaja, which is the Division #1 area. By the way, we started school in Jarkaken, but something happened, which led to the decision to leave the Chedepo area."

277

'Okay," I said.

Mr. Cholopray and I sat across from each other in his living room and stared at one another. Intermittently, I snuck quick looks at the family's photos, which were mounted on the walls around us. We sat on beige-colored couches that still had their original plastic coverings. Mrs. Cholopray and Melvin, the young man who accompanied me, sat off to the side. I asked Melvin to record our conversation, so he had my VHSC camcorder.

"The teacher did not like us," he picked up where he had left off. "The teacher did not like Paul and me for reasons we did not know."

"Who was the teacher?" I asked him.

"Mr. David Karwolo Swen was the teacher. No, the teacher was Geesay Doe," he corrected himself quickly. "You probably know him as Rev. James Doe Young. He had his church in Monrovia. Geesay Doe was the principal at the Jarkaken School. While he was there, Mr. David Karwolo Swen, who graduated a few years earlier, joined him and taught at the Jarkaken School. The two men, for some reasons, could not work well together, so the townspeople were trying to find a way to separate them. While the people were contemplating a solution, the people of Chedepo Geeken asked Mr. Swen to go to their town and teach. He agreed, and that was the solution; he went to Geeken and became the principal. The people who were in my student group," he continued, "who I named earlier went to Chedepo Geeken. Paul K. Winn and I left Jarkaken and enrolled at the school in Chedepo Geeken. (Isaac Swen joined us later.) When Geesay Doe realized that we had left the Jarkaken School, he stopped for a moment to assure me that he was an honest narrator.

278

"The things I am telling you have their basis in what I saw, what I heard, and what I did. This is not a rumor. Geesay Doe was not happy. He said Mr. Swen had effectively succeeded in stealing his students. But Mr. Swen had nothing to do with our decision to enroll at the school in Chedepo Geeken. We left Jarkaken because he [Geesay Doe] hated us with passion. He was so angry with us that he took us to court. While he was attending summer school in Nyaanke, where his brother, Pahchie, was a soldier, Geesay Doe pressed charges against Paul K. Winn and me. He told his brother that we broke into his home and took his personal properties. He accused me of entering his home and stealing his wife Lucy's sewing machine, which was a ridiculous charge. I am talking about the Rev. James Doe Young. He did all these things before God called him to serve."

We laughed.

"The commissioner in Nyaanke sent a soldier to get us. Mr. David K. Swen told us that Geesay Doe was doing all those things because of him [Mr. Swen], not because of anything we had done. So, Mr. Swen opted to go to court with Paul and me. When we arrived, we went to Quelley's house; he was a

279

Bocuwao man. Then we went to the courthouse the next day. I was not well versed in English, and I was not that articulate either. Even now, I am still not that articulate."

We laughed. Of course, Mr. Cholopray speaks fluent and coherent English. He merits better appraisal than what he gave himself.

Hon. William G. Cholopray, speaking at the Second Annual Jarkaken Family Reunion. This event was hosted by Mr. Wilfred K. Winn, Sr, and his wife, Mrs. Annie P. Winn in the city of Newport News, VA June 17-19, 2011

"When we arrived inside the courtroom, Paul spoke on our behalf. He spoke better English and articulated our issue well to the district commissioner, who, at the time, was D.C. Itoka. He asked if we were still attending school. We replied in the affirmative, and our response was supported by the presence of our school principal, Mr. David K. Swen. The D.C. told us to pack up our things. He said if the time of the day was good for traveling, we were free to go back the same day; otherwise, leave the next day. 'You have done nothing,' he told us. 'He is jealous of you.' We were happy with the court decision. We left the next day."

The two friends had had enough of the school politics in Chedepo, so they decided to try school in a distant land.

"Shortly after the court proceedings, we decided to leave both the Jarkaken and Geeken schools. That was how we ended up in Towaja, as I mentioned earlier in the conversation. While we were attending school there, we heard the locals were making a clandestine plot to kill us. They were angry with Chedepo, mainly Geeken. One of their sons was Mr. Harry Toe. He died a tragic death in Geeken while he was attending school there. A tree had accidentally fallen and killed him. So, his people wanted to get even, and once they realized who we were in their town, they started plotting to kill us tragically, too."

"Who-o!" Mrs. Cholopray reacted.

"Yes. Our older brothers heard the story before we did. So, Josiah S. Winn and my big brother, Brown Cholo Cholopray, made a quick stopover to us while they were going to Firestone. They explained the entire story to us, and then got us out of there. 'They are going to shop for us, so we are going with them,' was the way we chose to say our goodbye to the folks we had been staying with in the town. When we arrived in Firestone, I entered Jelatapo Government School, and Paul enrolled at Central Site. He did not like that school, so he came over to Jelatapo Government School, where we were. From there, we went to Pelloken. We were in Pelloken School when Paul left and went back home. Then, eventually, he left Jarkaken and went to Yekepa, Nimba County. Mr. Welayor Swen, Mr. Isaac Swen, Mr. Nyonpon, Mr. Isaac Doe, Mr. Josiah Jerbo ('Chebo Matieon')—all these people and I were in Pelloken together. I was there until I graduated from that school."

Mr. Cholopray went home after he graduated from the school in Pelloken. By that time, his father, old man Tylor Choloplay, had had enough with school. He wanted his son to settle down with a woman and to begin a teaching profession. But Mr. Cholopray had other plans.

"After I completed the school in Pelloken, I went to Jarkaken. And the people began to celebrate my educational achievement. My father called me and said, 'The level of school you have completed is sufficient.' He proposed that I take a wife and settle down. In fact, my parents had engaged a woman for me. They engaged the daughter of Kanmu—the brother of Chenapoh—for me to marry. 'You can be a teacher here in Jarkaken,' my father told me. While the town was still celebrating my educational achievement, my friend, Johnson Doe (Nyan), came to me at night. His people wanted him to go back to the Firestone area to continue school. He had not graduated yet. 'So, I want to go back to school again,' he told me. I told him that my people wanted me to settle down with a wife and teach at the local school, but I was not thrilled about such decisions either. Johnson Doe suggested that we find a way to hide and leave Jarkaken. I agreed. Therefore, while the town women were dancing in front of my father's house in Jarkaken, I left the town with my friend. My mother knew about my decision to leave quietly; my brother's wife, Snoh, knew about my departure, too. My father did not know because I was hiding from him; he was the one who wanted me to stop pursuing further education."

"All of this must have been a long trek," Mrs. Cholopray wondered. "Yes. There was very little car movement during this time; we walked

everywhere."

"How long did it take you to get to the Firestone area?"

"I do not know," he told his wife. "But travelers from Jarkaken usually slept in the town of Gbeapo Podloken, if they did not leave the town early enough. If they left early, the initial rest stop was well beyond the town of Podloken. But for our escape, we slept in Podloken. Then we trekked to the town of Towaja; we spent the night there. We resumed our journey the following day, and continued until we got to the village of Taeken, in the clan of Tienpo. The following day, we trekked from Tienpo Taeken until we got to the town of Karlorken, where we met a car. It carried us to the Firestone area. When we arrived, I went to Togbeh Nowinnie (Mr. John N.

Choloplay) in Jelatapo. I explained to him my reason for traveling to Firestone. He was happy to learn that I wanted to continue education—to enter high school. So, he took me to the city of Harper."

"So, the school you completed when your parents wanted you to remain in the town of Jarkaken, what level of graduation was it?" I asked him.

"9th Grade," both the husband and wife said, almost at the same time.

"That was in the year 1963," Mr. Cholopray added. "It was at the beginning of the year. School times fluctuated back then. Anyway, John N. Choloplay took me to Harper. He took me to Mr. Joseph S. Bush, who was the principal for Cape Palmas High School (CPHS). And he told him, 'This is my brother; I want him to be here and go to school.' I met Mr. Johnson S. Willabo at CPHS. I met Mr. Charles S. Nyan there, too. I doubt you know him."

"I know him," I told him, and added that I lived with him in the late 1980s in Zwedru. "He was the husband of Saratha Toe, my aunt."

"Okay," he continued. "I also met Mr. Robert Dewey there. It was this school that I graduated from in 1965. We attended CPHS with many people from Gbeapo, mainly from Kanweaken. In fact, after my graduation, I came home with many graduates from Gbeapo. When we arrived in the town of Kanweaken, we met many people there. They were in the town for a parade. They celebrated with the local graduates. My Kanweaken counterparts told the band leader that they had traveled with a Chedepo youth who was also a high school graduate. The band leader's name was Jones. Wiah Toe (Joe Weah) was there, too. He was the head of those who were in the town to parade. I do not know the fine details that led to

283

the decision to take me to Jarkaken with an escort band. But that was the decision. Mr. Jones and others told me the band was going with me to Jarkaken. And that was how I entered the town with the band."

"You were walking?" the wife asked him.

"Yes, we were trekking everywhere during this time." "So, the band was playing while you walked?"

"No, they carried their instruments as loads. But as we neared the town, the band began to play — thunderously. During that time, our people used to come out in their numbers whenever something happened. In the case of the band, however, they came out with anxieties. Many people did not quite know what to make of it. They did not know what was happening. So, some people were afraid when they heard the band. Once they'd realized the cheerful nature of the event, however, the people became calmed; they joined the festivities. When we entered the town, my brother Tuoh's wife, Snoh, was seriously sick. I am coming a lot closer to answering the original question, Wilfred," he told me, smiling. "She was very sick; she was barely alive, in fact. They took her to Worley's place, which was at the entrance of the town.

They'd tried all they could to restore her health, but nothing was working for her. Increasingly, her situation got worse. So, at Worley's place, they propped her door open and peeked in occasionally, just to check her status. When I arrived in the town, the townspeople noticed her absence from the fun events. So, they asked my brother about his wife. 'Snoh is too sick to make it to these events,' he told the townspeople. They told him, 'Your wife is healed; her sickness is no more. She needs to come and join us, so we can celebrate. Koah Gbeh [Mr. W. G. Cholopray] has graduated from high school, and we, the people of Chedepo Klosoken, are celebrating his

284

achievement.' To the surprise of many, the woman recovered. They went for her, and she walked to the town center. It was unbelievable; the people were stunned when they saw her participating in the merriments."

"When a man uses good words to wish another well—with God's blessing—such wishes will always come true," the wife said.

"Whoever bewitched her was probably scared," I said.

"My father stood up at the town center and said, 'On behalf of the Ponwaon family, I am killing that giant cow right there for the celebration of my son's graduation. He has completed the toughest of schools.' He ended his speech with a chant of 'Bati,' and the people responded thunderously. You asked me earlier to explain what Deateah was referring to in Jarkaken," he finally got around to the question I had asked at the very beginning of our conversation. "No one completed high school before me from the town of Jarkaken, River Gee," he said. "I was the first. I must say that that was the known fact when I graduated. However, when we dug a little deeper on the subject much later, it became apparent that I was not the first from the town to graduate from high school. Mr. John N. Choloplay, the man who helped me to enter Cape Palmas High School in Harper City, Maryland County, was technically Jarkaken's first high school graduate. But John Choloplay's graduation was uneventful. He did not go home to Jarkaken after his graduation. And so, no one knew about his graduation. He deliberately kept his graduation a secret. So, when I graduated, I was the only known high school graduate from the town. And that makes me officially the first Jarkaken person to graduate from high school. We celebrated high school graduates, but your generation is celebrating college and university graduates."

We laughed. He was not done with schooling yet. "You will hear something in

the not-too-distant future; I will invite you to my college graduation," he confided in me.

"Deateah, the son of Kentan, was in the town when I arrived with the band. He was there during the graduation celebration. And that was the reason he referenced that occasion when the town was planning to celebrate you as a warrior."

"I had a follow-up question, but you answered it in your narratives. After Mr. David K. Swen graduated, you said he joined Geesay Doe to teach in Jarkaken. My impression is that you were the first to graduate. So, what school did Mr. Swen complete?"

"He completed the school in Pelloken, or was it the Pleebo School? Either way, he graduated in the 8th Grade. That was the standard graduating class. Mr. Alfred Kenta, Mr. Jasper Chea, Mr. Charles Nyonpon, Mr. Isaac Doe, Mr. Isaac Dweh, and Mr. Albert Dweh—all these people graduated at the 8th Grade level. I was the first to graduate at the 9th Grade level in Jarkaken. When I completed the 9th Grade, it was a milestone achievement, too, in the town. It was immediately after my 9th Grade graduation that my father wanted me to go into teaching and forget about further education. But I hid from him and went to Harper, where I entered and completed high school."

He discussed his first job opportunity as a high school graduate.

"At that time, the Government of Liberia sent communications to county superintendents, asking them to send new high school graduates to Monrovia to be trained for positions in immigration and other national security sectors. The superintendent of Grand Gedeh County was Mr. Moses P.

Harris at that time. It was during this time that I completed high school. So, while we were still celebrating my triumph, Mr. Koon, a Webbo man, brought a letter to me from Zwedru. Mr. Koon was our son. His mother is from our area. I just cannot remember his full name. Anyway, Mr. Koon went to Zwedru to participate in a parade. While he was coming back, the superintendent gave him a letter for me. 'We want you to come to Zwedru; we will send you to Monrovia to work,' the letter said in a nutshell."

Mr. Cholopray's time in Jarkaken after high school was short. While the town was still rejoicing, he answered his country's call to service.

"I packed up my things and went to Zwedru. I started the trip with Mr. Johnson S. Willabo, but when we got to the town of Killepo Kanweaken, he got out of the vehicle. And I went on to Zwedru. When I arrived in Zwedru, I went to the superintendent's office. He was in his office with Mr. Samuel Davis, a Webbo man. He was the Debt Court Judge at the time. 'We want you to go to Monrovia. The government wants to train high school graduates for immigration and other security sector jobs. You are one of the recent graduates, so we want you to go and train for a post in the immigration service,' they told me. Then they called one man, a bus driver named Railroad. He was a Mandingo man. They told him to take me to Monrovia without charging me. They told him to take me straight to the home of Mr. Amos P. Young, which was on Ashmun Street. That was my destination."

Mr. Amos Pahchie Young was the brother of Mr. James Doe Young, the elementary school teacher of Mr. William G. Cholopray and his friend, Mr. Paul K. Winn, in the late 1950s to early 1960s. At the beginning of our conversation, Mr.

Cholopray told me that this teacher, who later became a renowned pastor in Clara Town, Bushrod Island, sued the two named students at a courthouse in Nyaanke, Maryland County. A few short years after the teacher-students court debacle, the brother of that teacher, Pahchie, was, ironically, the host for Mr. Cholopray. Mr. Young, the soldier, helped Mr. Cholopray to get around Monrovia in his effort to obtain an employment at the Bureau of Immigration.

"When I arrived in Monrovia," Mr. Cholopray continued, "Pahchie took me to the Bureau of Immigration. The superintendent of Grand Gedeh, Mr. Moses P. Harris, gave me a letter for the Bureau. So, when we entered, I gave it to the Commissioner of Immigration, who was Hon. E. Sumo Jones at the time. That was in the year 1966. The Bureau scheduled a test date for us, the candidates. And then we left. When the testing day arrived, a total of one hundred fifty candidates showed up and sat for the test. When the results came back, the candidates were split even—seventy-five applicants passed the test while the other seventy-five failed it. Thankfully, I was among the group that passed. In fact, I was one of the high scorers. Only one applicant scored higher. His name was Socree, a young man from Sarbo. He scored 85 percent. I took the second place with the score of 84 percent. Then the scores trickled down from there. But when we reported for interview a few days later, they revealed to us that Socree, the highest scorer on the test, was not at the testing site the day of the test. His older brother, who was a student at the University of Liberia, took the test on his behalf. So, I was effectively declared the highest scorer on the test. In fact, while we were going to do our PPD [purified protein derivative, a skin test agent for tuberculosis], we heard that Socree's name was removed from the list altogether. I took other civil servant tests while I was in Monrovia. I took a test for the police department. I also took a test for the Special Security Services. I passed all the tests that I took. My goal, really, was to obtain an employment at the

Executive Mansion. 'Stick to immigration; Grand Gedeh sent you here to be trained for a job at the Bureau,' Pahchie advised me. I agreed. Later, they sent us to the immigration training.

Upon completion, the government assigned me to Toe Town, Grand Gedeh County. By the way, shortly after my assignment, I made a way for your uncle, Mr. William P. Sayee. He took the test, passed it, and successfully completed the training. The two of us were assigned in Toe Town, Grand Gedeh County."

"What was your motivation?" I asked Mr. Cholopray. "What kept you going, especially in pursuit of education? Back then, for example, I am told that school was frowned upon in the rural country, but, somehow, school was a priority for you. While some of your peers were staying out of school because they had been conditioned to believe that school made people lazy, you kept pressing on. So, what was the push?"

"I knew early on that to earn more money in government, one had to know more books. There were different salaries for different educational levels. Those who completed 8th grade, for example, got paid salaries that suited that level. The same was true for those who completed 9th grade, high school, college, and university. When I was a youth, a

D.C. [district commissioner] did not walk long distances. He was hammocked to the places he wanted to go. I used to like that as a youth because I did not enjoy trekking at all. In fact, one of the reasons I took school seriously was the hope of one day obtaining employment as a district commissioner."

We laughed.

"You love Grebo traditional activities—you told me earlier—especially dancing. That tells me you must have spent a considerable period of your youth with our people. So, when exactly did you leave Chedepo Jarkaken? When did you stop doing these traditional activities?"

"I love our tradition. I am a good dancer, especially when it comes to ku-wleh [a modified war dance, the version Grebo dance when the country devil is in the village]. Ask your father, 'Saylee a peh,' about my dancing skills. He used to hate that nickname, especially when a member of our crowd called him as such. Ask him. He will tell you how good a dancer I am. In fact, when I was in school, Jarkaken was my only vacation spot. I used to go home frequently because of our culture. I can tap palm wine. I can do farm work. When it comes to 'Bati' [taking the floor as a traditional orator at the town center], I am good at that, too. I did all these things before I left the town. I can say I have never left because of my frequent visits there — once or twice a year while I was in school and while I was a government official, too. So, some people might think I have forgotten all these things, especially considering the period that has elapsed since I left the place. That is not true. Right now, if I get the opportunity, I will dance."

We laughed.

"I left Jarkaken in February 1966. And since that year, I have not lived there, but I am a regular visitor. The immigration training lasted for three months. After the training, and based on my performance at the academy, I received the rank of corporal (CPL).

Our general mandate, which was branded as Operation Tact, was to prevent illegal entry into the country. I was assigned to Toe Town, a border community in Grand Gedeh County. Several subversive activities were going on across Africa; that was the reason President Tubman instituted the Bureau. In December 1966, I went to Jarkaken for the Christmas of the year. By this time, I had on my uniforms, completed with badges and the Bureau's insignia. I have the picture I took during this visit in the room."

"You later went to Zwedru," I said.

"Yes. They transferred me to Zwedru in the year 1968; that was the same year street entered Jarkaken, the Putuken-Jarkaken road. Class B Corporal (CPL-B) was my first rank. In 1967, I received a promotion to the rank of Sergeant; that was due to my operations at the border. In 1969, I received promotion to the rank of Captain (CPT). We had paramilitary rank structures; but they had letters attached."

"So, you had Class B Captain," I said.

"Yes, but that was prior to President Samuel K. Doe's administration. We transitioned to complete, announced paramilitary rank structures under President Doe. When I received the lettered rank of Captain, my job was Border Inspector for Grand Gedeh County. With this rank, no one referred to me as an officer anymore. I was an Inspector. After that, I received a promotion to a full CPT. Then I received a promotion again to the rank of Major; my job title was County Commander. I was in this position when we returned to Monrovia for a refresher training. Upon the completion of that refresher training—during which I attained a certificate in criminal justice administration—I was promoted to the rank of Lieutenant Colonel (LTC). I was now a regional immigration administrator; my job title was Regional Commander. I was responsible for four counties: Grand Gedeh County, Sinoe County, Maryland County, and Grand Kru County. During the second or third month of my regional job, I received a memorandum from the Justice Ministry. It said a regional commander should hold the rank of Colonel (COL), not LTC. My friend, Robert Dewey, was promoted to COL as a

291

result of that Justice Ministry memorandum. My rank also changed to a colonel. Hon.

Winston Tubman was the Minister of Justice. The communication was disseminated

during his term (1982-1983).”

The regional position was Mr. Cholopray's last responsibility before the war broke out. He, like most Liberians, was impacted negatively, including the loss of his job. But, as the old saying goes, “an experienced player does not fight for jersey.” Mr. Cholopray was called back to service.

“I was a colonel until the war,” he continued. “When the war died down, the government called us back. I was appointed as the Chief of Protective and Internal Security Officer. This position handles sensitive issues, and it has the authority to investigate even the Commissioner of Immigration, the highest-ranking member of the paramilitary officers in the Bureau. That was the job I had. I reported directly to the Minister of Justice, who reported to the president of Liberia. Wilfred, at this level, I could

enter any government office in Monrovia without tapping on the door.”

We laughed.

“While I was in this position, the government sent me to the Republic of Ghana to carry out certain responsibilities. I went there, accomplished those tasks, and returned to Liberia. Because of the professional way I conducted myself and the duties of the office of Chief of Protective and Internal Security, I received another promotion. I was appointed as the Deputy Commissioner for Security Affairs. And at this level, I became a member of the National Joint Security. When the joint security met, I was one of the subject matter experts (SME) on issues involving Interpol, an international organization that facilitates worldwide police cooperation and crime control. I was the SME on deportation, for example. Deportation documents were prepared in my office. Then I got another promotion. I was appointed as the Chief Investigator for the Bureau of Immigration of Liberia. It was this job that I had when Taylor came.

Those of us who had not been on Taylor's side were removed from our positions. But in 1998, President Taylor wanted to reestablish the National Bureau of Immigration (NBI). So, his government was looking for people who were veterans in the field of immigration. In fact, he was looking for veteran police, immigration, and talents across all the security sectors. Hence, when I reported, I was selected to revitalize the entire NBI. My job title was Special Agent in Charge [of the NBI]. I retained the rank of Colonel, with the focus on preventing illegal entry into Liberia."

"And all of this was under Taylor, right?" the wife asked.

"Yes. This was Taylor's time. After he fired us, he later realized our importance to the security of the country, so he called us back. We just didn't have our previous job titles. He created new roles and responsibilities. I was at the NBI when I came to the United States."

"How did you survive the Charles Taylor war?" I asked him.

"I was reporting rebel activities directly to the Commissioner of Immigration at the time. The Commissioner of Immigration was reporting to the Justice Minister, who reported to the President of Liberia. That president was Samuel K. Doe. So, by the virtue of my assignment, I was in a serious dilemma when the Charles Taylor war came. Across the Bureau, we had Liberians from every county within the

293

country. And from their respective posts, they sent me critical national security information. I oversaw the borders. I collected national and international reports, which I compiled and sent up the leadership chain. Remember that Charles Taylor and his people were the 'rebels,' and I was charged to report their activities, which eventually went up to the president. Just think about that for a moment. Anyway, my position was among the first to go when Charles Taylor took over the country. And I was not safe at all. I was consistently on the move. I don't believe we stayed at one place for more than six months. My wife is right here as my witness. We started at 15th Street. Whenever we thought our lives were endangered at a particular location, we simply moved. Hence, from 15th Street, we moved to the 11th Street area. Then we relocated to Barnesville Estate. From there, we moved to Saint Paul Bridge, at Island Clinic."

"Yes, at God Blessed You," the wife added. "God Blessed You," I said, curiously.

"Yes, it used to be a very dangerous neighborhood," she told me. "Criminals ('Bojo people') used to chase the people in that area during the night hours. Whenever they'd failed in their pursuit—whenever the chased person outran them—they used to say, 'That God blessed you that is why we did not catch you.' And that was how the label started and remained to this date," she said.

"Then we went to Logan Town," Mr. Cholopray continued. "From Logan Town, we went to New Kru Town. That was our last neighborhood in Monrovia before I came to the United States."

"Have you been back to Jarkaken?" I asked Mr. Cholopray. "For example, to visit the local schools; to motivate the children and to provide some guidance. You do have very

294

powerful stories and life lessons. Have you used some of your time to visit schools, or the youth, to impact knowledge to them? Moreover, many women in our area did not go to school, particularly during the time you were in school. Why did that happen?"

"Our people had terrible stereotypes for people who were going to school. These stereotypes applied to both males and females. They were very effective, and that hurt the enrollment of both males and females. On females in particular, the ones who were trying to break what was largely a male school experience, if you like, were branded 'prostitutes.' Such a stereotype was the main reason many females remained out of school. And in a society where self-image and reputation mattered so much, no girl wanted to be seen as a prostitute. It was a very bad label (and still is) that was effective at keeping many females out of school. To some extent, I helped to change the perspectives of people in our area. One way I did it was to go home with some females who and I worked together. Of course, they used to dress in their uniforms, affixed with badges and matching insignias. And it was a powerful message to our girls.

That they, too, could enter school—regardless of the labels—and be just as accomplished. And, yes, I used to go to Jarkaken as a speaker. I went to many locations and spoke to different audiences. I went to Gbeapo Kanweaken, and I went to Jadeapo, too. People invited me routinely to speak on wide-ranging topics on different occasions. In 1984, I traveled to the United States and participated in joint security training with the Federal Bureau of Investigation. We also received antiterrorism training. When I returned to Liberia that year, an invitation was waiting for me. I got an invitation from the Zwedru Multilateral High School, asking me to present its graduates with certificates. I attended that commencement program, and I spoke on the topic of caring. It is important that we, as a people, care for one another. I used a boat analogy to drive my point home to the young graduates.

'How do we call the thing we use to cross a river?' I asked the students. 'Boat!' they answered.

'If you paddle your boat side-to-side, what will happen?' 'It will go straight.'

'Okay, what happens when you keep paddling on one side of your boat?' 'It will just keep turning around.'

"I associated 'bu-wah' with the sound that water makes when a boat paddle is applied. So, when I asked the graduates what would happen if they had kept paddling nonstop on one side of the boat, I was saying, 'bu-wah, bu-wah, bu-wah.' They thought that was funny, so they kept laughing. But here is the message that I left with the children: Every act of paddling represents a handout to someone; a gift to another; or service to people. Do not be the generous person who helps just one person or just one family. If you give something to one side, find something else to give to the other side, too. If you include God in it anything you want to do in this life, it will come to pass. It will come true."

He dived deeper.

"The sacrifices that some of us went through in Liberia before we ended up over here [USA], only God knows. I am blessed in this life, and I am grateful to God. But my life is not without misfortunes, downfalls, or regrets. My difficulties in government started in 1985, and in the runup to the election of that year. When President Doe was getting ready for the election, there was another party leader who wanted to be president, too. His name was Mr. Jackson F. Doe. He was a Gio man from Nimba County. His party was the Liberian Action Party or LAP, for short. But our people simply called it

296

'Koko-leo-ko' because its symbol was a rooster. Mr. Jackson F. Doe's party was very popular in our area. It was hard to find anyone in Chedepo who was not in LAP, or who did not support that party. Many people in my family were members of LAP. At first, I was not aware that some folks in my family were card-carrying members of LAP until I saw a few of their names in a local newspaper. They used to put the names of partisans in local newspapers to put them on the record. They did it to check the party loyalty of some Liberians. Some people used to be for one party on one day and then another party on the other day. My brother, Matthew Cholopray, had his name in the newspaper as member of LAP. My older brother, Brown Cholo Cholopray, and his wife were in the newspaper, too, for the LAP. So, when that newspaper got to Monrovia, and eventually to the Executive Mansion, members of the Mansion security saw it and took it to the President of Liberia. 'Cholopray,' they said, 'who we respect is putting his families in the other party. He thinks that man is going to win; so that is his contingency plan. He wants to go on that side.' They told President Doe. 'We used to say these things,' they continued. 'That the Grebo people are very bad. They are not loyal, but we still gave them key positions in the government.' I was almost arrested over this. They went for my friend, Robert Dewey, who is in Philadelphia as I speak. He was in Tuzon then. They got me, too. But one army man saved us. His name was COL Joloka. He did not do what the rest of the Krahn people were doing. He was very objective. He reportedly told President Doe that those who were making all the accusatory remarks about us were trying to ruin his government. 'They are not plotting anything, and if you take them from Grand Gedeh, which is a border county, this country will be vulnerable.' I was not there, but that was his advice to the President, we later learned. His swift intervention was the reason we were not arrested that night. But they got us the following morning, and we went to Tuzon. But from the period the names appeared in the

297

newspaper, we became targets of continuous surveillance. They could not find anything on me because there was nothing there to find."

Colonel Joloka did his part to calm the president and his closest advisers that Mr.

Cholopray and others were honest people who just wanted to do their jobs. But the stigma of disloyalty lingered. Mr. Cholopray and others were seen as unfaithful partisans, and there was very little anyone could do to change the minds of the Krahn people who had the President's ears. When General Thomas G. Quiwonkpa launched his failed coup d'état (1985), they said 'arrest all the people who were not for President Samuel K. Doe during the election.' I was in Gbarnga, Bong County at that time. In fact, it was because of the same suspicion raised by the names in the newspaper that they took me from Zwedru, where I oversaw four counties, to Gbarnga and put me in charge of three counties: Bong County, Nimba County and Lofa County. The regional headquarters was in Gbarnga. Anyway, they sent for us when the coup failed. And they put COL Pennue in charge of the operation to get me."

"COL Pennue who was that wicked!" the wife said.

"'Go and get him; whether he gets here dead or alive is up to you.' That was the message to COL Pennue," Mr. Cholopray continued. "So, he sent his personal bodyguards to get me; they were two men. Thankfully, he gave them strong warning not to hurt me. 'No one should put their hands on him.' On that same day, I just woke up and decided to go to Monrovia. So, I dressed up in my uniforms; of course, I always looked great in my uniforms."

We laughed.

298

"I had two bodyguards with me. The government gave me sirens by this time.

And whenever I am going anywhere for official duties, the police and immigration officers used to go on advance duty, in order to ensure the route was cleared and my destination was secured. The joint security team used to stay with me until my task was completed. Every time I visited a county, even the superintendent of that county came out to receive me. We were President Doe's leaders!" he said with a wide smile.

"Anyway, they came for me. They passed my vehicle on the highway, then they did a quick U-turn. So, I became concerned. I was wondering what was going on. We slowed down and stopped. They said they were going to get me. And when I asked who sent them, they told me it was Taye who sent them. Note that Taye and I had been friends for a very long time. 'Okay, let's go. I will continue in my vehicle.' I told them. So, we went straight to Taye's place. Then Taye's chief bodyguard entered the building. He looked at me and said, 'That's the man; we got him.' And before I knew it, he grabbed my button-up shirt and ripped it opened. My buttons went flying everywhere; they were gold-colored buttons. He took off my belt, and then he ripped my pants off, too. I was beyond shocked as he carried out these acts. I was completely speechless.

Wilfred, I was looking at him the way you are looking at me. I was totally

flabbergasted."

"So, Taye was doing this to you?" his wife asked.

"No. It was his chief bodyguard. His name was Robert. (He has since been dead though.) Then Taye entered. They told him, 'Chief, here is the man; we got him.' He

299

held his head down for a while, then he said, 'Take him to the Bureau of Immigration and lock him up.' And so, the guards took me. When we got to Sinkor Bye Pass..."

"Capital Bye Pass?" his wife asked.

"No, the airfield shortcut. The road that passes below there," he clarified. "That was the route they took me on. They stopped the car at that location, and one of them said, 'Let's take this man over there and execute him.' The other soldier said, 'No, that was not what Taye told us.' I was sitting there, listening as the soldiers debated each other over my fate. 'But Taye will not say go kill the man; once he said take him, all of that is implied.' They agreed not to take me out of the vehicle, and we passed the location. By the way, the guards were senselessly beating me. They were using the belt from my uniform to beat me. It was a huge cargo-strap belt, and it left a huge knot on my forehead. The knot was still on my forehead when I entered the United States. They beat me viciously until they were tired. When we got near the Executive Mansion, by the Unknown Soldier, the soldiers stopped again. They started another debate session. One wanted to take me to the Mansion, and the other wanted to stick to Taye's directives. We were there for a while. I was listening painfully as they tussled over my fate. Again, they chose to do what Taye had ordered. We passed the Executive Mansion compound.

Then they took me to the office, and jailed me."

Mr. Cholopray's long-time friend, Taye, came to the office the following morning.

And upon arrival, he made a heart-dropping decision about the prisoners.

"'Take them to Post Stocket to be executed,' Taye told the guards. Whether he had investigated our cases or not I do not know. But my name was on the list of those they had scheduled to be killed. And so, they took us to the Barclay Training Center (BTC), a military post. The Commanding General at the time was General Kolako. By the way, while I was at Gbarnga, General Kolako came through my gate. He was going to Lofa County, his home. He was going on a vacation. For us in the Immigration Bureau, it is almost a ritual to entertain visiting senior leaders of government. Hence, when he got to my gate, I filled the table with refreshments. I also told my subordinates to fuel-up his vehicles at my expense. Then he left Gbarnga and went to Lofa County.

No, he was attending Unification Day program. I followed up with him a few days later. That left a lasting impression. So, when the soldiers took us to BTC, he recognized me. He asked for my name, and I told him. Then he asked if I were the one at the Gbarnga regional office. I told him I was, and that was all the conversation I had with him. But instead of taking me to Post Stocket, where the executions were planned or scheduled, he gave the soldiers a strong order to take me to Central Prison instead. 'No one should go there to visit him,' he ordered."

"The man you did the good to was ordering the soldiers?" the wife asked.

"Yes. And he told the people that I was a kind and generous person. He said he was sure someone told a lie, which got me in trouble. I was not there when he reportedly made the comments, but I heard that later. Mr. Peter W. Johnson (Kanwea) [a former Liberian soldier] was there. The general did not know that Kanwea and I were from the same town. Kanwea had a Potupo girlfriend; she was a soldier, too. She was in the office when the general reportedly said the kind words about me. She was in the same office building as Amos Pahchie Young; she was on the upper floor. Anyway, while the other prisoners were going to Post Stocket, they took me to Central

301

Prison instead. I was there for a long time. But after the first week, the assumption was that I had been killed. 'They were executed last night,' people were reportedly saying. COL Pennue came to my location, and he said, 'Bring that man out!' We were many inside, including Mr. J. Rudolph Grime. He suggested that the guards tell COL Pennue I was not in there. I did not go along with that idea. I insisted to see COL Pennue because I knew they had a list of all the people who were inside. My name was on that list. So, I was aware that COL Pennue knew I was inside. But, as I was leaving to see COL Pennue, the guards called another person outside. His name was Mr. Isaac Gbatu. He was a Gio man, from Nimba County. He, too, was told to get outside and proceed to the colonel. During that time, a huge conflict was between Gio and Krahn tribal peoples because of the botched coup. So, when they called me and a Gio man out of the cell, my assumption was it was going to be over for me on that day. 'Do you know who brought you here?' COL Pennue asked me. I told him I did— that I was in there because Taye had ordered me to be in there. 'Why did he order you to be here?' he asked me again. This time I told him I had no idea. He laughed. 'When General Thomas G. Quiwonkpa launched his failed coup, you were rejoicing. You were celebrating and drinking. You were arresting people in Gbarnga.' When he was done naming the alleged acts for which I was in their custody, I asked him. 'Are you sure you are talking about me?' He said, with conviction, that he was. 'No, it had to be someone else, not me.' Then COL Pennue said, 'I know you. You could not have done the things that they are alleging.' COL Pennue told me that he had been telling Taye and others about jumping to conclusions. 'They are just lying on people,' he said. 'They are just killing people for no reasons. I have the power to free you right now,' he said. Then he asked for my thoughts on being set free. If he wanted to set me free, I advised him to consult with Taye first. If Taye was not aware, he would have thought I had escaped from

302

prison. He agreed. Then he reached in his pocket and gave me five dollars ($5); he gave the Gio man five dollars ($5), too."

It was not over yet. The two men—Mr. Cholopray and Mr. Gbatu—returned to their prison cells. For Mr. Cholopray, he was summoned at the end of the second week to report to the Bureau of Immigration.

"I was hand cuffed the entire time we were detained, but as we were going upstairs at the Bureau, they removed my cuffs. That simple act—removing the cuffs— saved my life that day. As we were going up the stairs, we saw many soldiers; they were all over the place. One of the soldiers aimed the butt of his riffle squarely at the back of my head. Of course, I couldn't see behind, so I did not see this coming. He sent a powerful butt stroke to my head, but missed—kind of—when I, by mere chance, moved my head. Hence, he did not land the butt of his riffle squarely at the back of my head, but the riffle rubbed the side of my head. It was a powerful hit, which torn my temple skin open. I started to bleed profusely. Had he landed it squarely in the back of my head, I would have died that day. But it was a powerful blow nevertheless. The blood was just gushing all over the place. The soldier who butt-stroked the side of my head was a Krahn man. Wilfred, I have not begun telling you about the beating marks that are left on my back and elsewhere on my body. To say 'I suffered' is an understatement. Ask your uncle, William Sayee," he told me. "And he was not spared either. If it weren't for the agonizing crying spree of his Krahn tribal woman, they would have killed William Sayee in Tuzon. In fact, they dug his grave while he was still alive, and they took him to the side of the hole. As I said, it was his Krahn woman's emotional plead that saved his life. They would have killed and buried him in the pit they dug for him. They did not even ask me what happened," he said of the butt stroke to the head. "No one asked why I was bleeding when we got upstairs. 'Okay, you will hear from us,' they told

303

us. Then they sent us back to BTC. I was at BTC for a month before they set me free. I went to the Bureau and received my letter of dismissal. 'No one gives him a job until President Doe's administration is over,' it said in a nutshell. I was set free in 1986. When I left BTC, I left Monrovia altogether. I went back to Gbarnga, Bong County. It was a calculated decision to remain in Gbarnga. If I had tried to go further east, they would have captured and taken me to Tuzon, Grand Gedeh County. Of course, they were waiting for me. My death would have been as simple as a missing person's report. If they had killed me, they would have gotten away with murder. Because they had set me free and had the records to prove that I was set free. That was the reason I stayed in Gbarnga."

In the ending pages below, Mr. Cholopray takes a moment and reflects on his life. He credits two simple truths for sparing his life, particularly during the turbulent national election year of 1985, and Gen. Thomas G. Quiwonkpa's foiled coup, which occurred later that same year. Mr. Cholopray suffered, especially after the failed coup.

Here is Mr. Cholopray, again:

"First, God Almighty blessed me through it all. I am very grateful to the Lord for His grace upon me and my family. Second, I am glad that God has given me a compassionate heart for others. I helped others and that may have helped, too. God blessed me for my good deeds towards other people. I used to help lots of students. In fact, at some point, the students had stopped going to the superintendent's office, which had been the traditional place for those seeking summer or temporary jobs and scholarships. They were going straight to my office. My office was like a local market.

The students were in and out of my office. And I gave them scholarships and temporary jobs while they were on their break

304

from school. Sometimes the companies did not have enough jobs, but they did not want to let me down whenever I asked for openings. So, they used to simply give me the money. 'Just pay the students and give us the receipts,' they used to tell me. So, some students did very little or no work over their break periods and still received money. I simply paid them and gave the payment receipts to the companies. I gave students scholarships from Gbeapo Kanweaken. I brought them to Zwedru, where they attended high schools of their choice. I did the same for students from Chedepo Putuken and across Chedepo."

Mr. Cholopray ended the conversation with a memorable advice for me, which I hope others can apply in their lives as well.

"Wilfred, doing good things for others is a godly thing. If someone asks for help from you, and you do not have it—what does red ant say? Red ant is deformed for a reason. It is deformed because the act of tactfulness is its area of specialty. It says, 'Being tactful to others is the reason I have a sagging back.' If someone asks for one dollar and you do not have it, give them the two cents you have. God will mark it for you. If they walk away without saying thank you, God will mark it still. Don't worry about not receiving their gratitude. You are a big government official; you are a big government official in this world. I am not talking about your stature." We laughed. "What I am saying has nothing to do with your size," he continued. "I am referring to your heart. Take your time. If someone steps on your foot, simply pull it back and wipe it off. If it is bruised, use warm water on it. Exercise patience."

Mr. Cholopray considers himself very lucky and blessed. He has given us a rearview into his extraordinary life's journey—a dual track that contains milestones and successes on one side and many trials and tribulations on the other. The initial pages give us the image of a successful and exemplary man, who all of us want to emulate. Those pages go from one minestrone to another, and from one high-ranking government job to another. These achievements, along with his Jarkaken values, made him a celebrated national leader.

Mr. Cholopray is one of the favorite sons of Jarkaken. He put the town of Jarkaken on the Liberian map more times than any other citizen from that community. In 1966, when Jarkaken was still a tiny dot in the Bush Grebo jungles (with no street connection), the superintendent of Grand Gedeh County (Moses P. Harris, Sr.) asked for him by name. He sent a courier to little known Jarkaken to get Mr. Cholopray. Note that Mr. Cholopray was the town's first person to complete 9th grade (all prior graduates completed at the 8th grade level); he was the town's first person to complete high school; and he is one of the accomplished government officials from the town. Hence, the people of Jarkaken could not be prouder and more appreciative for his numerous life-time achievements.

Later in this transcript, we see the heart-dropping calamities he had to endure. In one case, he was tortured by the body guards of his own friend (Taye). But it is important to set the record straight. Mr. Cholopray's political troubles had nothing to do with what he did, or what he failed to do, for that matter. His "misfortunes" had their origin from the period his family members carried out some simple acts of patriotism. What exactly did they do? His younger brother, Mathew Cholopray, and older brother, Brown Cholopray (along with his wife), did what many Liberians were doing in the year 1985. They registered their names in a political party of their choice, with the hope of participating in the presidential election of that year.

The simple patriotic duties carried out by the few members in Mr. Cholopray's family were not seen as simple by the influential personnel within the ruling party, which was the National Democratic Party of Liberia (NDPL). Mr. Cholopray, then a high- ranking immigration leader in Liberia and member of the NDPL, was accused and blamed for registering his family members in a party that was competing with the NDPL as a contingency move. That if the NDPL did not win the presidential election, he, Mr.

Cholopray, could ride the gravy train to LAP, the formidable party of Mr. Jackson F. Doe.

The above fabrications were the basis for some leaders within President Doe's political party to question the party loyalty of Mr. Cholopray. COL Joloka, a renowned military leader within the NDPL, forcefully and promptly debunked the tales as erroneous and having no merit. The good colonel may have saved Mr. Cholopray and others' lives. They were not even arrested over the issues; granted, they still had to proceed to Tuzon, where the matters were discussed civilly.

But the damage to Mr. Cholopray's reputation would endure for a prolonged period. He found himself among the most scrutinized; he was a subject of continuous surveillance. Those who were questioning his loyalty were too busy trying to find any inkling of truth, which they could employ to validate their false charges. They wanted to link him to the opposition party, where his kinsmen were members. "They could not find anything on me because there was nothing there to find," Mr. Cholopray said. I agree with the statesman from the land of Chedepo Jarkaken, River Gee.

Chapter XIII:
The Killepo War

Every clan has someone who stands out for extraordinary acts. It could be an individual who exhibits extraordinary physical strength, say at traditional wrestling matches. It could be a great hunter, a farmer, or even a warfighter. The latter recalls the oral narratives of my uncle, Mr. Newton Gbeh Chea Nyanley Winn, a veteran classroom teacher and a career educator who was trained at one of Liberia's preeminent teacher training institutions: the Kakata Rural Teacher Training Institute.

He is an oral historian, too, proven by this and other stories mentioned elsewhere in this book. In this piece, our reliable narrator puts the act of gallantry on a pedestal by highlighting the heroes of a little-known war that took place between two neighboring in what is today's western River Gee: Killepo and Chedepo clans. Their heroic acts did not know anything about the luxuries of today's communication devices: social media, and so on.

Here is my uncle, Mr. Newton Nyanley Winn:

"We have extraordinary warriors in this place, people who fought for this land.

There are many warriors in the history of this area, but very little is known about some of

our giants because of the tendency of oral narratives to fade or die out over time," he said.

"There was a warrior in the clan of Killepo. He hailed from the town of Killepo Kanweaken, which is now a key population center in River Gee, Liberia. He was the pride son of that land, even to this day. He reigns, even in death, as a famous fore relative for the entire land of Killepo. His name was Bayor ['Warrior'] Fenyi Jahowl. Admired greatly, the people of Killepo have coined a lengthy epithet for their land, 'Fenyi Jahowl Wailaya,' or 'Fenyi Jahowl's resting place.'

There was a warrior in the clan of Chedepo, too. Like the Killepo's Fenyi Jahowl, the Chedepo hero was the epitome of warriors. His name was Bayor ['Warrior'] Pah, and he was the proud son of Chedepo Geeken, a town in Chedepo District. Interchangeably, the people of Chedepo refer to him as Gbeyee Pah because his mother, herself a powerful force multiplier on the battlefield, as Gbeyee. Gbeyee Pah was the type of hero who stood above the rest. He was a great warrior ['Bayor suwa']. While he enjoyed a slew of acclamations, praise phrases and nicknames, his preference was 'Tajigba Pah.' The term 'Tajigba' means 'war face.' He earned it on the battlefield."

Anyway, the two warriors discussed above—Bayor ['Warrior'] Fenyi Jahowl and Tajigba Pah—came to prominence in the run-up to the Killepo-Chedepo war, which Chedepo refers to simply as the Killepo War. The two men heard of each other. One warrior would hear that the other was mightier, and he would disagree and send a rebuttal, proclaiming the opposite. The two sent threats and counterthreats across clan lines. They sent challenges and counterchallenges. Soon, a war broke out between the clans, and the chatty Fenyi Jahowl sent a message to his counterpart: Chedepo's Gbeyee Pah. His message to the Chedepo hero was this, 'I have been hearing so much nonsense from you. I have had enough of you. We will meet soon on the battlefield, and I will have your head to use as a pillar case. Overtime, I will use your skull as a makeshift cup from which I will drink.'

But Bayor Pah was not deterred. He sent his rebuttal to Killepo Kanweaken, 'The day you and I meet on the battlefield, I will not waste a bullet on you. I will grab you by the hand and bring you to the land of Chedepo alive. I will take you to the traditional center of town, and I will dismember you into tiny segments.' So, the two men flexed their warring muscles during the initial days of the war, sending and receiving threats."

Eventually, the war reached a critical stage. And the two men had their day on the battlefield. Before Gbeyee Pah left Chedepo Geeken, his mother warned him that Jahowl was no small child. Pah's mother was a very powerful lady. Pah's father, too, was a powerful man. On the day Pah was setting out for the battlefield to meet Fenyi Jahowl, his mother, Gbeyee, was the primary force multiplier. She told him, 'I will not just let you go. I am just as prepared to protect you. I will not drink a sip of water the entire time you will be on the battlefield. I will drink only palm wine. No food will enter my mouth. Consider yourself fortified. I protect you. Your spirit is in my custody. I will remain seated on this fine piece of wood ('tukolo') until you come back to me. You will be elusive to Fenyi Jahowl because I am sitting on your spirit.'"

He described the powers of the warriors in that era.

"Even though improved roads have rerouted some, the roads have not changed that

much, practically speaking. In terms of distance of travel, it remains essentially the same. Some powerful warriors took minutes to get to places like Gbeapo Kanweaken. Warriors, by their nature, are fast, but back then they were using 'juju.'

A 'juju' is an object that has been intentionally infused with magical power or the magical power itself; it also can refer to the belief system involving the use of juju. Juju is practiced in many West African counties, such as Liberia, where some juju involves the use of magical objects, spells, and rituals.

"So, they were extraordinarily fast," he said about the movement of the traditional Grebo warriors.

"Some of them used to fly in the dark. Gbeyee Pah's mother called him and said, 'Tajigba Pah, Fenyi Jahowl is waiting for you. When you on the battle field, I will be here [in Gbayee Pah's home, Geeken] until you come back.' Whenever he got on the battlefield, his battlefield name was 'Tajigba Pah.' And, for Bayor Jahowl, his father was Fenyi, who was the proud son of the land of Killepo as well. When the two men met on the battlefield, the Killepo warrior did everything he could to evade being captured by the warrior from Chedepo. It was a man-to-man battle. The battle went on for some time, with both warriors trading magical powers. But soon, Tajigba Pah realized he needed to take the Killepo warrior out by any means necessary; hence, he ditched his earlier goal of apprehending or grabbing the Killepo fighter. This was a tough decision. But he made it reluctantly based on unforeseen battlefield conditions. The people in his native Chedepo, particularly Geeken, his hometown, were anticipating seeing a captured Fenyi Jahowl because Tajigba Pah told the people in Chedepo Geeken to expect such outcomes.

Anyway, Tajigba Pah reached for a rifle, took aim and fired a fatal shot at Bayor Fenyi Jahowl. The warrior from Killepo had no chance; he succumbed immediately to the

injuries he had sustained on the battlefield."

It was a triumphant moment, and the warrior from took some time to celebrate his accomplishment. Here is uncle, again:

"And that was how Bayor Pah killed Fenyi Jahowl. After the warrior's death, Tajigba Pah went over his body on the battlefield and did a war cry; he basically ranted— saying: 'My dear friend, didn't I tell you that you couldn't do anything to me? I earned the name Tajigba (the face of war) because I am

312

an accomplished warrior.' He did not get the name because his father was Tajigba. He embodied a warrior, and that was evident, even on his face. He was quick-tempered. He was a fighter. He did hand-to-hand combat on the battlefield. He was an extremely physical person. He was in perfect shape; he was very strong. He had the tendency to jump up and grab tree limbs. He was a hard headed person. These were some of the reasons he was re-named Tajigba.

The death of Killepo's proud son triggered yet another war," Uncle continued, "this time it bore the semblance of a cold war because it was a war of words, jujus, and magics between the neighboring clans. The powerful mother of Jahowl was clearly not thrilled about losing her son, and more so because she felt she did not apply herself more (magically) during the battle of the warriors. Had she applied herself more, her son's spirit would have been just as elusive as Bayor Pah's, whose mother helped him to triumph over his opponent."

Uncle continued the story.

"After he killed Bayor Fenyi Jahowl, he came home to Chedepo Geeken. Mere weeks after the death of the Killepo hero, word got to Geeken that someone was planning to retaliate his death. Who could it be (not that it mattered to Tajigba Pah)? It was the mother of the dead hero. She was obviously not happy for the death of her son. She wanted to see or meet Gbeyee Pah. They told her in Killepo that if she wanted to meet the Chedepo hero, she had to go to Chedepo Geeken, his hometown. The warrior was indeed a Geeken man; he was a member of the Kaytiao family."

The woman who wanted to revenge her son's death was not planning to enter Chedepo with guns blazing. In fact, she was not coming to overrun Chedepo, not even the small town of Geeken. Instead, it was an eye-for-eye revenge—the clash of jujus or voodoos. She was coming for the Chedepo hero, and only the Chedepo hero.

"'Go there, if you want to see him,' they told her in Killepo. So, she left Killepo several weeks later to meet her son's killer. She wanted to creep on him. She wanted to surprise him by doing something he wasn't expecting or prepared for. In other words, she planned to suddenly appear and catch him off guard. As established earlier, Bayor Pah's mother, Gbeyee, was a powerful woman. She was the caliber of witchcraft we call 'waidiorsuwa.' She was in a category of her own when it came to juju and voodoo activities, which was characteristic of the latest war. She used to see in the future; in other words, she was a witch who could foretell events—long before they came to fruition.

When Gbeyee woke up from her sleep, she went to her, Pah, and ordered him to don or put on his full battle gear. 'Assemble everything you use on the battlefield,' she said to him. 'There is a stranger on the way—heading to us. In fact, she is coming to you. Get your effects ready, so I can protect you. She is not coming on a date; she is not just coming to visit you. She is furious. You killed her son. I have been seeing her; in fact, she is getting very close to us.' He complied and received his mother's protection."

Uncle went over the woman's instructions to her son.

"Bayor Pah's mother told him to go back to the town hut, where he was when she called and informed him that a stranger was in route to him. 'Be there [to the back of the town hut] and hang out with your friends. I will know when she enters the town. Go back and resume the playing of the dugout drums. She will go to the town center when she enters the town. Do not approach her; just stay inside the town hut. As I said, I will know when she enters the town. At that time, I will

314

call you to come. And you will get in your full battle rattle. I will be with you, carrying your battlefield bag. Only at that time she will be welcomed to meet you. Since seeing you is her priority (and since she wants to admire your presence), she will be welcomed at that time. She will be able to see you."

Before Pah could leave, the mother said the battle was hers. In another words, she had assumed the battled.

"I am prepared; she and I will go at it. It is a challenge. I am ready for her. In fact,

the fight you had with her son—the one between you and her son—has long been over. Her son is dead. That happened why our children were at play. Our children's fight is behind us now. So, the fight she wants is between me and her. It is woman to woman now."

The Chedepo warrior did as his mother had ordered.

"Pah went to his peers at the town center. Then, predictably, the woman entered the town of Chedepo Geeken. And the people said to Pah, 'You have a stranger. You have a stranger.' She went to the traditional town center. Imagine that—the town center and sat in the spot reserved for the elders (korgbaeken). As soon as she sat down, Pah's mother, Gbeyee, called her son. As she had told him earlier, Pah knew not to approach the lady without his mother. That would have been the end of Pah, Chedepo's Tajigba. He knew better not to disrespect his mother. So, he got out on the other side of the town hut. And he ran to his mother. 'Put on your warrior's effects,' she said upon seeing the Chedepo's warrior. 'Grab your large animal skin.' He did, and he wrapped it around as fast as a warrior of his caliber would. She was barking commands, and the braved warrior kept up with his mother. His life was on the line, and not carrying out his mother's commands would have been detrimental to him. He knew better. 'Grab your sword from

315

the hut ceiling! Grab your pouch—the one that contains your voodoo!' Then she ordered him to tie it around his waist, as if it were a belt."

The warrior told his mother that he had secured or obtained everything she had ordered.

"'You will not sit on the elders' spot at the town center, where the woman is seated,' she told her son. 'Take your traditional chair ('gbesaid'). She told the people of Geeken who were playing the town's dugout drums to play 'Klor-tu,' which is a powerful sounds of war cries; the types of sounds the woman asked for were recognized readily as the undisputable sounds of on-going battles. 'Klor-tu! Klor-tu! Klor-tu! Klor-tu!' the people sounded the drums. Then she told the drummers to switch from 'Klor-tu! to 'Popo-wleo. Tol!' and they did. 'That's enough!' she told the people. As soon the drums seized, Tajigba Pah (Bayor Pah, Gbeyee Pah) gallantly stormed out!"

He continued the story.

"Then Tajigba Pah told the people to resume the sounds from the dugout drums: 'Klor-tu! Klor-tu! Klor-tu! Klor-tu!' Then the sounds changed to 'Popo-wleo tol! Popo- wleo tol! Popo-wleo tol!' Pah continued to pace around. He was gallantly walking from one side of the town center to the other. It was the same way he had walked on the battlefield with Fenyi Jahowl when the Killepo warrior successfully evaded captivity, which prompted Pah to use his rifle. Originally, Pah wanted to capture him alive and return him to Chedepo Geeken before killing him at the same town center, where the mother the dead warrior was seated, with the hope that Pah would die upon seeing her there. She was beyond brave. But she had a lot to learn."

He returned to the actions of Tajigba Pah at the town center:

316

"Bayor Pah was gallantly pacing around, as I said earlier; people were pouring cold fire-place ashes all over his body. He walked up to her [to the dead warrior's mother], and he held out his hand for a handshake. She extended hers, too. At this point, the woman's juju was reduced to nothing. She had hoped the power of her juju would have done the job of killing the Chedepo warrior at the point he laid his eyes on her. But the Chedepo warrior did not die when he saw her."

With his mother standing behind him, Uncle said, Tajigba Pah began to taunt the visiting witchcraft.

"He greeted the woman, 'Tato! I am Bayor Pah. I am the handsome and fine Chedepo Warrior. I am the warrior who killed your son, Fenyi Jahowl. And if that makes you angry, I will kill you, too. After I kill you, I will kill anyone from Killepo who wants to revenge for you. If your people come in drove to revenge your killing, I will kill them, too. And I will continue to kill them until I will live out my days here in Chedepo Geeken. You are here to see me, right? Here I am.' Then he sat down in his tiny bamboo chair ('gbesaid')."

"That was a powerful scene," Nelson [Targiour Winn] said, taking it all in. "Our people were truly powerful. Obviously, we do not see such caliber of our people nowadays."

"'So, you wanted to see me? Here I am,' he continued the taunting. 'My mother is

right here. I am the one who killed your son. No one else was involved. I did it alone. Well, my mother sat on my spirit, which was the reason your son could not see me. Your son is dead. My mother is alive, and she is here. If you are angry and want to do anything to me, it will be to your detriment. I will never apology to you. We are a people above whom the owl flies. It is good that you have come, so you will not compare me to a feckless warrior. I am Pah. My mother is from the land

317

of the people of Blorpo [a variant of the Kru tribe in Sinoe County, Liberia]. She is not a local woman. She is here. Do you want to see her, too? She is ready. She is capable to face you—to look you dare in the face. Here she is. Tajigba Pah told his mother to shake hands with the Killepo woman. And then he asked her, 'Are you happy now? If you have a relative here in Chedepo Geeken, they can feed you. My mother and I have nothing for us even though you are our guest.

You came with the intent to bewitch my mother and me, but the voodoo you brought to this land did not (and will never) work. The people of Chedepo call me Tajigba Pah. When I am going into battle, I fly. I do not walk. I am ready to fly for the land of Chedepo. So, as you watch, I am going home.' And, puff! They left the stranger at the town center and went home."

And that was how he concluded the story.

Chapter XIV:
How the People of Chedepo Count Money

Before the arrival of western influence, there was no money in our area, the greater River Gee area. Our people were using the goods-for-goods or service-for-service—also called barter—method to trade. Then, the monetary system, as we know it today, came with the "influence."

I am not sure when civilization came to Chedepo. But old man Gbeh Chea Nyanley gives us a clue. He said when "civilized people" (by which he meant westerners) came to the land now called Liberia, they built and lived along the water (the Atlantic Ocean), and then, slowly, they moved inward into the hinterlands. But they picked where they wanted to venture, so not all areas had the so-called civilized people. People who did not have the civilized among them were craving the civilizations (such as western style education opportunities) that other communities had. So, they decided to find ways to bring the civilized to their rural countryside. In other words, those who wanted or liked certain elements of the civilization, had to go to the water to invite the civilization, which came in the form of Christianity.

Here is old man on Christianity and civilization:

Chedepo and Christianity: In 1928, the people of Chedepo requested Christianity, which was the only way schools and civilization came to the rural areas. They wanted mission schools for the Chedepo region. The request for Christianity and the written form of education transpired during the reign of Kolobah [Chief] Gbagba Toe in the ancient Chedepo town of Klosoken. Kolobah Gbagba Toe was a member of the Magwulu family, which is one of five family groups in the Kaytoken area. [The others are Bowionpo, Ponwaon, Bocuwao, Dowao, and Kaytiao.]

The people of Chedepo, mainly from the towns of Putuken and Klosoken, met in the town of Putuken, which is a main-road [Zwedru-Harper Highway] community, and decided to send two people to the City of Harper, Maryland County, Liberia. They wanted to appeal to the government of Liberia for schools in the greater Chedepo area. They specifically told their representatives to communicate directly with Mr. Allen N. Yancy [1881-1941]. Mr. Yancy was the Vice President for President Charles Dunbar Burgess King (1875-1961).

In Chedepo, the people, especially those in the towns of Putuken and Klosoken, called the Vice President 'Mennee Yanseh,' which literally means "Civilized Yancy. The missionaries were reluctant to go to what is now River Gee County, Liberia. They did not want to go too far from the ocean. So, ironically, the local people were the ones who used to go to Harper, Maryland (and other coastal areas) to request that missionaries go into their remote locations. In other words, instead of the missionaries going out in the forest, where many indigenous people were living in order to spread their Christian religion and civilization, the locals were the ones looking for them. It is worth mentioning that the people really wanted schools into their areas, and, during that time, to get school, you had to embrace Christianity. You couldn't have one without the other in the remote forest areas. That was the reason the people in what is now Chedepo District met and decided to send two people to Harper City, Maryland County—one from the Kaytoken section of

Chedepo, and the other from Nyenawleken section of Chedcpo –to petition for schools and Christianity.

320

The people in the Kaytoken area agreed to send Jaylee Pah. He was their representative. Pah was the son of Kolobah [Chief] Welleh [also a Magwulu family man] and his wife, Nyenaon Jaylee (a Bocuwao woman). When Nyenaon Jaylee's firs husband—Kolobah [Chief] Welleh—died, she remarried Chief Gbagba Toe. So, Jaylee Pah was a stepson of Chief Gbagba Toe. As for the people from the Nyenawleken section of Chedepo, they sent Tuweli—that was his name—and he was a native of Chedepo Putuken. These two men went to 'Mennee Yanseh' and requested a missionary. He complied and sent a white missionary to the Chedepo region of today's River Gee. It was a challenge to have white people come into the forest.

Anyway, that was how the woman went Chedepo. Her name was Ms. Carson, a native of Missouri, which is an American State. In Klosoken, they built a hut for her on the outskirts of the town because they feared the collision of local and western religious values. So, her church—'mission town'— was built just beyond where my brother's house is [Winnville] now in Jarkaken. We call the area Soklotogbe [Cassava Hill]. That was the location of her house. Today, breadfruit trees are growing on that spot.

Anyway, the arrival of western influence meant the arrival of physical money. In other words, there was no money in our area before the arrival of the western influence. Our people were using the goods-for-goods or service-for-service—also called barter— method to trade. And since our people never had this form of monetary system, they used the original units within the western monetary system to count the new money. They, however, coined Grebo's equivalence to some of the western terms.

- Penny, for example, became *"cenjowel."*

- Nickel became *"tolorporce."*

321

- Dime became ***"sayporce."***

- Fifteen cents became ***"naporce."***

- And twenty cents became ***"sayley".***

As the counting got higher, our people felt a need to revamp the whole process. They did this by settling on two key sets of numbers. They opted for "a set of twenty," which they used mainly to count smaller sums—from a penny to one dollar. They also chose "a set of four," which they used to count much larger sums of money. These selections made it easy, relatively, to count money in Grebo. It is even easier to count money in Chedepo, provided you understand and follow the basic concept outlined below. It is important to first understand the basic units in a dollar, as outlined below:

- Penny is Cenjowel

- Nickel is Tolorporce

- Dime is Sayporce

- Fifteen cents is Naporce

- Twenty cents is Sayley (sing.) Seali (Plural)

You should know basic numbers in Grebo, too:

- 1 (One) = Dole

- 2 (Two) = Son

- 3 (Three) = Tan

- 4 (Four) = Heln

- 5 (Five) = Mm

- 6 (Six) = Mowondole

- 7 (Seven) = Nyeyentan

- 8 (Eight) = Nyenyhen

- 9 (Nine) = Seayidole

- 10 (Ten) =Pu

How would you say "eighty-five cents" in Grebo (Chedepo)? To say eighty-five cents in the Chedepo language, you have to know or understand how many sets of twenty cents can be found within the sum. The answer, of course, is four. There are four sets of "twenty cents" in "eighty-five cents," with Nickel— "Tolorporce"—as a remainder. Therefore, "eighty-five cents" is "Seali heln tolorporce," literally four sets of twenty cents plus five cents.

Here are the basic units in a dollar:

- Penny = Cenjowel

- Nickel = Tolorporce

- Dime = Sayporce

- Fifteen cents = Naporce

- Twenty cents = Sayley (sing.)

- Twenty-five cents = Sayley tolorporce (*one set of twenty plus nickel*)

- Thirty cents = Sayley sayporce (*one set of twenty plus dime*)

- Thirty-five cents = Sayley naporce (*one set of twenty plus fifteen cents*)

323

- Forty cents = Seali son (*two sets of twenty cents*)

- Forty-five cents = Seali son tolorporce

- Fifty cents = Seali son sayporce

- Fifty-five cents = Seali son naporce

- Sixty cents = Seali tan

- Sixty-five cents = Seali tan tolorporce

- Seventy cents = Seali tan sayporce

- Seventy-five cents = Seali tan naporce

- Eighty cents = Seali heln

- Eighty-five cents = Seali heln tolorporce

- Ninety cents = Seali heln sayporce

- Ninety-five cents = Seali heln naporce

- One Dollar = Seali mn

Since one dollar is "Seali mm" (or five sets of twenty cents), we can rightly imply that two dollars is "Seali pu" (or ten sets of twenty cents); three dollars, therefore, has to be Seali pu tuo mm (literally "fifteen sets of twenty cents; **tuo** means "add"). And we could go on forever, but, as you can see, it will get a little complicated as the figures grow. There will be way too many sets of twenty cents in the large figures, so our people go to the set of four.

For four dollars, if you had suggested "Seali wolo" or twenty sets of twenty cents, you, technically, will be correct. However, our people choose another monetary unit for four dollars: Ponwun (sing.) Penyi (Plural). Ponwun stands for twenty sets of twenty cents. In other words, instead of saying "twenty sets of twenty cents" every time, it is convenient to simply say Ponwun. So, five dollars becomes Ponwun seali mn; six dollars becomes Ponwun seali pu and seven dollars becomes Ponwun seali pu tuo mm. Eight dollars, however, is not Ponwun seali wolo (which will be correct, technically, if you had guessed it). Eight dollars is Penyi son (or two sets of four dollars).

- Nine dollars = Penyi son seali mm

- Ten dollars = Penyi son seali pu

- Eleven dollars = Penyi son seali pu tuo mm

- Twelve dollars = Penyi tan

- Thirteen dollars = Penyi tan seali mm

- Fourteen dollars = Penyi tan seali pu

- Fifteen dollars = Penyi tan seali pu tuo mm

- Sixteen dollars = Penyi heln

- Seventeen dollars = Penyi heln seali mm

- Eighteen dollars = Penyi heln seali pu

- Nineteen dollars = Penyi heln seali pu tuo mm

- Twenty dollars ($20) is Penyi mm

- Thirty dollars ($30) is Penyi Nyeyentan seali pu

- Forty dollars ($40) is Penyi pu

- Fifty dollars ($50) is Penyi pu tuo son seali pu

The above is all the information needed to count as high as possible. For example, if you want to count to sixty dollars ($60), count the sets of fours in sixty. In other words, have four ($4) divide sixty (60). That will be fifteen (15) times. Hence, sixty dollars ($60) in Chedepo is "Penyi pu tuo mm."

Don't get frustrated, if you do not get it initially. You might want to go over it a few times to get it. This should be fairly easy though for all *E-Je Grebo variants. E-Je literally means "I say." Certain variants of the Grebo language say "I say" exactly the same way. So, we call them "E-je Grebos."

Chapter XV:
Bride Price Presentation Between two Jarkaken Families: Bowionpo and Bocuwao

Mr. Annie P. Winn ("Bowionpo Girl") and Wilfred K. Winn, Sr ("Bocuwao Boy"),

the Bride and the Groom

On November 9, 2018, a few members of the family of Bocuwao gathered at the home of Teaty Kpadeh in Chedepo

Jarkaken, a town in River Gee County, Liberia. It was an impromptu meeting, hastily called to welcome Saylee Komoh, one of their sons, who had traveled home from the United States. (Only three elders made it to the meeting: Kpateah, Tuwleh and Dokpeh.) Old man Dokpeh was fatally shot the day after the presentation by his own son. The same was true for the young men who showed up. Only six were in attendance—Woday, Sayjela, Kpadeh, Sayjolo, Seabo and Komoh, the guest.

Saylee Sayjolo stood up and sounded off with a popular local chant, "Bocuwao, ah bati'o!"

"Bati!" The audience of mostly males responded.

A lone woman, uninvited, not expected and most importantly not ask to leave was at the men's gathering, which was called to plan or draw up some agenda points for an upcoming bride price presentation.

"He is here to visit us. He told us something of enormous importance. This is why we made the hasty call to inform you. Before we begin the discussion, our tradition demands that we offer you a kola nut," Sayjolo said.

"Accept the kola, so we can eat it," Elder Tuwleh told Seabo. It was the elder's way

of designating Seabo as the spokesperson for the event.

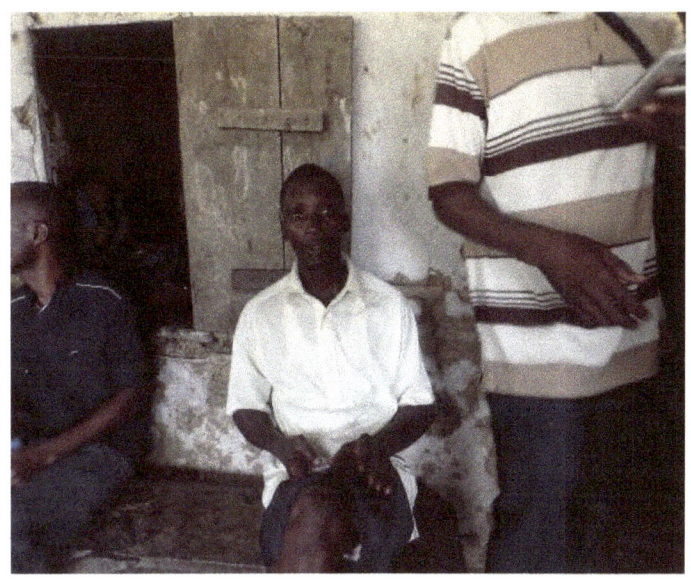

"Accept the kola, so we can eat it," Elder Tuwleh told Seabo [in the middle]. This was the

elder's way of designating Seabo as the spokesperson for the event.

"And pray for it," Sayjolo told Seabo, also a local pastor.

"Our good God," the pastor began his prayer, "for our brother who have flown through the skies just to get us, we give you a big thank-you for his safety. Whether for good or for bad we will continue to praise you. We present this kola to you. Bless it, so it becomes food for our nourishment and therapeutic for health. Give us common understanding as we deliberate here as a family. Let all of this be in your name."

"Amen!" the people responded.

"By tradition, kola is accompanied by a drink," Sayjolo said. "We present this

$2,000 in Liberian dollars (LD), for your drink. Let us deliberate over the kola and the

drink."

"I am just taking a piece of kola," Woday jokingly said, as he reached over a stack

of local bills on a small table. The family laughed.

"Thank you for the money. Thank you," the spokesman said. Then, quickly, he turned to the guest. "Do you remember the last time you ate a cassava?" The family used improvised kola—a bowl of raw pieces of cassava, a starchy root of a tropical plant the locals used as food.

"We have cassava in the United States," the guest told the pastor. "But our cassava is not as fresh as yours."

"Bati'o!" Sayjolo chanted again. "Bati!"

"You are asking Komoh, 'Why did you call us?' He has come to...well, he is here.

Maybe it is best to hear the message directly from the source."

"Deliver your message in our local dialect..." Elder Tuwleh said.

"Before you stand up," the speaker interjected. "I want to make something very clear. We, as a family, should have come uninvited and presented a kola to you. But you are in a hurry, so that will not happen this time around. This is the hut of Teaty Kpadeh [brother of the guest]. He is a prominent member of our Bocuwao family. So, in a way, the family has called you. We will do a better job next time. The family should have called you. And, at that gathering, the family would have had proper standing to ask you the reason for your travel.

330

Forgive us. You are in a hurry, as I said earlier, so we won't get the opportunity to get it right. On behalf of our greater Bocuwao family, I say welcome. As you know, we use a kola to inquire of a stranger's reason for traveling. So, you have the floor."

"Thank you, Mr. Speaker," the guest said. "I left this place a long time ago. I was not here when my oldest sister, Gbasay, died. I was not here when my mother, Bolju, died. I was not here when my father, Saylee, died. I am here to see family members following these tragedies, and others I did not list. Thank you. I saw all your pictures and videos, especially when my parents passed away. Also, the woman I have at home in the United States is a member of the Bowionpo family. I want you to present a bride price to the family of Bowionpo for my woman. We met overseas; we both want to honor our traditions. So, I want you to engage her and present the bride price later."

"So, this is what he said," the speaker took the floor and reiterated the guest's comments to the family. "The reasons he flew through all that danger—through all those snakes and tigers—to get to us are the tragedies that befell us while he was away. He did see some images on the television screen, which is not same as being there. He has come to see us. He has come so we can console one another. His wife is Paytee, the daughter of Paytee Jarbo. She is with him overseas. He has come to marry her the traditional way. He wants us to do our duty as his family and present a bride price to the people of Bowionpo. This is the other reason that compelled him to come. Because he is in a hurry, he wants us to conduct the dowry ceremony today. If there are other issues, I am sure he will tell us later, but that is all he wants you to know. Komoh," he faced the traveled son. "We say thank you. The reasons that brought you are good. In this life, we are here only for a very brief period. When your time comes, you go. It is true. We lost the relatives

331

you listed— plus more. Their times came, so they left us. My own wife, who was here the last time you came to us, has gone, too. But we are here—all of us. On behalf of the family of Bocuwao, we say thank you. We saw all the tragedies, but you didn't. It makes your pain more unbearable. You only saw the events on videos; you cannot shake hands with people in videos. We interacted with one another. Suhsuh, your older sister, was here. We went to her, and we hugged her. We cried together. You missed all of that," he said.

The family concluded their meeting at Kpadeh's place and walked a short distance

to the Bowionpo side of town.

The meeting took place at Elder Fulton Sayon Pah's home.

Elder Fulton Sayon Pah, Annie Paytee Winn's paternal uncle, prepared his courtyard for the meeting. The family of Bowionpo were there in their numbers. Several members of Bocuwao were at the courtyard when the men arrived from the huddle at Kpadeh's place.

"Our father, Nowinniegbe, has asked me to call you," Sayon Pah told members of his Bowionpo family. "We have strangers in our midst."

"Sayon Pah has called us, along with our father, because he has strangers," Swen Martin, Bowionpo's spokesperson, echoed Sayon Pah's message. We the family of Bowionpo have visitors. That is why he has called us. Isn't that what you said, Sayon Pah?"

"You echoed my message correctly. Thank you."

"On behalf of us, the Bowion," Swen Martin continued, "I want to thank you, Sayon Pah, and our father, Nowinniegbe, for the call. We are here. We are complete. We are looking forward to hearing from you."

"Here is a kola," Sayon Pah presented a kola to the visitors.

"Jaybloforpo [Bocuwao], ah bati'o!" Seabo rendered a chant, and, before the family could response, a young woman got up and ran up and down the courtyard, where the two families had gathered—with chants of her own:

"We are here! We are here! Jaybloforpo, we are here!" "We are here!"

"Do it! Do it! Jaybloforpo, do it! "Do it!

"The spokesperson Bocuwao brought to this ceremony is our own son," Fredrick Saylo Wesseh said. "He is a Bowionpo woman's son. And the woman who is running up and down this courtyard—with these chants—is also our own daughter, too. We need to keep our eyes on them. If they manage and grab any items from us, we will not be able to

get them back, according to our custom." Seabo, the speaker of Bocuwao, got up. "Jaybloforpo, ah bati'o!"

333

"Bati!"

"Bowionpo, ah bati'o!" "Bati!"

"We accept the kola," the speaker said. "Thank you for your hospitality. Kola cures a stranger's hunger. We also know the kola inquires about the reason for our coming to your house. 'Why are we here?' Well, we have come to you because of a very serious reason.

We have come for an enormous reason."

"We are not here for a bad reason; we are here for a very good reason," Sayjolo

clarified.

"We are relieved," replied one, and the crowd laughed.

"Our son, Komoh, who lives overseas, is the reason we are here," Seabo said. "He has come and is here with us. Komoh and your daughter, Paytee, have expressed interests in one another. And, when you have a family's daughter, our tradition requires that you go to the family, engage their daughter and subsequently pay a bride price to her family.

This is why we are here. We have come to engage your daughter. We have come to

present Paytee's dowry money to the family of Bowionpo on behalf of our son, Komoh."

"Komoh kidnapped our daughter and carried her overseas," Saylo joked. "Seabo," Sayon Pah called. "I called your name because you are the spokesperson

for the family of Bocuwao. We are looking up to you. For everyone here, including all of you who are standing, I want to

334

thank you on behalf of the Bowionpo family. Today is Sunday. So, I want to appeal to the pastors here to adjust your church schedules today. This occasion will cut into your regular times."

Swen Martin stood up from the Bowionpo side:

"Bocuwao, ah bati'o!" "Bati!"

"Bowionpo, ah bati'o!" "Bati!"

"We have all listened to the family of Bocuwao. They are strangers here because their son, Komoh wants to engage and pay dowry for our daughter, Paytee. Let's do it one at a time. Engage her first, then we can go to the bride price presentation later."

Seabo stood up: "Jaybloforpo, ah bati'o!" "Bati!"

"Bowionpo, ah bati'o!" "Bati!"

"Seabo, I am sitting in your seat; you are here for my daughter," a middle-aged comedian and member of Bowionpo said. Clearly, he wanted the people to laugh, but the joke lacked its desired punchline; it did not materialize.

"No, get up!" one elder said. Come to the Bowionpo side. You are the host; you have to provide a seat for Seabo."

"I apologized," the comedian said.

"We are presenting US$50 to engage your daughter, Paytee, for our son, Komoh." "Paytee has to receive that sum and take it to her mother. Since she is not here to

receive this money, we need someone to play Paytee's role. This is for ceremonious

335

purposes only."

"I am a Paytee," Nyonotenya, the wife of Paytee's brother, Darkpe Chea,

volunteered for the role.

"Paytee, do you accept the engagement request from Komoh?" Swen Martin asked

the role-player.

"Yes," she said almost instantaneously. The crowd laughed as she walked the

money to the mother.

"Paytee's mother," the speaker faced the mother, "do you accept the money and do you understand that it is for the engagement of your daughter?" Swen Martin asked the mother, herself a role player.

"Yes. I accept it. She is engaged. We accept him."

Bocuwao applauded.

"Komoh," Tetoe Saylo called me, "Susannah Nyonotenya Chea is not Paytee. She

is just playing a role. Do not come here later and take her with you, too."

A thunderous laughter ensued.

"We are happy, too," Swen Martin said. "The token for the engagement goes to the mother. She has it. We, the family of Bowionpo, have nothing to do with it. Bocuwao, come forward and present the bride price (dowry) for Paytee."

He continued, "Start by presenting the mother-in-law's goat *[Nyenenaewle]*."

"You are requesting Nyenenaewle before the dowry. We want you to know that that is the sequence. You are not wrong. But we want an exception to the norm here, please. Let us present the dowry now. The norm is an actual goat, so we do not want to use a monetary value for the goat, so we appeal to you to give us some time to look for a live goat," Seabo requested.

"Mother-in-Law, you have heard the family of Bocuwao. They do not forget you;

they want to get it right. We want to hear from you," Swen Martin asked. "I accept the postponement of the goat payment."

"Since you have agreed, we agreed, too," Martin took his seat.

"Look at all the members of Bocuwao here, but you are having our own son (Seabo) speaking to us," Bowionpo' s oldest family member, Mr. Albert Nowinniegbe Dweh, said. "He is a 50-50; half Bocuwao and half Bowionpo. If I wanted to be technical, I would have insisted that you change your speaker. But since this is a joyous event, we are pleased to hear from you, Seabo."

Laughed.

"We would have rejected Sayjolo and Seabo, too—on the ground that both are

Bowionpo female children," Nyemah Komoh said.

"Thank you, old man. You have to accept me," Seabo said. "I am Bocuwao to the core; I am the one the family has selected

337

to speak. "In my hand, is US$40. I am presenting this as the *Gelorwle,* the actual price for the bride. LD$500 as the *Wlegborkolar* ["Goat Money"] ..."

But Swen Martin did not like the order in which the items that constitute the traditional bride price were being presented.

"I am seeing something here this afternoon that I have never seen before. I have been to ceremonies during which my family was a receiver of the bride prices. I have been to ceremonies where we presented the bride prices. My point is this: we have to be careful so we do not deviate from what has been the tradition. We do not want to teach something that is totally different from our norms. We have to do this the right way. Granted that we have settled the Nyenenaewle [mother in law's goat] issue, however, for proper sequence, Nyenenaewle is the first to be presented. Once that is presented, all the other items are presented as a package. We call that bundle of items *Wlegborkolar.* Wlegborkolar is not a separate goat that is chained and presented; it is the name of everything else that is to be presented or displayed after the mother-in-law's goat (Nyenenaewle)..."

"Hold on, Swen Martin," old man Nowinniegbe interjected. He attempted to go around the table behind which he sat, perhaps to get in the middle of the two families, where the speakers were standing. He changed his mind, stood in place and continued, "You are correct. But the package you are talking about is *Kpajor,* not Wlegborkolar"

"Exactly!" Martin said.

"We were just looking at the Bocuwao speaker," Oldman Nowinniegbe (the oldest of the families) continued. "He has the items, but he did not talk about how they are categorized. Inside the Kpajor are many items—a machete (a cutlass) is there; the father's blanket is in it. The point is, they are usually

338

combined and presented as one, as in a package. 'This is the Kpajor' and we will know exactly what should be in it. After the blanket, is the Tanson [salt]. Sorwelyee Kpakpor [tobacco] is in there, too."

There were more seasoned Bowionpo elders than were elders from Bocuwao family; moreover, the atmosphere at Sayon Pah's courtyard, where the two families gathered, was peaceful, warm and very friendly. There were plenty of opportunities to learn, and the family of Bocuwao did not feel trampled upon with multiple interjections from elements within the Bowionpo family.

"Thank you for the corrections," Seabo said to the two Bowionpo elders. "We will get it right. In fact, we are not wrong—at least not terribly—because we have the items here. We just have to focus on the sequence and how we group them," he said.

And then he went back to the presentation of the contents within the Kpajor. Seabo did exactly what the elders wanted to see, and they were pleased—with intermittent applauses as Seabo weaved through what was clearly a challenge.

"Here is the *Ju Gbeyee Dafueh*," he placed a white blanket on the table. I said it was for the father-in-law.

"Here is the *Tanson*," he placed two bags of salt on the table.

"Yes, that is it!" an elder on the receiving side of the bride price could not contain

his approval.

"Here is the *Pantin*," Seabo placed a cutlass on the table.

Note that the two families agreed on the monetary value for items they could not obtain physically due to time constraints.

339

So, Seabo did not physically put a cutlass on the table. He lay on the table a cash amount equivalent to the market value of the items in the local area.

"Here is the **Sorwelyee Kpakpor**," he placed a cash amount (equaled to the market value) on the table for tobacco.

"Here is the **Kporkay**," he placed a figure on the table.

I did not know the meaning of Kporkay. Like several items, this item was not tangible. So, I asked my good friend, Saylo (Frederick S. Wesseh), to talk about it.

"It is a cup in which the elder puts his drink. It is about a kilo. The old man in the family will store some palm wine in it for any unexpected visitor or anyone who may want to get the old man's blessing after the sharing of the wine," Tetoe Saylo told me.

At one point during the presentation of the items, Seabo sought clarity from Swen Martin, the elder who was the first to identify the sequential and grouping irregularities. This tradition-rich ceremony was incredibly straight. In fact, the receiving family refused to take any excess. So, when Seabo considered placing LD$500 on the table for **Wlegborkolar**, he was cautioned against doing so.

"No, we do not want that!" the Bowionpo elder told Seabo. We watched Seabo put the extra money back in his pocket. "Here is the US$40 for the **Gelorwle**."

The above amount is the actual bride price—the dowry money—that the family of Bocuwao presented to the family of Bowionpo. The other items inside the "Kpajor" package are required kind gestures towards the family of the wife to be (Paytee's family, in this case).

340

The Gelorwle figure was the last of the items that were presented. As usual, the deliberations were dominated by the spokespersons. And so, the speaker of Bowionpo, Swen Martin, took the floor:

"On behalf the family of Bowionpo, I want to say thanks to the family of Bocuwao.

From time immemorial, the bride price has always been the figure you have presented today for Paytee. But times are hard now. We are adding something to it. We are adding US$10 to the US$40. Add it up to US$50 before we can accept it," he said.

This was not expected. The family of Bocuwao thought it had met all the requirements to present a bride price to Bowionpo for their son's wife—Paytee. In fact, before meeting the wife's family, members of Bocuwao gathered at Teaty Kpadeh's house. The family listed all the items they thought they would need at the ensuing ceremony.

They consolidated the physical items at Kpadeh's place, and, for the ones they could not obtain in tangible forms, the family determined their values in the local areas—and in the local currency. Thus, when the family of Bocuwao presented the items to the wife's family, we saw a combination of physical materials and segregated sums of money. The two families, for several generations, had set bride price (a symbolic matrimonial gesture) at US$40. That was the reason Seabo presented that amount to the wife's family, but, to Bocuwao's surprise, the wife's family requested an increase. This gave Seabo the chance to regurgitate the words he had swallowed earlier while he struggled over sequence and grouping. "We have to be careful so we do not deviate from what has been the tradition," Swen Martin told Seabo.

"Jaybloforpo, ah bati'o!" Seabo stood up. "Bati!"

341

"Bowionpo, ah bati'o!" "Bati!"

"You are requesting an extra US$10 before you can accept the dowry from our son, Komoh. The dowry exchanges between our two families have remained constant over decades. It has always been US$40 dollars. We have to do what our fathers have taught us. I want to remind you, the family of Bowionpo, about our most recent bridal exchanges, and the figure that we paid in dowries to one another. Our daughter, Kaynyonoh (Togbe Bafeh's daughter), is married in the family of Bowionpo (married to Klay). Bowionpo gave us a bride price of US$40. Gbayee Duhl's daughter is married to your son, Sankon Badior; she received US$40 from the Bowionpo family. I, the chosen speaker at this ceremony, married a Bowionpo daughter (even though she passed away); she received US$40 as a bride price. But, today, it has come to Paytee. You want Bocuwao to add US$10 as a condition for accepting the dowry."

He took his seat.

"When I spoke earlier, I said from 'time immemorial' the bride price has always been the sum you presented today," Swen Martin offered a firmed rebuttal. "Didn't I say that? These are hard times. Times have changed. The price has gone up. We will accept US$50. In fact, the man [groom] has not done any labor [as in farming work] for the family of Bowionpo, if you want us to go down that route. If we say 'add US$10 more,' add US$10 more."

For a few minutes, the speakers [both the Bocuwao and Bowionpo speakers) were off the stage. The families on both sides went into their corners to deliberate on the unusual request from the family of Bowionpo. Bocuwao wanted to reach a compromise with the family of the wife, but serious consideration had to be made. It was not hard to find an additional US$10; that was not the issue. But any decisions made here between the families were going to affect to dowry exchanges of between the town families. Bocuwao's reluctance to adding US$10 to the standard bride price was forward-looking. If Bocuwao had agreed to adding to the bride price, that act would have affected all future bridal exchanges between the two families. Instead of the long tradition of US$40, the new bride price would have increased to US$50 between Bocuwao and Bowionpo.

They reached a decision, and both families agreed to keep the price at US$40, which had been the standard.

"Thank you for accepting the US$40 as Paytee's dowry," Bocuwao's speaker,

Seabo, broke the long pulse.

And both families applauded.

"When my son-in-law came to me last night," old man Sayon said, "he called his wife on the telephone. I had an opportunity to talk to her. She asked me to make a list of young Bowionpo men, so she can pick 'who will eat her money.' I have the list. I will give it to the husband, so he can call and read out the names. So, we can know her choice."

Seabo got up. His face was lit up with a bright smile, "For accepting the bride price, we, the family of Bocuwao, also known as 'Jay bloforpo kwi mininedeh u ton neh,' present LD$2,000 to you for your refreshment." The 'Jay bloforpo' phrase means, "Pioneers who purchased what the civilized played with," essentially a toy. It was coined for the family of Bocuwao long ago in the ancient community of Kaytoken, where Wiah Chie, a renowned Bocuwao's pioneer purchased an expensive, fragile toy so that Kaytoken's kids could play with it. The merchants charged a chow, and the town appealed

343

to its people of means to find reasons to buy it, or risk losing it to another town. Wiah Chie give the merchants their asking price, and the children in Kaytoken had, what was then, a modern baby-like toy; hence, "Jay bloforpo kwi mininedeh u ton neh." Anyway, a few years later, Wiah Chie, broke the toy on the grave of his son, Kopeh Nowinnie. It was his way of paying a tribute to his son. The family use the epithet in their proudest moment, and Seabo used it because the family, which is labeled in Jarkaken and elsewhere as stingy or mean, was being generous to the family of Bowionpo.

"We are happy," Swen Martin said. "Let's celebrate a successful bride payment ceremony. I know this ceremony falls on Sunday, which means some people have to go to church. But I want you—all of you—to know that this is not a child's play. This is a joyous event. Yes, it is a source for intense debates and arguments. But the message we are going home with is our daughter, Paytee, is now married to your son, Komoh. We accept the LD$2,000. But this is not over yet. Paytee is not here. Your son and our daughter did not meet here. They met abroad, where she is now. We want him to call her right now.

Her husband has given us a bride price. Does she want us to accept it? Let us hear from

her."

The husband's family placed a call and gave the phone to Swen Martin. "Bodior ju," he called the bride. "We, the family of Bowionpo, are here. Albert

Dweh (Nowinniegbe) is here. Jacob Nyenpan (Chilean) is here. Fulton Pah (Sayon) is here. Chenekan (Jowa Chenekan) is here. I, Swen Martin (Wilson Swen), am here. And Saylo — all of us are here: Wiah Sleh, Bihepo...we are many here. We, the family of Bowionpo, have just received your bride price. It

344

is on the table right now. Do you want us to accept it? Bocuwao, keep the noise down. In fact, she says no," he joked.

Families laughed.

"She is smiling," Swen Martin tells the families.

"I want you to accept the bride pride," Paytee said on a speaker phone. Swen Martin held the phone to his ear, but the bride's voice was not only audible but clear, too. So, the groom's family started to celebrate before swen Martin could relay her message.

"Bocuwao, you are celebrating," Martin said. "Wait for me to relay her message.

She said no."

The families laughed.

"Bodior ju," Swen Martin called the bride. "We say a big thank-you to you. Since you told us to accept the money, we accept it. A woman is supposed to receive a bride price. So, she can be respected in the community. If a woman finds a man in a far-away land, she is supposed to tell him, 'Let's go and see my parents.' This is what you have done. You have honored us. May God bless you and your husband."

"Thank you for receiving the bride pride," Paytee said. "We have the names," Swen Martin told her.

By this time, the folks had been deliberating for well over two hours, mostly peaceful, with sounds of crackling laughter. But someone on the Bocuwao side thought the decision to pick who the recipient of the money should have been made with only a Bowionpo audience. But, clearly, the words from the Bocuwao's side of the courtyard infuriated elements within the family of Bowionpo.

"That decision does not belong here," a loud voice was heard coming from the Bocuwao side, suggesting that the family of Bowionpo needed to discuss much later—in the absent of their guests (the Bocuwao members)—who among them [the Bowionpo family] was qualified or fitting to receive and use the dowry. Personally, I thought it was a good and valid point, which the voice from the Bocuwao side presented without any tact. So, it stuck a nerve; the family of Bowionpo was not pleased at all with such an utterance.

Many of them were visibly furious, including Tetoe Saylo, a powerful Bowionpo influencer at the gathering. He was a middle-aged man, and did not waste any time:

"Really!" Saylo was alarmed. "Go to your homes!" Saylo told members of the Bocuwao family; the guests at the presentation. "This is our home; it [what the voice protested] belongs here. Don't tell us what to do; if you don't like how we are making decisions here—decisions that affect our family, and decisions we are making in our own house—then go back to your homes. Get out of here!"

346

"This is not Bocuwao's quarter," another powerful Bowionpo elder, Swen Martin, older than the earlier speaker, was equally alarmed by the comments from the Bocuwao side. "We are in our house."

Soon, calm returned, and Saylo read out the names of those in the Bowionpo family. They believed they were technically qualified to receive and use the dowry, but they needed the input of the bride to pick who was the most qualified. Note that all the people on the list were men, young men who were either not married yet or whose had not conducted the traditional dowry payment for their partners. A western style marriage, while acceptable in the area, does not replace the traditional version. So, a proper marriage here must encompass both to satisfy the government (or the secular society) and the traditions in the village. The list below was presented; it was read out loud at the dowry payment for members of the Bowionpo families to deliberate.

1. Livingstone Tabla Darkpe Dweh, son of Isaac Dweh

2. Fulton Sayon Pah, Jr., son of Sayon Pah

3. Abenego C. Dweh, son of Isaac Dweh

4. Napoleon Q. Nagbe, son of William Nagbe

5. Isaac Wallace, son of Bafeh Nagbe

6. Vasco Nagbe, another son of Bafeh Nagbe

We learned that the bride had to either make a decision on the names or agree with any personnel choice the family made. The bride was not physically at the meeting; she was in the United States, but she participated telephonically. In situations where she had to be physically present, the families agreed for one of the young ladies at the occasion to represent her.

347

"Livingstone should not be on the list," the bride said. And some of the elders from her family were nodding in agreement. Clearly, she had done her homework. "He [Livingstone Tabla Darkpe Dweh] should not be the recipient of my bride price because he and I are maternal cousins. Our mothers are sisters—from the Ponwaon family quarter." She went down the list; it was overwhelming for her. She could not make an on-the-spot decision.

The family of Bowionpo realized that she needed time and counsel to make a choice. So, the family decided to table the selection process. Apparently, what the voice said on the Bocuwao's side, which had infuriated the host family, was correct after all. The voice, which almost got us [the Bocuwao family members] kicked off Sayon Pah's property, was clearly in line with the Bowionpo's decision.

"Where is Fulton Pah? The bride asked for her father, whose premises we were using to conduct the tradition. "Let me talk to him."

And that was how we got to the conclusion. We heard later—long after we had left the meeting place—that Paytee [the bride] selected her paternal cousin, Fulton Sayon Pah, Jr to receive her bride price.

In theory, the next time he spends that US$40, it will not be in his father's courtyard. In fact, it will not be at the courtyard of any Bowionpo family member. Fulton Sayon Pah, Jr is expected to present it, along with a well-vetted **Kpajor** [total bride pride] package, to the family of his future wife.

About the Author

Wilfred Komoh Winn, Sr. was born in Puwaiken, a few-hut settlement located in the Dilamo Reservation, a huge farming reserve (Sonjigba) outside Chedepo Jarkaken, River Gee County, Liberia. He grew up in nearby Wodaiken village (a farming settlement) and in Jarkaken proper.

Mr. Winn is a product of Kaytoken Junior High School (KJHS), Jarkaken; Antoinette Tubman Day (A.T. Day), and later Robert Baker Richardson Baptist High School (RBRS), both in Zwedru, Grand Gedeh County, Liberia. He escaped to the Ivory Coast in the early 1990s due to the Liberian Civil War (the so-called "Charles Taylor War") and attended a United Nation High Commission for Refugees High School in the western Ivorian town of Tabou, which is between Harper City, Liberia and San Pedro, the Ivory Coast.

In 1994, Mr. Winn immigrated to the United States of America. It was in the USA where he got a chance to complete his high school. In fact, he is a recipient of General Education Diploma (GED), a US-based education program that gives

349

adults the chance to complete high school. He received his High School Equivalency Diploma from the University of the State of New York Education Department in September 1997. Mr. Winn briefly attended Interboro Institute, a Business-Centered College in Midtown Manhattan before enrolling at Maria de Hostos Community College of the City University of New York (CUNY) in the south of the Bronx, New York City [1999-2000], in New York City, where he obtained an Associate degree in Liberial Arts and Science. Mr. Winn was a student of English—with a focus on Literary Criticism and Politics— at Drury University, St. Robert, Missouri.

Other areas of studies include Heating, Ventilation, and Air Conditioning at Virginia Technical Academy, Newport News, VA.

Mr. Winn, a veteran of the United States military, holds a Demonstrated Senior Logistics Certificate from The United States Army Logistics University, at Fort Gregg- Adams, VA, formally Fort Lee, Virginia.

Back Cover Summary

When an oral historians die, countless stories die with the storytellers; this is an example of oral history being prone to rapid death. The stories of the Chedepo people in northwestern River Gee County, Liberia, do not go too far back in the past. The stories die out fast because they are not written. Transgenerational communication, therefore, consists of word-of-mouth narratives that depend on the memory power of the narrators.

The intent of this book, therefore, is to serve as a pioneer, if you like, in the quest to slow

the "rapid death" of our stories through the text form.

Find among other attention-grabbing contents in this book, to include the profile of Chedepo District. Learn about ancient Chedepo communities, such as Nyenawleken and Kaytoken. Learn about Chedepo's peer culture—how the groups are formed, refined, and inducted, and how they become a highly structured Gbor stage (elder).

Learn about Jumayee dance, a youth dance. How it started, and how Mr. Sam Chebo Weah used it (the dance) as "a tool of diplomacy." You will learn about Mr.

Wilson Swen and others, particularly how they stood up and promoted the dance when an army of community elders, local educators, and religious authorities fought to silence it.

Readers will learn also that the land of Chedepo (the entire land of Chedepo) belongs to one family in Chedepo Jarkaken (a symbolic gesture).

In the early 1990s, Jarkaken lost many citizens during the Liberian civil war. War in Jarkaken extensively covered rebels' activities, from their entry to how they employed their brutalities. Learn about the town's martyr men—the likes of Fala Seakor Quayee, Tutu Quayee, Johnson Finakan Quayee, Shannon Juty Toe, Wesley Toe, and more—who gave their lives while fighting as members of the Jarkaken Defense Force (JDF), a self-help force that emerged after core rebel fighters left Chedepo.

www.ingramcontent.com/pod-product-compliance
Lightning Source LLC
Chambersburg PA
CBHW051131120626
46547CB00012B/763